A tiny family after the war

Three generations: my mother, my son, and me

William Saroyan in the army

Lucy and Aram Saroyan, 1957

Oona O'Neill—before Charlie

Oona and Charlie Chaplin, 1943

Gloria's wedding to Pat di Cicco

With Gloria and Sidney Lumet at their wedding

On a cold winter day, a group of porcupines huddled together closely to save themselves by their mutual warmth from freezing. But soon they felt the mutual quills and drew apart. Whenever the need for warmth brought them closer together again, this second evil was repeated, so that they were tossed back and forth between these two kinds of suffering until they discovered a moderate distance that proved most tolerable.— Thus the need for company, born of the emptiness and monotony inside them, drives men together; but their many revolting qualities and intolerable faults repel them again. The medium distance that they finally discover and that makes association possible is politeness and good manners. Whoever does not keep this distance is told, among the British: keep your distance!—To be sure, this only permits imperfect satisfaction of the need for mutual warmth, but it also keeps one from feeling the prick of the quills.—But whoever possesses much inner warmth of his own will prefer to avoid company lest he cause or suffer annoyance.

—Schopenhauer

Among the Porcupines

Among the Porcupines

A MEMOIR

Carol Matthau

TURTLE BAY BOOKS
A DIVISION OF RANDOM HOUSE
NEW YORK
1992

Photograph credits:

Waking up: Harold Halma/author's collection. Three generations: È
Maillard Tesslère/author's collection. William Saroyan: Sgt. William E.
Hamilton/author's collection. Lucy and Aram Saroyan: copyright ©
1957 by Richard Avedon. Oona O'Neill: AP/Wide World Photos.
Oona and Charlie Chaplin: AP/Wide World Photos. Gloria's wedding
to Pat di Cicco: AP/Wide World Photos. With Gloria and Sidney
Lumet: UPI/Bettmann. Finally, an Avedon: copyright © 1954 by
Richard Avedon. With Eli Wallach: UPI/Bettman. Total happiness:
Bill Ray/*Life* magazine © Time Warner Inc. Wrestling for Oscar:
AP/Wide World Photos. In Southampton: Nick Machalaba/*WWD*.

All other photographs are from the author's collection.

Library of Congress Cataloging-in-Publication Data

Matthau, Carol.
Among the porcupines: a memoir / Carol Matthau.—1st ed.
p.   cm.
ISBN 0-394-58266-7
1. Matthau, Carol.   2. United States—Biography.   I. Title.
CT275.M46447A3   1992
973—dc20   90-52892

This book is dedicated to you, Walter.
I love you today with the same passion
as when I fell in love with you—
all those many years ago.

Contents

Among the Porcupines

Wuthering Heights in Maryland

I was the youngest girl at National Park Seminary in Forest Glen, Maryland. I lived in a suite over the ballroom with a rich girl from Houston, Texas, who had pimples. It is now part of Walter Reade Hospital: The suite I was in has been turned into a padded cell. There are armed guards around. Then it was a finishing school, with girls from all over the country. When there were dances, the boys from Georgetown University were invited and always came. All the girls wore lipstick. I always watched from the balcony—the school thought I was too young to go to a dance. And I wasn't allowed to wear lipstick.

I was thirteen and seeing a cross section of the United States for the first time. My parents were in Europe that year, and my mother thought our house in New York would be too lonely for me while they were gone. I liked the school because it had horses, and I liked to ride. I rode every morning before breakfast for an hour, and again in the late afternoon. I was taught jumping and form (English saddle, naturally).

I hated every single girl in that school except for Marcella Arias and her cousin Hilda Vallarino. They were both from Panama (Marcella was the daughter of the president) and they were so beautiful.

During the holidays, when everyone else went home for a week or more, I spent the day at the movies. There were two movie houses in Forest Glen. On one holiday, *Wuthering Heights* was playing at one theater and *Dark Victory* at the other.

I could not make up my mind which one to see first. I'd always admired the way Bette Davis strutted through her parts, so I decided to save that fun for the evening and spend the afternoon with Emily Brontë, watching *Wuthering Heights*. But the main event was Laurence Olivier.

I went into that movie theater and I never came out. I am still there. Nothing in my heart has changed since that day.

If you were a very young girl and you went to see *Wuthering Heights,* it became engraved between your shoulder blades. Olivier's strength, combined with his exotic weakness, helped create that deep, deep love that so few are capable of and so many want. He really was the one who gave us the scent of it, the wish for it, the deep desire for it, the feeling of not being able to live without it.

I saw love—passionate love—for the very first time in my life. It just about killed me. I cried and cried and stayed through three showings until the theater closed late that night. I came in the next morning and cried and cried and stayed and stayed. It happened the next day and the next after that and to this very day. It took hold of me in a way that nothing else I have ever seen or read has. It's a part of me now.

In that movie, I saw what I believed love to be. I know now that most people don't love that way; they don't die in each other's arms with beautiful music and tender kisses and unforgettable words. Our society is anti-love. Love is considered childish. Why else would people say, "What a man will do to one woman, he'll do to another"? Or "Love is for the birds." Or "Sexual love doesn't last." I have learned the whole litany of "life goes on" without it. I know it isn't true. I don't think it does go on. I think it stops. I don't think you survive anything. You simply continue.

But as a very young girl, never having even held a boy's hand, I knew everything I really wanted out of life—big, big love. To this day, that is how I think. I know I won't change, not only because I'm older—but because if life is not about passionate poetic celestial incredulous aching thrilling totally beautiful love, then life is not worth living.

Three on a Match

My mother was sixteen when she got pregnant with me and her mother threw her out of the house. I never knew who my father was.

She was very beautiful, and sometime later she met a man who fell in love with her and married her. After awhile she became pregnant again. The night they brought my half-sister home from the hospital, I was in a corner in a crib. The man pointed at me and said, "Now we can put that one up for adoption." My mother said, "Hold the baby just for a minute." She got her coat and her purse and lots of blankets, wrapped me up, carried me out, and never went back. She left my sister with her father, who immediately put her in a foster home.

My mother worked in a hat factory and boarded me out in foster homes. They were bleak and ugly places—impoverished Depression families doing the best they could, faceless people who scared me. I knew instinctively not to be any trouble. I waited for my mother to come to see me. I learned how not to be where I was.

The year I turned eight, I was taken to visit my mother. A man was sitting in a big armchair, waiting for her to dress. He was tall and distinguished-looking. When he saw me, he stood up to shake my hand. "You must be Carol," he said, and I said, "Yes."

The way the sun was slanting into the room made me think he was smiling at me. But I wasn't sure. In my hand was a little square beanbag I'd made myself, out of burlap and lima beans.

When I was positive the man was smiling, I threw the beanbag to him. He caught it and threw it back and I caught it. And that was the real beginning of my life.

He was Charles Marcus, the great aviation pioneer who with Vincent Bendix had formed the Bendix Corporation. My mother had met him on a blind date. I called him Daddy.

Going from foster homes to living with Daddy was like going to sleep in Dickensian squalor and awakening to sit in the queen's box on the opening day of the Ascot races near London. After my mother married Daddy, we lived in an eighteen-room duplex at 1107 Fifth Avenue, the same building in which Mrs. Marjorie Post Merriweather lived, as well as many other rich and famous people of the day. We had two chefs, butlers, and every rug was an Aubusson. Daddy bought my mother the most beautiful jewelry I have ever seen, including a pink diamond and a red diamond. She had a dressing room that was all mirrored and carpeted in gray silk. She had as many coats as other women had blouses, some of them ermine lined in sable.

Years later, my mother used to tell me that I was the only reason Daddy married her and he would say, "Of course. You made my life, darlin'."

I no longer had hour-by-hour fears, but I worried that this glittering world would suddenly vanish.

Three friends—Oona, Gloria, and I. We were really children when we met. We remained children. All those unlived years, those early years. We knew each other in the dark. We had an unbreakable tie: the desire and the need for the only thing we cared about—love. We gave that to each other. We didn't have fathers, each in a different way. We were orphans and our mothers were orphans. We spent our lives making up for it. It doesn't always work, but it worked sometimes. And when it did, we knew how to fly. We flew and we laughed and we lived and we cried. And now, one of us has died. The tie is still unbreakable.

It's the orphan bond: no father, no father, no father. Gloria grieves for her father. She believes she remembers him, believes she remembers the moment he died even though she was an infant. She always knew that her father loved her.

Oona did not think her father loved her. She knew her father and was fatherless. Eugene O'Neill, the famous playwright, left Agnes Boulton, Oona's beautiful mother, for Broadway actress Carlotta Monterey. Oona was no more than a baby when her father left, and she almost never saw him again.

I was the luckiest of the three.

· ·

Truman in the Transom

· ·

Truman Capote. I had never heard a name like Truman Capote. He was my age, about thirteen. He and another boy came every afternoon, after school, to visit my sister, Elinor. I told everyone that she was the older sister but she continued to sign her letters "Baby Sister." She moved in about two years after I did. It took Mother longer to confess to Daddy that she had another daughter. Elinor had been blessed, though. She loved the people who had taken her. She came home so pretty and plump. She looked like Snow White.

I would arrive home from school, go directly to my books and study frantically like a little robot, and then run a bath and change for dinner. I did the same thing every single day.

Once in a while I thought I heard a noise as I would come out naked after my bath. Then I would decide I hadn't really heard anything. But late one afternoon I definitely heard a noise, looked up, and saw a face framed by the transom window. It was a face with yellow hair and pink cheeks and the bluest blue blue eyes—a perfect Cupid.

I screamed. I didn't know whether to grab one of the covers off the bed or go back into the bath and get a terry robe to cover myself. And as I was deciding, making moves in both directions, he spoke.

"Stop! Stop!" he said. It really was an appeal, a strong one. "Please don't move. Please. You are *directly* from the moon. I have never seen anyone look like you. Your skin is made of moonbeams. You are lit from within. No, no. Don't move. Stay as you are exactly. Please, I ask you this with all my heart."

I was stunned, wavering between getting something to put on and the pleasure of hearing myself described as a moonbeam, so I managed with all my energy to do nothing.

"You must never forget that you do not belong here," he said quickly. "You can see it yourself if you look in the mirror. You are moonlight. No question about it. That's where you are from. I have watched you for so many afternoons, just to see moonbeams. You are directly from the moon. How did you ever get here?"

At which point, I said, "Wait. Please wait." I ran in and grabbed a robe and put it on and went to unlock the door. As I did, I saw there was a huge ladder going up to the transom and Truman was sitting on top of it. He came down slowly, staring at every part of me (although I was now covered) as I backed into the room.

"Oh, how could you?" he said. "How could you? You look so incredible without that robe."

"You hate my robe?"

"Oh, no. It's very beautiful. Even from a distance, one can see that it's all handmade and how it suits you with all those little rosebuds."

He came into the room directly to me. He looked at my face very closely and said, "Oh, yes, oh, my, you are the moon, you are. What skin. And those little baby rosy cheeks. I've never seen anything like it. You really should go out like that all the time."

I was obviously flattered, but beyond that, I was fascinated with the way he said the things he said. I had never heard anyone speak that way.

After that, Truman came to see me almost every day. We took walks and he'd say, "You are magic" and "It's like a valentine to be near you"—the sweetest things. Sometimes he'd come and sit with me for the evening. We'd put the radio on and dance to the Hit Parade. He was a terrific dancer. I was sure of that although I hadn't danced with anyone else before.

"Have you ever been in love?" he asked one night. "Have you ever kissed a boy?"

"No," I said. "But I'd like to kiss you."

"Let's kiss," he said. And, very innocently, we did.

That was the beginning of what was to be a deep and lasting friendship. As the years passed, he never forgot to greet me with "Yes, sweetness, you're still from the moon."

Our friendship lasted all his life. I told him all my secrets. He told me some of his.

· ·

A Visit to the Pharmacist

· ·

I didn't get my period until I had just turned fourteen. Before that, it seemed that all the girls at Dalton, where I went to school, were getting their periods and talking about it. I didn't want to be left out. It was called "the Curse."

"Oh, yes," I would say, "I got my period," about which I knew nothing.

One Saturday afternoon, I saw three drops of blood on my panties. I was so thrilled. I can't tell you how happy and relieved I was. That surely had to be the Curse. That had to be what they were all talking about.

I was so excited. I jumped into the bathtub. I didn't know exactly where the blood was coming from. After the bath, I got all dressed up for the event of buying Kotex at the drugstore—the same one I'd been going to for many years.

I proudly proclaimed that I needed ten boxes of Kotex.

The pharmacist smiled at me.

"Here, you'll need this too," he said. And he gave me a belt, which I hadn't even thought of. "So you finally grew up. We were wondering when you would."

"Oh, I've had it for forever," I almost started to say to him, but I took a look and realized he was too smart for that.

"Look," he said, "I think we'll deliver these to your apartment. You can't walk on the street with ten boxes of Kotex."

"Oh, but I need one immediately."

So I took one box and the crazy belt home, and went to the loo to see if anything more had happened. And I got a little nervous because it seemed that nothing had.

I followed the instructions that came with the belt and now I was ready to be a woman. I couldn't call up anyone to tell them what had happened because I had told everyone I had gotten "it" long before. But I was truly delighted.

The three little spots grew and I actually did have it for about three days, possibly four. Suddenly, it stopped. I couldn't understand it. I didn't know what had happened. No one had ever told me that once you got it, you didn't have it all the time. I thought maybe I had some very rare exotic disease and no one must know. So I continued shopping at the drugstore.

"Ten more boxes, please," I'd say every five or six days.

"Are you sure you need this many?" the pharmacist said.

"Oh, yes, and six more belts."

This went on for about two months. (After the first month, the blood came back and I was so happy because I thought I was normal, but then it went away again after a few days.)

One day, I went into the drugstore looking for perfume and the pharmacist said, "Please excuse me for this, but I've known you since you were a little girl and I have to ask you something."

"Is there anything wrong?" I said.

"I don't know. That's why I want to talk to you. I want you to be honest with me."

"That's a terrible thing to say."

"Well, you know what I mean. Have you had your period all the time for these past two months?"

I was trying to think of some wonderful lie to tell him when he continued on.

"Because, you see, you are only supposed to get it once a month or let's say, every twenty-eight days for three or four days. Now if you have been bleeding for all this time, you must see a doctor immediately because it is not normal."

"Tell me that thing about twenty-eight days again."

And then he explained what he meant. He also took out a little book from another kind of Kotex.

"Doesn't your mother tell you anything?"

"My mother is extremely modest about all physical things and she does not like to have discussions about that kind of thing."

It was then that I realized there might be other things I didn't know, so I went about the business of catching up.

. . . .

We Didn't Know We Were Girls

. . . .

Gloria and I met at a party she gave at her aunt's house in Westbury, Long Island. She went to boarding school at Miss Wheeler's in Rhode Island. She was more sophisticated than Oona and I were. When I saw her I was reminded of the stories I loved to read in the Red and Blue fairy tale books. She looked just like the Snow Queen, with "lips as red as blood, skin as white as snow, hair as black as ebony." It seemed that Vanderbilt was a big word in America. I don't think Gloria had any friends either. She had been the victim of a famous custody battle between her mother and her aunt. I sensed the same thing I did about Oona, I felt that sadness; we became friends. She was lovely, tenderhearted, and sweet. She was away most of the time but we would try to catch up on the telephone. Still, I always missed her.

Oona and I went to different schools—she to Brearley, I to Dalton. We met because our mothers had signed us up for activities considered proper for those our age, ridiculous little junior proms given for embarrassed young people twelve, thirteen, and fourteen years old. We were wallflowers. When we went home we would cry and lose ourselves in our books. We met after school each day on a Park Avenue corner and we would walk down to Fifty-fifth Street, where we were living at that time (at 420 Park Avenue). Oona's mother had an apartment in Greenwich Village, but she said it was all right for Oona to spend much of her time with me. We began to live together for quite a long time in my family's apartment.

Both Oona and I were extremely academic, with our noses in

books. We did our homework together and would spend hours deliberating various theories about writers and writing. If I was doing a paper on T. S. Eliot she'd say, "You're wasting your time with him. He's an anti-Semite." Then there was Hemingway with "the fake hair on his chest." I did not read Saroyan because I thought he was very boring. I also thought he was dead.

Oona and I were not in the least competitive. We both wanted to know everything the other knew and arrive at, perhaps, some conclusion that had never been arrived at before. We loved learning things and speculating on the state of the world as we were finding out about it. Oona was the most brilliant person I've ever known in all my life. She had a mind like a lime crystal, clear as a bell, very level-headed about the practicalities of life. She was light about things; she didn't kill you with the truth. Oona wouldn't buy anything she didn't look well in just because it was in style. She was very much her own person always.

That Christmas, Oona and I went to a dance. Those boys, with their acne and their sweaty palms and embarrassing shyness, tried to attract girls by ignoring them. But this time we went with a plan. It was mostly Oona's idea. We went to Klein's (it was the cheapest place to buy dresses in New York City). Oona picked out identical dresses. One in white tulle and one in black tulle. They were strapless and for us that was very daring. We bought the sexiest, trashiest lingerie that we could find. We thought we were the ultimate in sophistication.

We became known at all the cosmetic counters of all the department stores in New York. Instead of studying, we spent the afternoons in drugstores, having sodas, buying face cream and movie magazines and wondering whether the boys would fall in love with us.

We did each other's hair in styles we saw in those magazines. We bought lots of perfume and told each other how supremely beautiful we were. Every day. In fact, we decided we were much more beautiful than brilliant. We were totally taken with ourselves, our newly discovered looks, our clothes, our various scents, our silk stockings and silk lingerie. We tried to redesign ourselves to look like Gloria. We even darkened our eyebrows.

We would practice ways to look over a boy's shoulder when we were dancing with him. Oona and I would do this in front of a mirror, taking turns at playing the boy. We watched ourselves and realized how effective we were when we dropped our eyelids. We learned how to flirt in front of the mirror by simply ignoring the person we were flirting with.

The night of the dance we walked into the ballroom hand in hand and all of our dreams came true. The boys were falling all over themselves trying to get in at least a minute of dancing before another boy cut in. We had planned to laugh and flirt and look slightly bored as we twirled and twirled; it all came so naturally. We thought, This is what we were made for. The girls at school suddenly wanted to be our friends because we had become the belles of the ball. From that moment on we never relinquished our positions.

That June, we graduated from high school. Despite our recent self-infatuation, both Dalton and Brearley had to recognize the academic records we had accumulated. We had our pick of colleges, but more education was the furthest thing from our minds. We wanted to have a good time, all the time—every day, every night. We no longer knew anything of sadness or loneliness. All the boys fell in love with us. We slept late and took hours to dress and went out all night.

That September I turned fifteen.

. . . .

The Eve of the War

. . . .

There was a swirling split second on the eve of the war that summer, before December 7, 1941. There was never a New York like that. Everything was heightened—fears, joys, dreams. Although it was not said, it was understood by most people that we were going to be part of the war. The parties got bigger and more frantic. There were tea dances in the hotels.

I swirled through the black velvet sky filled with diamond stars, all through the night, night after night. There were big, big coming-out parties, held either at the Waldorf or the St. Regis or any of the best ballrooms in New York. Between dancing and flirting, we ate caviar in those beautiful rooms that were made up to suit the fancies of the girls who were coming out. One girl had the whole room done in white doves—a symbol of peace. Another girl had a rose garden, which all in all turned out to be a better choice than the one who had a room of gardenias. That girl's mother fainted when the scent became too much for her. It was the best part of the evening for her daughter.

While Gloria had gone out to California to spend the summer, Oona and I actually wore out our dancing shoes. Each night we had to choose between invitations.

Our dresses were made to look like flower petals and stars. Strapless tulle evening dresses and long white gloves. And hair down to the shoulders like Veronica Lake's, a movie star of the day.

And the nights went on longer as the war was drawing closer. In fact, my mother planned my own coming-out party, with the Cinderella Ball as its theme. It had been scheduled for late December, but it was immediately canceled, as were all the others, on December 7.

Gloria's first beau was Geoffrey Jones. In November of 1941, he was a senior at Princeton. His class was putting on the world premiere of a new play by William Saroyan called *Jim Dandy*. They needed two girls, and Geoff knew I wanted to be an actress, so I ended up with a part that had only one line: "No talking in the public library." But I had to say it many, many times. The boys in the audience hooted and howled when they saw a girl onstage. "I think you're going to make it as an actress," Geoff said. "They love you." I was never happier.

There was another line in the play that attached me to Saroyan to this day. "He knew the truth and was looking for something better." I waited every night to hear it. That line for me, to this day, represented what I feel about truth.

His Manly Grace

One late October afternoon in 1941, Gloria telephoned me from California, where she had gone to spend the summer with her mother, who was thrilled to have some time with her daughter. Gloria had blossomed into a beautiful, luminescent young girl and she needed a mother. And she wanted her very own man to love. Gloria told me that she had met the man of her dreams and that they were going to get married in December. She told me how much it would mean to her if I would come out to be one of her bridesmaids.

I said, "How wonderful. Who is he? Tell me everything. My God, how exciting! I want to know everything."

She told me his name was Pat di Cicco and that he worked for Howard Hughes. I had heard his name before. Gloria told me he was a very handsome, romantic man. I wondered what had happened to Howard Hughes. She had been dating him and she thought he was "divine."

But one night she stood him up to go out with Pat di Cicco and that was the end of Mr. Hughes, she said. She was very young. We talked for only a few minutes because she was dressing for one of life's big evenings where she was going to announce her engagement to Pat di Cicco.

As it turned out, I flew to California with Big Gloria, Gloria's mother, and her twin sister, Thelma Lady Furness, who'd been a big pal of the Prince of Wales, but had asked Wallis Simpson to look after him when she left London for New York to help Big Gloria in the custody case. Gloria always described her mother as very passive, and she was, but she was passive in a lovely way. She was beautiful and sweet. She loved me to try on her clothes. I was very, very frivolous. All I wondered about was what to wear. It was wonderful not to have any depth or sensitivity, just to go with the wind and be wafted through life and not be fearful.

When I woke up in Big Gloria's house in Beverly Hills, I got up to look around. I looked out onto the front lawn and across the street. I looked at the gardens. The grass was the wrong color green.

I'd lived in New York and Maryland and taken vacation trips to New England and England, so I was used to that first-spring-blade-of-grass-color green which is so fresh-looking and signals the coming of all kinds of wonders—roses, white lilacs, peonies, all the beautiful flowers. It meant holidays to me, times that are in a sense put in parentheses and taken out of your life—special kinds of time.

So I couldn't help but notice how strange the color green looked in Beverly Hills. It didn't look fresh and new. It had a lot of yellow and brown in it. It wasn't grass at all—it looked like an old rug. It was my first impression and it has never left me. I have never gotten used to it. When I complained about it, I was asked a few times what I meant by the wrong color green. Was I making a comment on the money made out here? I was not. There is no wrong color money.

The wedding was on December 28, 1941, in Santa Barbara. There was a whole series of parties, and one's clothes had to be perfect for each event. The ushers were all the handsomest men in Hollywood, actors and very famous people. They were Pat di Cicco's friends. My escort for all the wedding festivities was Errol Flynn, at his swashbuckling peak, so cavalier. I had a big crush on him. I felt I had definitely stopped being a little girl and I wanted to be a woman. I wanted to fall in love. I had been told that I was beautiful and that's what counted in this privileged world. I was delighted to be so popular, knowing Gloria would be proud of me. But to be truthful about Gloria, she would have been proud of me anyway. I wanted to do everything Gloria did, no matter what. Whatever she did was the okay thing to do.

Gloria was a miraculously beautiful bride. I have never seen anybody look like that, so filled with hope and love and pleasure and happiness. She came to that occasion, the most beautiful moment in her life, the best. She was a perfect heroine.

I caught the bridal bouquet and thought it really meant something. I believed in everything, anything you can grab out of the air to believe in. Santa Claus. The Easter bunny. The bluebirds of happiness. I felt I had been born and died and woke up in a situation of great good fortune. I didn't want to waste it. I was just absolutely ready to live.

After the wedding, my mother joined me to spend time in Los Angeles. We took a big terraced apartment at the Sunset Towers in a huge penthouse that was built into a hill.

My mother's best friend was Lee Wylie, a very good singer of the popular songs of that day. One night Mother and Lee told me they were going to go out to dinner with Artie Shaw. When I heard the name, I nearly fainted. In those days bandleaders were such big heroes, you have no idea.

He came to pick them up and he said, "Oh, who are you?"

"I'm her daughter."

"What are you doing in California?"

"I am going to be a good actress, or a star."

"Have you ever acted?"

"Yes, I just finished a play before I came out here: *Jim Dandy* by William Saroyan."

"He's my best friend. Did you know he's out here now?"

"William Saroyan?"

"Yes."

"Not dead?"

"Not dead. Definitely not dead."

He told me what a terrific person Bill was and how he'd be very interested in meeting me. Artie himself began calling me to have dinner, but for so early in the evening that I fully expected the next time we'd have dinner would be at 3:00 in the afternoon. I'd always ask him, "Who's your real date tonight?" I knew he just considered me a child.

About a week later, I was out with some people at the Players

Club, a Hollywood restaurant. Artie came over to our table and said, "I'm with Bill over there in the corner. I just told him all about you; why don't you come over and say hello?"

I turned to my friends and said, "I'm going over to meet William Saroyan. Did you know he's still living?" I was very happy, I felt I was really entering the adult world I so longed to get to. It was February 20, Gloria's birthday. I didn't know I was about to fall in love with William Saroyan, and that from that moment on, he would become my life.

Suddenly, there he was. He stood up; he looked me right in the eye. He was intense-looking, romantic, with black hair and burning black eyes. He was the best thing I had ever seen: brooding, poetic, passionate—very passionate. Was there a whisper of something back at that movie theater in Forest Glen, Maryland? He was like that man, an echo, a haunting whisper of my first scent of love. I kept thinking—is he?—maybe?

"Oh, Artie," I said, "you didn't tell me he was so handsome." That endeared me to Saroyan no end. He wore very simple, expensive clothes—gray flannel suits and black turtleneck sweaters. He looked like a gangster, sinister and dark. Oooh, I thought. He's rotten. It's wonderful.

Not only that, he was old. That was the most glamorous thing of all. He didn't have acne or sweaty palms. He was thirty-three years old. I was sixteen. His hand was cool when we were introduced, and he said, "You look like vanilla ice cream and pink rose petals. I heard your performance was wonderful. What did you think of the play?"

"It's the most beautiful play I've ever seen in my life," I said, because somehow, instinctively, I knew that was the only thing one could possibly say to him.

The minute I met Bill, I knew that my life would never be the same again, and he later told me that he, too, knew the same about his. I've heard about these things happening. I've heard that they never happen. But I know that they do and it did.

He didn't sit down again. He took me by the hand and led me out of the restaurant right then. I hoped Artie would be glad. Bill had just bought a car, a sky-blue Cadillac convertible with white leather seats, and we drove around. He was not the gentleman

Artie was. He wanted to go to bed. I was willing. I went to his room, but I didn't know what to do. He knew I was scared, and he said, "You're just a kid. Come on, let's go. I'll take you out to lunch tomorrow."

"Are you involved with someone?" I asked.

"Yes," he said. "You." This, in retrospect, turned out to be one of the nicer moments I ever had with him.

I loved him the next day and the day after and the day after that. I loved his looks, like velvet, and his very fresh skin. I loved the scent of him, but more than anything, I loved his words. Words of love and poetry—unforgettable words said with limpid black eyes and at times a boyish countenance. I'd never heard anyone— except Truman—use words in that way, and they became engraved in my bone marrow for the rest of my life.

He was quick to laugh—at himself, at anything. He loved to laugh. I had the feeling, even then, that he had not laughed a lot in his life.

After about a month, I went back to New York with my mother. I didn't think I'd ever hear from Bill again. He really needed a girl who he could sleep with and I was too scared to be that girl. One night, when I was out dancing at the Stork Club a waiter said, "There's a call for you." A voice said, "Hi" and I said, "Bill! Where are you?" He said, "I'm in the Cub Room," which was the room next door, not for people who were going to dance. I told whoever I was with that the call was from my mother and I had to go home. Instead I went and waited in the lobby. He came out and we went to Toots Shor's, a very different kind of place, filled with sportswriters. He still looked like a gangster and I still found him thrilling.

A few days later I was walking home from the library thinking about what to wear that night, a date I had made before Bill came to New York. When I reached our apartment on Fifty-fifth and Park, there standing in the doorway waiting for me was Saroyan, along with another man. I thought I would die. We had no date. I was in bobby socks and a raincoat and a plain skirt and a sweater with my string of pearls. I didn't have a drop of makeup on.

Oh, my God, I thought. I had lied to him about my age, making myself two years older, but in my real clothes I looked even younger than I was. I didn't know enough to know that that would enchant him. I thought that men wanted to see a sophisticated Joan Crawford all in white in a big-shouldered Adrian evening dress. But Bill really fell in love with me. He never did see me old. There's a certain pleasure for me in that, I don't know why. But at that moment, there was no pleasure in his seeing me so young.

"Hiya, kid," he said. He never called me anything but kid. "I want you to meet George Jean Nathan." He turned to a man standing beside him who was old and dazzling.

"How nice to meet you," I said. I knew he was the most famous drama critic. Trying to hold my own, I said, "Would you like to come up and have a drink?"

"You mean a mint julep," Bill said, alluding to one of our first dates. When asked by a waiter what I would like to drink, I said the only drink I had ever heard of, a mint julep. Bill did a very sweet thing—he ordered one too. He did rise to certain occasions.

"Oh no," I said to Bill and George Jean Nathan. "Let's have Cokes—I mean, champagne."

And so up they came.

Daddy was already home, resting and listening to Mozart's Twenty-seventh Piano Concerto. He came into the living room to see what I had wrought, and was rather amazed that I was making a fuss about two old men, as he later described them.

"Actually, Carol," Bill said, "we've come here to invite you to have dinner with us at 21."

"Oh, how wonderful. I would love it. But I will need time to dress."

"If you go as you look now, you will never be forgotten," George Jean Nathan said. He loved women who looked like schoolgirls or nuns.

"Yes, but somehow I would just feel terrible that way. I'll go in and rush. Please make yourselves at home."

Which I suppose wasn't the easiest thing for them to do with Daddy looking them over as if through a microscope. He was wondering where I had found these old people, because George Jean Nathan was easily old enough to have been Bill's father. But Daddy had great manners, and I knew he wouldn't be impolite.

Upstairs, I raided my mother's closet and put on tons of makeup.

When I came down, they seemed rather startled. Except for Daddy, who looked amused. We went off to 21, and I conveniently tried to forget the young man I'd just stood up to go out with Bill.

As the years went by, I often thought of that young man. And as they really went by, I thought, How could I have done that? I thought to myself, how unfeeling, how untender, how selfish.

I think the reason I've always remembered that night is not just because of what I did, but because of the kind of person I did it to—a young, sensitive, introverted boy. It's funny, but it still makes me sad. When that happened, I was sixteen years old. Even so, I knew better. Even so, I didn't care. But that is so long ago and long ago is long ago.

And as long ago as long ago is, there's still that tinge of regret. Because I'll always remember the way he'd kissed me once before, so quickly, so shyly.

Looking back, I realize I was never as passive as I seemed to be. I knew what I wanted. I always feel that my actual personality counterpoints that sudden, unexpected kiss on the mouth.

Three Little Pieces

On one of my first dates with Bill in New York, he took me to a party that was being given by a very famous and very good poet from the Philippine Islands whose name I cannot remember. It was in the middle of the New York City summer and it was between 5:00 and 8:00, so people were dropping in and out. We got there around 7:00. It was still very light outside and somewhat cooled off from the very hot afternoon it had been. As we arrived (the front door to the apartment was open—I guess to try to keep it a little cooler), I looked directly into the apartment. A long, long hallway opened up into a room, and there, straight ahead of us, was a love seat with three people sitting on it.

On one side of the love seat was a huge woman, in a big black silk dress, with her arms around the side and top of the love seat. On the other side, looking toward and up to the lady that looked like a great big black bat, was a tiny, bony, wrinkled, birdlike woman whose head was covered in a turban with lots of diamond pins all over it. She talked to the big black bat, using her long, bony fingers. In the center sat a very pretty woman in a beautiful garden-party dress, wearing a summer hat made of lace and flowers and ribbons. The colors of the hat matched her dress. What I loved most was that she was wearing darling little silk shoes of the same sky blue as the dress. She had snow-white hair, dreamy blue eyes, and pink cheeks, and she wore a touch of pink lipstick. She would have been a sight anywhere—but here, between a big black bat and a tiny, bony bird turbaned with diamond pins, the beauty of this garden flower was somewhat overpowered.

As we walked into the apartment and past this trio to greet the host, the big black bat boomed out in a very upper-class English accent, "Saroyan, come over here."

"Yes, Saroyan," peeped the little ebony bird. "Do, do come over here. Bring that little beauty over here to see us."

The garden flower looked at us and smiled and made a gesture as if to say, "Please do come and sit with us."

Bill introduced me to the host, then took me directly to meet the three ladies. The big black bat was Edith Sitwell, an English writer later made Dame of the British empire. The tiny, bony bird was the Baroness Karen Blixen, who wrote under the name Isak Dinesen. The flower in the middle was Marianne Moore. In Bill's words, "one of our best poets." He told me she wrote about baseball.

After the introductions, Bill motioned for me to come with him and meet all the other people.

"No, Saroyan," Edith Sitwell said. "Go and mingle yourself. Leave the little girl. What are you doing with such a young little girl? What's the matter with you? Just leave her here."

He looked at her and laughed.

"It's all right," he said. "I'm going to marry her."

"What makes you think that's all right?" Edith Sitwell said.

And off he went.

I sat on the floor looking up at the three ladies, who were making little curls with my hair and playing with my dress and shoes and looking into my purse.

They were fascinated by me. I didn't really know why.

"What are you doing with that old man?" Dame Edith said. "You are just a little girl."

"Not at all. We're getting married. And I'm in love with him."

Karen Blixen's long, bony fingers went ruffling through the air.

"Oh, no, no, no," she said. "No, no, no, oh, darling, no, please don't say that again. Don't even think about marriage. Don't even think about it, love. Those aren't things you should think about. Have you finished school?"

"Yes."

"Go on to even higher education," she said. "Do anything but marry. Sleep with someone else. Sleep with someone wonderful."

"He is wonderful and I love him."

At which point Marianne Moore said, "Oh, my poor darling. Oh, you poor baby. You're in love? It's the most terrible thing I've ever heard. Oh, darling."

"Oh, dear," Karen Blixen said. "It's a total tragedy."

"No, no," Edith Sitwell said. "You just come to England with me. We're leaving tomorrow. We live in a great castle and you can have your own apartment in it and you simply must meet more people before you decide what you are going to do. You can live with us forever, and then after you've met some men, you can make a true decision."

"Oh," I said. "But I've been out with boys before. I've been out with many boys. I've had lots of beaus."

"Of course you have," said Marianne Moore. "But you do know how different it is to have a beau than it is to get married? They're very different things. And they deserve some thought. I have a feeling that you have not thought about these things enough. Do you think I'm right?"

"Yes," I said. "I haven't given it a lot of thought, but it's because I haven't wanted to be with anyone else. I love to be with him."

"Why, dear?" asked the big black bat. "Does he tell you pretty things?"

"Of course he tells her very beautiful things," said the bony bird.

"Very compelling, very appealing, very poetic things. Can you imagine the effect this has on this child? She probably never heard such things before."

"But what is he doing with such a little girl?" asked the flower in the middle.

The big black bat said, "Take a look at her and answer your own question, my dear."

"Oh, I see."

The three of them continued to ask me many questions, and I answered them as well as I could. I tried to be unusual, never realizing that it was my usualness that they found so unusual.

Finally, Bill was ready to leave.

"You know, you haven't met all the people here," he said.

"I know, but I've had a wonderful time and I've been invited to England."

"You've also been invited to be my wife."

At which point the big black bat grunted and said, "Good God, Saroyan, stop that."

"Oh, how dreadful," said the bony bird.

"There's no way of telling," said the flower in the middle.

I kissed all three good-bye. As I bent over to them, still seated on the love seat, each surreptitiously handed me a tiny piece of paper.

During the rest of the evening, I forgot about the three pieces of paper but when I got home very late that night and opened my purse for my key, I saw them. And I read them. They had each written out their full names, addresses, and telephone numbers. And each had written a little note, just a few words saying, "You can come and stay with me always. You don't have to stay with him." They thought I could only possibly be with Bill because I was a waif with no place to go.

They were really darling, totally diverse, each one so special, each one so proper. And they seemed to know things about Saroyan that I did not.

I saw a lot of Karen Blixen many years later, after being twice married and twice divorced from Bill. She remembered our first meeting very clearly and said a very sweet thing to me: "Why Carol, you didn't grow up."

And she, too, had not changed, I'm sorry to say, because she looked so old and sick when I first met her and she still did.

She told me she was dying—that the years since I had met her had brought her only grief. But she knew the one thing that made life worth living was love.

"I knew it the last time I saw you and I know it now. Carol, dear, you are successful at love. It's very important to remain that way because you need it even more when you get older."

I told her all about Walter Matthau and how much I loved him and how it didn't matter to me that he was married.

"If he loves you," she said, "it will matter to him." And she was right.

I told her all about the tough years with Bill. She said that's what she and Edith Sitwell and Marianne Moore were trying to convey the day I met them. They were trying to tell me that there was no way he could ever be happy—or that I could ever be happy, knowing he could never be.

She's one of the few people I have ever met who was utterly memorable.

She was extremely delicate but she had great physical strength. One afternoon I was waiting for the superintendent to come and help me move a piano. I had left Bill and was living with the children on East Ninety-third Street. Karen was coming to spend the afternoon with me. I was proud of my new apartment. I thought I'd made it very pretty. I did it the way I wanted to because I wasn't married, with the money I made from modeling, the theater, and some magazine writing for *Collier's*.

As she came in, I took her coat and hat and she looked around.

"Whatever is the piano doing *there*, darling?"

"Isn't it awful? I've been trying to move it over to that corner all day and I can't get it to budge."

"Of course not. It will take two of us."

"Oh, no, you mustn't even think of it. The superintendent will be coming at any moment."

"No, let's not even think about him. You'll have to give him a big tip and he'll ruin our afternoon." By now she had rolled up her sleeves, so to speak.

"We want the piano here," she said, "that is correct, yes?"

"Yes."

And pushing it with her was a piece of cake. I don't know whether it was because we were at opposite ends or because she was so strong. I have never quite figured it out.

She always wore a turban. I never saw her without it. She varied the pins—diamonds, rubies, emeralds, all incredibly beautiful, and she always wore at least five or six of them.

In contrast, her skin looked moldy—like an old moat near a castle. Crusty. Even though she wore makeup, that very sallow color could never be covered. She wore tons of lipstick and tons of eye makeup, but you still saw a rather terrible-looking complexion.

Yet when I would go to kiss her hello or good-bye, it was like falling into a flower garden. She was so fragrant. Her scent was soap and water and white lilacs and lilies of the valley. Fresh and clean. It was incredible. She was the essence of cleanliness. It was such a delicate scent that you had to be very close to her to be aware of it.

She always had a fresh white lace handkerchief with her. Her clothes looked as though they'd all come from Paris. She usually wore black silk. And she wore beautiful coats—cloth coats. Some were lined with sable and others fur.

She was extremely elegant in both manner and dress. Despite this, at first glance her clothes simply seemed to hang much too loosely on her.

She always had such an elegant way of thinking.

"You know," I once said. "I'm very flattered, Karen, that you would want to come and visit me. I'm probably the poorest person you know." I was, at that time.

"Oh, no, dear. I like to hear you laugh. I like to look at you. Life does things to people's faces. You know, people finally show up on their own faces. And as I look around your little apartment, so incredibly pretty but more than that, so clean—I know who cleaned it. I know by your hands."

"Oh, isn't that awful? The arthritis is so awful."

"Yes. No one knows better than I."

And of course, the first thing you saw when you saw her were her hands, so riddled with arthritis. I had it, too. It had started when I was only twenty-six.

"Wasn't Marianne delicious-looking?" she said to me later that day, referring to Marianne Moore.

"Oh, yes, she was like a dream."

"She was indeed. And do you know that she was really an old maid? She never slept with a man."

"No, I don't believe that. How can you believe that?"

"I do. I believe it. I don't know why. But I do. It's most believable."

During her last stay in New York, Karen saw a great deal of Truman, who had helped plan her trip. And Gloria really went out of her way to show her a good time. She gave luncheons with fascinating people. And if Karen displayed any casual interest when someone's name was mentioned, Gloria would invite that person to the next luncheon. Karen was really very thrilled by that and thought it was incredibly sweet of Gloria, which it was.

One day, at a little tea, Karen said outright, "I would rather meet Marilyn Monroe than anyone else in the world."

"And so you shall," Gloria said.

Gloria arranged a luncheon and Marilyn, of course, came. I think Gloria filled her in about the Baroness Blixen—Karen—Isak Dinesen. Marilyn was actually smart, but did not seem to register this information. I don't know why, exactly, but she didn't.

Still, she arrived at the luncheon and was absolutely charming and the whole thing went off rather well.

Later that day, Truman Capote called me. Since he had taken Karen home, I asked him what she had thought of Marilyn.

"Do you really want to know?" he asked.

"Yes, I do."

" 'Well,' she said, 'she's a sweet little thing, isn't she? Of course, she didn't have much to say, but I suppose she's shy, just as we all are. But there's something about her that seems to be counterfeit.' "

Truman went on to say he couldn't stop laughing and had said, "Karen, you didn't expect her to be the way she is in the movies?"

"Oh," Karen had said. "Of course not. Actually, the whole thing was wonderful. She was nice, the luncheon was nice, and Gloria as always was divine. But my dear, I'm sorry. I'm so tired. I must go to sleep for a while. I can't talk anymore."

So Truman had seen her to her door and hadn't gone in to talk a bit as he usually did.

When he told me this, he couldn't stop laughing.

"You know," he said, "I love Karen. And you know, more than anything else, I love that kind of naivete she has. She thought that if she could meet Marilyn Monroe, that that was absolutely the cat's ass. Can you imagine being so naive? And yet, think how sweet that is."

"That's what I can't help liking about her. She's like a young girl. She puts her brilliance away and goes out and meets people. Then, when she knows she is alone, allows herself her self again."

That day was the last time I actually saw Karen. She, like Edith Sitwell and Marianne Moore, became faded memories.

It seems strange that everyone I'm writing about was very famous. I wonder about it, too. Didn't I ever find anyone interesting who was not famous? Actually, no, I didn't.

· ·

Starry-eyed

· ·

Bill and I went out together every night. He was in New York to produce two one-act plays: *Across the Board on Tomorrow Morning* and *Talking to You*. I went to all sorts of places and met all kinds of people. Quite often we would go out during the day and have a picnic in the park or go to one of the beaches. And one night in Bill's room at the Hampshire House, after all the nights, we made it, and I felt that for him it was great in bed and I knew that was a big thing for him.

I felt uneasily close to him. I actually began to know him a little, though in those early days I didn't suspect his darker side. He was fascinating. I thought he loved me. He knew how to say it—and it's a wonderful feeling to be loved by someone who knows how to tell it to you. He spoke of his past, his family's poverty, and the orphanage he had been in for a little while after his father died. He spoke of growing up Armenian in Fresno, California, and the terrible objections his immigrant family had to his being a writer, and how he knew, even before he'd become famous for his story "The Daring Young Man on the Flying Trapeze" and won the Pulitzer Prize for his play *The Time of Your Life,* that he could not possibly spend his life doing anything else. He knew it was something he could do brilliantly if he set his mind to it, and he worked at it every day of his life for as long as I knew him.

Bill also made very clear what he felt about women—total distrust. It was almost as if he'd been brought up to hate them.

"Why do you feel like that?" I asked.

"It's the nature of the beast."

I must have looked unhappy. He started to laugh and said, "I don't mean you. You're just a little girl. Of course, I don't mean you. Would I be with you night and day if I thought that about you?"

I laughed and said, "Yes, you would," and I kissed him and kissed him.

We always had a very good time together, and I must say that even during the two disastrous marriages and the two divine divorces, we had fun, too. On a superficial, social level, I don't think there was a more charming man. He was funny, articulate, and you could never guess what he was going to say next. One to one, hour to hour, minute to minute—walking on the street holding hands, going to the movies, going to the theater, going out to dinner, going to parties, meeting his friends (I hid all of mine because they were too young)—there was something wonderful about just being together. He really talked to me and I was really able to talk to him—of people, the world. I learned from him. That is what we had that summer, but soon the war would change everything in the world, especially Bill.

In the early fall of 1942, Bill was drafted. When his sister telephoned to tell him of the notice, his teeth were clenched, and from then on they stayed clenched in what I finally realized was rage. How could they take the world's finest artist and do this to him? The phenomenal success that he'd had as a young writer—the great reviews and the money he'd made from the productions of his plays—had not only made him one of the richest of writers, it had destroyed his feeling for the world and its people. He thought he was immune to everyday life. He just couldn't take the idea of any authority imposed on him and he thought the entire war was an attempt to keep him miserable. He couldn't see beyond his name, "William Saroyan." He saw himself as the artist, the poet, the recipient of a Pulitzer Prize, not a soldier or a politician. "Let *them* go to war," he said. "I don't want to go to war, I don't want to kill anybody." I had never seen a rage like it before, and it was never to leave him. And somehow he made me feel it was my fault.

"Bill," I said, "the war will not go on forever. It will be over soon. Things will be different and you will come back to who and what you are and no one will tell you what or who to be."

"I will never be the same," he said. And he wasn't. He never got over the war. It ruined his life.

All I could think about was that he would be gone. It had only been a few weeks before that we had finally really slept together, and that was all I had thought about since. Sleeping with him meant I had to marry him, because in those days no one nice would ever marry you if you weren't a virgin. I felt I had done something that was terribly wrong, and yet feeling as I did about him, how wrong could it be?

By this time, I was so in love with him that I couldn't speak. I'd do things like poking my fingers in the holes of the telephone dial, spelling out his name. I thought if I did that sixteen times it would ring. I thought of taking a walk and maybe meeting him on the street, but I was afraid to leave the telephone. One of the things he loved about me was that I was so quiet. One of the reasons I was so quiet was that I couldn't think of anything good enough to say to this great man I had once thought was dead.

On his last day in New York, we spent the day in bed together at his suite in the Hampshire House. He was leaving by car the next morning for California and his army induction.

We said good-bye at about 4:00 in the morning and I rang for the elevator. It came, but I decided not to get into it. I sat on a little bench in the foyer and began to cry. I couldn't stop—all the grief I had ever known welled up in me at that moment.

I don't know how long I was there, but suddenly his door opened. I was shocked. He was shocked to see me crying like that. Neither of us could stand it. We embraced, and he said, "I love you."

I went home and cried for hours. I didn't think that Bill realized what sleeping together meant in the world I lived in, and I just didn't want to tell him and make things more difficult than they seemed to be. I was sure he wanted to marry me because of what we did.

There it was—love. You can't see it, you can't touch it, but it permeates every cell of your being, no matter what the consequences.

Worst of all, it was first love. There's no love like that. I don't wish it on a soul. I don't hate anyone enough.

· ·

Still Starry-eyed

· ·

The day Bill left to drive to basic training in Sacramento, California, the pain of knowing he was going, going, gone was more than I could bear. I didn't want to do anything or see anybody or know anything. I just knew that I loved him and I had had an affair with him—and I felt as though my heart would break.

Bill telephoned that night from Pittsburgh and said he had been thinking of me every minute of the drive. "Kid, I'm not going to make it without you," he said. "I love you. We were made for each other. I'm an old guy and going into the army, I thought I ought to leave you alone, but I see my only chance is you. I want to talk to your mother and see if she'll send you out to meet my family so you and I can get married. There's no one like you."

I began to breathe again. I put my mother on the line and he knew just what to say to her. My mother was very impressed with fame.

"Oh," she said, "you want your family to pass judgment?"

"Of course not. I don't care what they think of her, but I think it's a nice gesture."

My mother paused and said, "Well, Bill, if you're really that serious about Carol—"

"Has anyone not been serious about Carol?" He was wonderful about me to her.

"My God, my daughter is such a femme fatale!"

"Oh, she is. She could get into a lot of trouble. She should get married."

My mother promised to talk it over with Daddy. "Of course," she said to me, "I'd have to send a chaperone with you."

"Mother," I said, "I have already slept with Bill. Please don't tell Daddy." Her face went blank. I think she was counting his money. Whatever she may have been thinking, the news that we slept together made the future airtight. Not only did I have her consent, I suspected she'd kill me if I didn't marry him. But she still wanted someone to go with me, however, and Oona agreed to go.

It seemed like the whole army was on our train. Oona and I had our own compartment, but whenever we tried to leave it to go to the dining car, the soldiers would hoot and howl and follow us. We would talk and sing songs and dance with them.

It was strange because, despite all the gaiety, there was the underlying truth of what the future held for them. Ordinarily we would never have talked to strange men, and yet with the feeling that these very young boys might be dead soon, we forgot all that kind of decorum and we sang and we danced in the aisles.

I told them I was going to meet the family of the man I was going to marry. There was a slow moan, and Oona picked up on it and said she was doing the same thing. We didn't want to have any problems. We wanted the chance to sing a song or two, make jokes, play games, get to know them a little, and then forget them. But when we got back to our compartment, we would always cry, realizing that we would most likely have a lifetime ahead of us and they might not.

Bill said he would pick us up at the stop just before San Francisco, the train's final destination. He was there waiting as we unboarded, while every single soldier (there didn't seem to be any other women on the train) began to sing and throw kisses and say what great girls we were and what lucky sons of bitches the men we were going to marry were while *they* were going off maybe to die for their country. They kept singing, "The most beautiful girls in the world, ta da dum dum . . ." and other songs of the day. They also helped us with our luggage, which I think made Bill forgive them a little.

We got to the car, and Bill said rather meanly, "Well, you girls had quite a time, didn't you?"

"We had an awful time," Oona said softly and firmly.

"It didn't look that way from where I was. There wasn't a soldier on that train who wasn't insane about you."

And then Oona said the most peculiar thing.

"They were crazy about Carol," she said. "Not me."

Bill wanted to shoot Oona, he wanted to shoot me, he wanted to shoot all three of us. But Oona was so annoyed at his attitude that she couldn't help but let him have it. She wanted to let him know right away how honored he should have been that I had decided to come out there to see him. As I look back now, I think how wonderful she was, how much she knew—despite how little she said.

Bill dropped us off at the hotel.

Oona looked at me.

"Do you really love him?" she asked.

I gave her what I thought to be my best answer at the time.

"Can a duck swim?"

"But you're so smart. You see through him, don't you?"

"No, I don't."

"God, you do know that he's a madman, don't you?" she said. "It's okay to have an affair with him, but you want to marry him. I wouldn't even have dinner with him if it weren't for you. He's not very nice."

"I can't help it," I said. "I know you're right. You're smarter than anybody. But there's something about him."

"I know what it is. You like the way he talks, the things he says.

He's just plying his trade. You keep forgetting that's what he is—a writer. That's the one thing—the only thing—he can really do."

When Bill came back into the room, he made some small talk and then turned to Oona.

"Oona, I'm going crazy. If I can't have Carol now, I'm just going to go crazy."

"Good," she said. "I was just going to get some things from the drugstore. Of course, Bill, I know it doesn't take you too long. But feel free to take more time than you usually do."

She winked at him.

"Thanks, kid," he said. Oona left and then we said our very real hellos.

When Oona came back, Bill said, "I've got a few things to do. Why don't I pick you girls up later?" He left.

"Oona, guess what?"

"What?"

"He asked me to marry him."

"When?"

"Well, there's a little hitch, but I wouldn't even call it a hitch."

"What?"

"Well, you know—he's Armenian."

"Yes, Carol, I know he's Armenian," she said, and couldn't stop laughing. (You could not spend more than five minutes with Bill without knowing not only that he was Armenian, but that he was *the* Armenian. You learned in a half hour the entire history of the Armenian people and even a few words of their language. "I just wouldn't want anyone not to know that," is what he would always say.)

"Oona, listen. Bill said to me, 'I know that you know how much I love you and how much I want you to be my wife. But you also know that I'm an Armenian; my family's from the old country, and marriage to us means children. I know you can have children. Nobody could look at you and not know that you're just bursting. You're like a piece of fruit. But I must be sure. I know this sounds strange, but it's my background. If you were pregnant before we married, I would be happier.' And I said, 'Oh, of course.' "

"That," Oona said, "is the most ridiculous—and by the way, Carol, insulting—request I have ever heard."

There was always something major about Oona, about all of her—her mind, her beauty, her outlook, her taste, the way in which she divided that which she would hold dear and that which she would not. Bill was definitely a not. She begged me not to marry him. But I had fallen in love and nothing else seemed to matter.

. . . .

Telephone Calls

. . . .

In Sacramento, Oona decided to call her father, Eugene O'Neill, where he lived in Contra Costa County with his third wife, Carlotta Monterey. She put it off each day, but I encouraged her to make the effort once and for all just in case her father answered the phone and might, miraculously, make things all right. Carlotta did not like Eugene O'Neill's children and seemingly kept them from him. I always wondered, though, if those decisions were his and not hers. Like the characters in *The Country Girl*, where the husband made the spitballs and the wife threw them.

Oona and I never talked about our private pains, knowing that once we gave them voice, they would never go away. Whenever I asked Oona about Eugene O'Neill, she would only tell me that he was angry with her and her older brother for not going to college. But bravely, this day, she made the call.

The wrong one answered. My heart sank, and I could feel Oona's shoulders trembling beneath my hands, for I was holding them to lend support.

"Hello, Carlotta, this is Oona. How are you? I'm in Sacramento, and I would love to see you and my father while I'm here if it's convenient." Very formal. Carlotta said, "Just a minute," left the phone, and came back in much less than a minute and much too soon to have had a conversation with anybody.

"Oona," she said, "I'm so sorry to tell you this, but your father would prefer not to see you. There's really no point in calling and he's asked that you please not telephone anymore."

"Thank you, Carlotta," Oona said, and hung up. I quickly ran to the loo to give Oona some space and stayed as long as I could. When I came out she was still sitting by the phone. We kept all of our books under the bed, and, feigning interest in some particular title, I crawled under. After awhile, Oona's face appeared on the other side. "I'm okay. You can come out now," she said.

We never spoke about it again.

. . . .

A Visit to the Doctor

. . . .

My body began to feel strange to me. I missed my monthly happening. I began to think that I was pregnant. By the time I was close to missing it a second time, I got very scared. I confided all this to Gloria.

She said, "There is nothing to worry about. We'll find out right away."

She made an appointment to take me to her gynecologist. She introduced me as her cousin Cornelia Whitney—Mrs. Whitney, from Lake Forest, Illinois. I wore a turban to cover all of my hair, dark sunglasses, and very dark makeup so that I did not look the way I normally looked.

Everything about it was terrifying to me except the doctor, who was so nice. He told me I was in very good health and that he would give me the results as soon as he got them.

When we got out of the office I told Gloria that I would be happy if I were pregnant. I knew that Bill was in love with me, but I knew how much having a baby meant to him.

As I think back now I cannot imagine why he ever wanted any children. He simply was not cut out to be anybody's father. He wanted to remain a "daring young man."

I couldn't wait for the results. Gloria called and told me to call the doctor right away (I had given the doctor Gloria's address and telephone number as my New York address). I telephoned the doctor.

He said, "Yes, you are having a baby and I know you are very happy."

I said, "Yes, I am."

I telephoned Bill immediately and gave him the news. I must say that his voice sounded happier than I had ever heard and happier than I was to ever hear it again.

He wanted to know every detail. This, of course, included the doctor's name, et cetera. Being as distrustful as he was, I'm sure that he visited the doctor himself as Mr. Whitney from Lake Forest, Illinois. The reason I'm so sure is that many months later Gloria went in for her annual exam. As she was leaving the office the doctor said, "Oh, Mrs. di Cicco, be sure to send my very best to Mrs. Saroyan."

Gloria, dying of embarrassment, smiled sweetly and said, "Yes, I will."

Counting Snowflakes

Bill was restationed in Dayton, Ohio, and I remember being in a taxicab taking him to the train. It was very early in the morning, still dark. As I sat with him in the car, he suddenly turned to me, and with real feeling he held me and said, "Are you going to be all right? Are you going to be all right?" I'll never forget that. It's one of the few real moments we had together. It was one of the few moments he was tender.

Daddy still didn't want us to get married. "He's not a good male," he said to me. "A good male's first instinct toward the woman he loves is protectiveness. He'll never protect you. He'll take the floor away from under you. I really feel terrible that you're marrying him. Why don't you wait till you're twenty-one?" I couldn't tell him I was pregnant.

Bill and I were married in Dayton on February 20, 1943, exactly one year after we met. Nobody was at the ceremony except my mother and anyone they could filter out of the courthouse for a witness. Oona was in California and Gloria was in Kansas where Pat had been stationed. Daddy wasn't there because of a trip to England; however, I don't think he would have come. I must have sensed that the marriage was already over when it began. I felt a little heartbroken for no reason that I can tell you.

I remember every hour of my wedding night. I was always trying to figure out what it meant to get married. Romance means everything to me, but marriage sometimes felt like nothing but a lot of trouble. I'm a great courtesan, but I'm not by nature a good wife. I make myself be.

It was snowing. Bill looked very serious as we got into bed, man and wife. I had bought a beautiful nightgown and robe for the occasion. It was ice-blue satin embroidered with flowers. Bill had brought a book, *Gulliver's Travels* by Jonathan Swift. He started reading.

An hour or so later, he turned the light out. He had not even looked at me once. I watched the falling snow.

. . . .

I Invented It

. . . .

We were in Dayton for about a month or two and then came back to New York. Bill was stationed in Astoria, Queens. We took a penthouse apartment at 2 Sutton Place South, paid for by Bill's royalties. I fixed it up to look exactly like the place we'd had our first affair in: his suite at the Hampshire House, decorated by Dorothy Draper. It was all big red and pink cabbage roses and green leaves and candy stripes. The apartment had a beautiful terrace overlooking the river. I put a red and white striped awning over it and painted the terrace floor a dark shiny green. There was wrought iron furniture and bright red geraniums growing everywhere. We had breakfast there and very often dinner, too. From the terrace, I would watch Bill walk across the bridge to Astoria each morning.

I wanted the apartment to be completely finished before I had the baby. During one of my regular appointments with the doctor, he told me that Bill and I could not have sex in the eighth and ninth month of pregnancy.

I was very worried about it because Bill liked to have lots and lots of sex, night after night, morning after morning. And even though it made me tired sometimes, I was happy to have the intimacy with him.

"What will I do?" I asked the doctor. "What will happen to my husband?"

"He's having the baby, too. He'll wait."

"Yes, but he'll be very unhappy. He's a man who loves to have sex all the time. We do it all night and, a lot of the time, all day."

"You'll work it out. Don't worry about it."

I realized he was not going to be of any help.

What am I going to do? I wondered.

As the seventh month was nearly over, I told Bill how sorry I was that I wasn't going to be able to sleep with him next month. I said I would miss him terribly.

In truth, I felt so encumbered by the baby at this point that I knew most of the hardship was going to be on him.

During the first part of the eighth month, we would be in bed in each other's arms. We would sort of hold each other and kiss and he would touch my stomach to see if the baby was doing anything. But, being so close to him, I could feel this terrible thing that he had, so big and like a rock.

I felt sorry for him and didn't know what to do.

He left very early in the morning and, of course, would return late at night, very tired. So at least this helped the situation somewhat.

But all of a sudden he showed up with a three-day pass. And I remembered the last time he'd done that we'd stayed in bed for the whole three days having a wonderful time.

But what could we possibly do this time?

I was trying to think of stories to amuse him, jokes I could tell, music I could play. I got theater tickets—seeing *Oklahoma* suddenly seemed very important. I was cooking lots of Armenian food. I just did every single thing I could think of to divert him.

But the nights had to fall anyway, followed by very pretty mornings. And he was a morning *and* night *and* middle-of-the-day man.

My nerves were just stretched to their limits.

On the first night of the three-day pass, I was just looking at the ceiling and away from his thing. I was acting as if I was half asleep and not noticing anything.

"Sleeping?" he asked.

At first I didn't answer. But I was in over my head. He asked again.

"Sleeping?" he said, a little louder.

"No, no of course I'm not sleeping," I finally had to say. I couldn't let him try to fall asleep with that big hard thing. It just isn't fair, I thought.

And all of a sudden, the answer came to me straight from heaven. There it was right in my head. I knew exactly what to do. And I did it.

I kissed him on the mouth. Then all over his face and ears and neck and all over his body, skipping Armageddon.

Until I knew there was no way I wouldn't. And what a brilliant idea it was. If nothing else, I knew it would show him that he had a brilliant wife. I don't think I have ever been that proud of myself before or since.

I didn't know *exactly* the way to go about it, but I learned by trying. He never said a word. He never moved. But Armageddon came. Then he pulled my head up and kissed me.

"You didn't know I was a creative genius, did you?" I said.

"No, I didn't."

"I can't believe it. Imagine, in all this wonderful world, no one thought of this until today. It was worrying me terribly what we could do this month. I was worried about your well-being."

"I always told you you were a genius," he said. "No one looks like you and no one thinks like you."

As we were falling asleep, I thought to myself, my God, no one in the world could have thought of that. But somehow it just came to me, and I couldn't have been more pleased with myself.

. . . .

"Tell Us More and More: Everything You Know"

. . . .

When I left Oona in L.A., we wrote to each other all the time. She told me about all the people she had met: Orson Welles and other movie stars, all of whom wanted to take her out, give her jobs, and, she added, "They want to sleep with me. It makes me nervous."

One day I got a letter, and at the end she wrote, "P.S. I just met Charlie Chaplin."

On June 1, 1943, Oona and Charlie were married. He was fifty-four, she was eighteen. I was so happy, but I didn't get to meet him until almost exactly a year later. In the meantime, my son Aram had been born and Bill had been posted to London.

I met Charlie Chaplin for the first time on D-Day, June 6, 1944. Oona and Charlie took me to lunch at 21. We stayed until 5:00, talking and laughing and talking. Charlie turned out to be not only articulate and well-spoken, but very good-looking, with the best skin and the bluest eyes I ever saw. He adored to laugh. It wasn't haw-haw, a big ridiculous laugh; it was light, natural laughter, like a part of his speech. He never stopped laughing, because Oona had the best wit in the world.

In Oona, Charlie really did marry the girl of his dreams. He was the most in-love man I ever saw. He couldn't take his eyes off her. Her looks were his perfect looks, and though she had all the depth and emotion you could want, her manner was very soft, very light, like Mozart. She was it for him.

But Charlie was the most jealous man who ever lived. Even during that lunch at 21, and the ones we had there every day afterward, it was obvious. For a lot of Oona's and my old beaus were still around New York, and every once in a while one of these kids would come up to our table and say, "Oona! Carol!" They'd want us to dance or go see Glenn Miller. And Charlie would go mad.

"Who are these boys?" he'd demand. "What are you two up to? Carol, I'm going to tell Bill on you." He was so old-fashioned. My God, what were we supposed to do? Pretend we'd never met them? They were sweet. They liked us. And they were always nice. We had no reason not to say hello to them, even if we were married. I think all men in love are insanely jealous. I know all women are, even those who don't admit it. That's part of love. There can be no great love without exclusivity.

Oona was pregnant with Geraldine then, and she could only eat certain things. So we met for lunch every day at 21 and had nothing but smoked salmon and napoleons. One day Oona said to me, "Tomorrow I've invited a friend of mine from California to join us. She's fucked everyone you ever heard of, and she'll tell us everything."

"Terrific," I said. I was never so excited.

The woman turned out to be petite and very pristine, and Oona guided her right down to hell. Clark Gable, Tyrone Power, Errol Flynn, this woman had had them all, and more. Some were terrific, she said, others "just liked to pop off their guns." Oona and I were so fascinated, we could have stayed and listened to her for the rest of our lives.

Eventually we'd run out of everyone famous, and, not wanting to go too far down the list, we asked who was the best ever.

"Irwin Shaw," she said, not skipping a beat.

"Irwin Shaw? He's like a prosperous butcher on the Grand Concourse in the Bronx. Are you sure?"

"Don't question that. I know. He's very male—romantic, tender, strong. Nothing compares to Irwin Shaw."

Then came the fatal blow. Oona wanted to know who was the worst. This the woman refused to tell us, and Oona went crazy.

"What do you mean you won't say," she insisted. "You owe it to us."

"Don't ask me again. I'm not telling you."

"Yes, you are, or I'll never speak to you again."

"Well, all right. It was Bill Saroyan."

My heart fell. I remembered all the times I'd told Oona how wonderful he was. Oona took my hand and squeezed it. She knew I was dying inside.

"A lot of men," she told me, "when they don't love someone, it's different."

I was grateful, but not entirely convinced. How could I be?

. . . .
Diamond Earrings
. . . .

On Gloria's twenty-first birthday, her marriage to Pat di Cicco was virtually over. He was mean and played cards a lot and didn't have any money and wasn't terribly nice to her. He was no longer her beau, he was her husband. And he wanted a good Italian wife cooking spaghetti in the kitchen. Which Gloria definitely was not. I had no idea things were going wrong until the day she told me they were getting a divorce. Gloria has an uncanny ability not to tell things until she has dealt with them already.

Bill was still overseas. I loved him so much, and I was lonely. Of course, I had one baby and we went to the park on the East River every day. But we both were lonely for Bill. So when Gloria turned twenty-one, I decided to give her a birthday party. It was always fun to plan things for Gloria because she saw everything, she noticed every detail, no matter where she was. She had an artist's eye and making any little effort on her behalf was always so appreciated that it used to break my heart. I wondered why everyone didn't always make an effort for her. She always did for them.

I bought her twenty-two presents—one for good luck. Gloria's favorite song was "I Could Write a Book" from *Pal Joey,* so I ordered a cake in the shape of an open book with pages of very white icing. On the left page it said, "I could write a book about the way you walk and whisper and look" in pink icing. On the right page, it said "Happy Birthday, darling" in sky-blue icing, and sprinkled underneath were little flowers shaped into clusters of 21, 21, 21, 21. The little flowers were in all different colors and had green leaves. And in very tiny writing on the bottom of the right side of the cake, I wrote, "I could write a preface and it would say, 'Gloria, I love you, Carol.'" Gloria's name was written in gold icing.

After she opened my twenty-two presents—all handmade silk and lace lingerie—she thanked me for the twenty-second time and then did something unbelievable.

"I have a present for you," she said.

"Oh, no, it's *your* birthday."

"I know, but it's my twenty-first birthday and I am now independent and this is what I designed for you."

At which point Gloria went into the coat closet and came back with a small package and a rather large envelope that said, "I love you Carol, darling." I opened the envelope and in it was a drawing made by Gloria. It was a bunch of grapes with leaves on the top. The grapes on top were very big and then they gradually got smaller the way a bunch narrows at the bottom. The drawing was simply beautiful.

And then I opened the box from Van Cleef & Arpels and there they were—the most beautiful diamond earrings I have ever seen in my life. Each earring was a replica of the drawing—the leaves were pavéed and the grapes hung from them. Each grape was a diamond and each grape moved and they were big and blindingly beautiful. The effect was indescribable, and I could have lived for the rest of my life off what they must have cost. But better still, they had been designed by Gloria for me, and she'd meant it in the sweetest way.

There was a lovely note enclosed that said that she knew how much the symbol of grapes meant to Bill as well as to me and that was why she'd chosen that design. And Bill did love everything about grapes. He felt they were a wonderful symbol of the life of the refugee Armenians who'd settled in Fresno, where there were many, many vineyards. Even more, he loved the twisting and turning of the vines in winter when they were bare. A vine was one of the more beautiful things in the world to him.

Still, I just looked at Gloria. I was stunned.

"You cannot give me these. You must keep them for yourself, because in every way they belong to you. It's too much to take."

And she said laughingly, "How can you be so ordinary? You usually are not."

"You're right," I said. "I love them." I put them on instantly. The doorbell rang and the party began.

We spent the evening dancing and talking and remembering, knowing that the war was just about over. We talked of what we would be doing a year from now or two or ten years from now.

The next day it was raining, but as darkness fell it got colder and then began to snow. The whole East River—the bridge, everything—was covered in white.

The telephone rang. Bill was coming home.

Later in the evening, after he had played with Aram, bathed, and luxuriated in bed, I brought him a tray of food that I knew he loved. We talked. And after that, while playing with the bubbles in my bath, feeling so happy, I decided to come out naked, wearing the diamond earrings. I must have looked like a car with headlights, because I saw Bill blinking.

When I got into the bed, he sat up and said, "What the hell are those?"

"Those are my big, beautiful boobs—or do you mean the diamond earrings?"

When he didn't respond, I said, "Grapes, the thing you like most of all. Gloria designed them just for us."

Bill just looked at me. Whatever he normally felt about grapes, it wasn't apparent at this moment.

"She gave them to you as a gift on her birthday? And you, you little beggar girl with the tin cup, just accepted them without any thought to their possible monetary value?"

I was silent.

"You're going to give them back," he said, then closed his eyes and fell into a sleep of total exhaustion.

I really didn't want to do that, and I felt it was a terrible thing to do to Gloria. I said, "Let me throw them in the East River, so that you'll know it has nothing to do with money. But I don't want to put her in that position." But Bill was adamant.

"If you ever get anything like that, it has to be because I give it to you," he said. "And I won't ever give you anything like that, because I don't think that way." Finally, after eating earrings for breakfast, lunch, and dinner for the next year and a half, I summoned up the courage to return them to her.

"Darling," I said, "there's something you have to understand. The present that you gave me when you were twenty-one will be with me all my life. I will never forget it. It will always give me pleasure just to think about it and remember it, but I must tell you that the actual objects themselves must be kept by you—not only because of their enormous value, but because they were made by you and they must stay with you."

Gloria looked at me lovingly and said, "Carol, I know that Bill doesn't want you to have them. I know that you love him, I understand the whole thing. I don't ever want you to think about it again, and I won't either."

They were now in my hand and I gave them to Gloria. She put them in her purse. I was very relieved. Whatever she may have been feeling, her main concern at that moment was for me not to feel terrible. She knew that I'd been put up to this, and she didn't want me to feel more rotten than she knew I already felt.

. . . .

The Night I Slept in an Orange

. . . .

Between the time I received the earrings and when I returned them, I spent a night in an orange. We were out on the West Coast, because Bill said he had to live near San Francisco—that's where he felt happy. "I need my environment," he said. "Our marriage is going to have my environment."

I said what I always said: "Fine."

With the war over, Bill had to drive up from the Bay Area to Fort Lewis, Washington, to be officially discharged from the army. We left the baby with Bill's mother and sister. I was pregnant again. We were hoping for a girl this time.

It was a very long and arduous drive, particularly because Bill got angry if I wanted to stop for any reason at all. I didn't want my pregnancy to irritate him, so I tried not to ask him to stop so I could use the bathroom. On the other hand, I knew my pregnancy was the thing he wanted most on earth; he wanted eleven children, an entire football team. I still had morning sickness, which was also simply not allowed, and we drove and drove and drove. I knew that pretty soon he would need some gas and that was going to save me.

When we stopped for gas, I tinkled and threw up in the loo. We then drove for many more hours, and after I practically begged, he agreed to stop for dinner. We ended up at a truck stop (those were his favorite places) where a jukebox played Peggy Lee and Duke Ellington songs like "Why Don't You Do Right?" and "Do Nothin' Till You Hear From Me." The joint was really jumping. Then the jukebox played "The River Seine" and Bill looked at me.

"I used to hear that in Paris when we got over there," he said. "It always made me think of you."

I felt suddenly warmed by this bit of friendliness. Also the steak had kicked in. So I took the risk of making conversation.

"Bill, don't look this minute, but when it seems right, look to your left two tables away and I think you will find that Lon Chaney, Jr., is sitting there."

At which point, Bill went into a total, uncontrollable rage. His rages, which I had been seeing more and more of since he came back from the army, always came out of nowhere. It was like being in a dark room you'd never been in before and not knowing where anything is. I didn't know when or where or how it would happen.

"What the fuck do I care if Lon Chaney, Jr., is sitting two tables away? Why are you telling me this? First of all, you're lying."

"I am not lying. That is definitely Lon Chaney, Jr. I know it."

This really exasperated him.

"I care nothing about Lon Chaney, Jr. What I care about is why you are a liar, a total, miserable liar."

"Bill, all you have to do is turn your head a little to your left and you will see him, too."

Now he blew up completely and began screaming.

"You are crazy. You are lying. Why are you making this stupid thing up?"

The worst part was that he refused to look, insisting over and over again that I was a sick liar. He asked for the check.

"What about dessert?" I asked.

"What about it?" he snarled.

"We ordered it and it's coming."

"Oh," he said, somewhat calmly. "I had no idea. Why don't you give the dessert to Lon Chaney, Jr.?" He was snarling again. "I'll go back to the car."

"All right, I'm coming. I just have to go to the loo."

"Of course you do. Everybody knows that."

I went to the loo, where I cried my eyes out. Then I went to the car, where Bill was waiting, seething with rage. Whereupon he began a litany of abuse not to be believed, starting with:

"You think because you are beautiful, you can lie and lie and lie and lie every time you open your mouth. That's all you do—lie. You are a congenital liar. You know it. I know it. Everyone knows it and you must do something about it. You must stop it. I don't want to hear about Lon Chaney, Jr., and people you make up seeing in restaurants. I don't want to know about these things. Don't you understand, I have just come back from the war? Don't you understand what I have been through—that my entire nervous system was turned upside down by the war? I have been through hell and you are sitting there finding people in the movies in restaurants. You think that's something, to find Lon Chaney, Jr.? Is that where your head is? Is it? Is that where your head is? Tell me. Tell me. *Tell me!*"

"Yes. That's where it is. That's where it's staying and it's never going to move. If I had a place to go, I'd go. If I see a place to go, I'll go to it. I hate you. I hate you like poison. You're cruel, you're inhuman, you're poisonous. You're sick in the head. You should do something about it. If you weren't so sick in the head, you'd become the best writer that ever was, but you won't."

"I am the best writer that ever was."

"No, you're not. You have written a few wonderful things. Period. You never will again. You don't have a heart. You have taught me hate and fear. I'm afraid of you. But you have driven me to the point where I don't care what you do or what you think. You are a bully boy."

"Listen, kid, you don't have to take everything so seriously."

That sentence was like a stick of dynamite that blew me apart.

"Stop the car," I said. "I want to get out."

"Don't be ridiculous. How can you get out in the middle of nowhere?"

"It's better than in the middle of here. I'm getting out. If you don't stop the car, I'll get out anyway."

"Look," he murmured, making a 180-degree turn in mood, "I know you're just a kid. I understand. It's not important."

"Bill, don't use that word 'important' ever to me. I want to leave you right now, right here. Stop the car."

Although he didn't stop the car, it seemed to me that in the last minute or two he had slowed down a bit. When I saw that he was in the lane nearest the grass, I opened the door. We slowed down even more and I jumped out, landing on my feet.

I heard the door slam and the car drive away. For that little amount of time on the grass in the dark, I felt good again. I simply didn't care about anything. I hoped he would drive to the North Pole and get lost. I sat down and took my mirror out of my purse to put on a little lipstick. I refreshed myself with a little perfume that was in my bag. I was getting cold, but I was still happier than I had been in the car.

After a while, I got up and started to walk. After walking a mile, I thought I saw something very odd across the road. It seemed to be a great big orange—an orange as big as a house. Of course, I knew there couldn't be a thing like that anywhere. But as I looked more closely, I saw that it couldn't be anything else.

Oh, my God, I thought. I'm so sleepy that I'm just seeing things. I decided to look at it anyway. I went across the road and walked around the orange, and there was what should have been a place for a door without a door, so I walked right in. All around the inside of the orange there was a wooden ledge to sit on.

I don't need him, I thought. I had found a place to be without him. I love this orange. I don't want anything more than this—a place to sit, a place to sleep, a place to stand.

I then curled up on the wooden ledge and put my purse under my head. There was a tiny drop of moonlight coming in from what seemed to be some counterlike thing with an opening—a window without glass. With my head on my purse, by the little bit of light from the moon, I fell asleep.

I don't know when I woke up, but when I did, I found Bill curled up on another part of the ledge. He had taken his jacket off and put it around me. This did soften me toward him somewhat. I was even wondering if he was cold. But as morning came and some sunlight shone in, it became rather warm in the orange (and I also wanted to show some independence), so I threw the jacket in the middle of the orange as if I hadn't used it to keep warm for the last few hours. I simply didn't want him to have the satisfaction of knowing it had been a comfort. In fact, I didn't want him to have any satisfaction. He was just too mean.

He woke up and I pretended to still be asleep. He found his jacket in the middle of the orange, dusted it off, and put it on. He looked at his watch and woke me up.

"Time to get going," he said in a gently gruff way.

"What are you talking about? It's time for you to get going. I'm not going with you. I—"

"Don't be silly. How many people in this world do you think have spent the night in an orange? It's a bond between us. Anyway, we're practically there, so let's go. I looked all over for you on the road, and when I didn't find you I went crazy."

"No, you went crazy long before."

"No. No, I wasn't. You mean everything to me."

"I know I do, Bill. When you have me down on the ground like this, then I mean everything to you. But when I walk around like any other person, I mean nothing."

He put his arm around me and sort of kissed me on the ear and whispered, "There's a drink called orange passion. We're in the middle of nowhere. No one's coming here. Let this be our orange."

"No, Bill. I don't want to. I don't like you anymore. I know you're trying to be nice because you want to make this orange yours, but it doesn't make any difference. You are something less than human. I don't know what you are. But I know you are not human. I think people will be coming here any minute."

"It's off-season. This is an orange stand where they sell Orange Julius in the summertime."

"Orange Julius? What's that?"

"I don't know. That's the name of the drink. It's written above the counter, outside. You couldn't see it in the dark."

Bill kept insisting that we make love, until finally I said, "Oh, Bill, this would be so wonderful, if you really loved me—if you could really love."

"I do," he said. And we did.

Afterward, Bill said, "Of course, as I drove around looking for you, the minute I saw the orange I knew you were in it. It was a perfect place for you, a perfect place for you to be."

"No, it wasn't. A perfect place would have been a four-poster bed with a fireplace going and snow falling and falling outside—a silent snow, a secret snow, like the name of the short story that Conrad Aiken wrote."

"C'mon kid, let's get in the car. Let's go."

And we went.

A Very New Language

I didn't really care where in the San Francisco area Bill and I lived, but I knew that unless we lived where he wanted, I was going to be in big trouble. Otherwise, he would feel that he was being led around by the nose.

After much searching, we found a house with lots of acreage. It was in Los Gatos, way south of the city, and it belonged to violinist Yehudi Menuhin. It was very pretty, with old trees, and well priced. But what Bill loved most was all that extra land.

"You see, kid," he said, "the reason I'm stuck on this house is we can have the kind of life that I've always dreamed of."

"What were you dreaming of, Bill?"

"First, we're going to have a lot more kids. I still want that football team, you know. And this would be a great place for them. They could live in a house with my mother and sister to take care of them. Then you and I could build a dream house just for the two of us on a piece of the property. We could have all our privacy, I could work and know that you are close by, and the children of course would be fine with Ma."

"You're joking, aren't you?"

"No, why? Why are you saying that?"

"I'm not giving the children away to someone else."

"It isn't someone else. It's my mother."

"Your mother, before she is anything, is someone else."

"I didn't know your feelings about it would be that strong. Families take care of each other. There's nothing unusual about that."

"Unusual is not what I would call it. It's the most frighteningly insane thing I have ever heard. I'm not going to cook and pop babies for your family. I'm going to cook and pop them for us, if you're still around and you're loving enough, because you cannot be crazy with children."

Of course, it was easy to say that, but another matter to make it the truth.

"Oh," Bill said, "I never heard you so strong and definite about anything. Where's that sweet little thumbsucking baby I married?"

Bill stopped speaking to me for about a week. I was very happy to have the rest.

We ended up taking a little house on Taraval Street in San Francisco. A streetcar went right by it; I loved the sound. Lucy, our second child, was born there, on January 17, 1946. We knew almost no one, and all I ever really saw in San Francisco were Bill's relatives and the washing machine. Now for the first time I got to see the backwardness of his family, their distrust of anything but their own blood. Bill's mother and father were cousins. They were immigrants, and they never expected anything out of life after they got to America.

While Bill was overseas, one of the things I did to feel close to him was take Armenian lessons from a very old Armenian lady in New York. She came every day at 4:00 P.M. for over a year. On his birthday, I wrote him a very long letter using the Armenian alphabet, never realizing that though he spoke the language, he couldn't read those letters. And once he got back, he never spoke of it.

Before Bill had left, his mother and sister had visited us in New York, and now that he was living in San Francisco, they came for an extended stay. "They haven't seen me for so long," Bill said. "It's easier for my mother to stay here," and I said, "Of course." They never suspected I could speak Armenian, and Bill had forgotten. So night after night at dinner on Taraval Street, I listened as they slapped me in the face. I couldn't believe that anyone in the world would say rotten things about me to the man who was supposed to love me in a language that I supposedly couldn't understand while I was sitting right there. But they did. I got so I couldn't wait for dinner every night. It gave me the true picture of what I was into, because I also heard Bill's replies.

"Natural blonde?" they asked.

"Oh, yes. You want to see?"

"No, believe. Why does she speak that way? Is she English?"

"No, American. She speaks perfect American speech."

"Why do you like her?"

"Well, it's not for her cooking."

"We know. She can't sew your buttons on, either. She's a princess. What do you want that for?"

"That's what I wanted."

"You think she flirt with other men?"

"No. Her manner is flirtatious, but she is pure. Very pure."

"You think she love you or the money? What?"

"No, no, no. Her family has money that would make your head spin. You never saw money like where she lived."

Finally, one night, they said, "She's too pale. Too white, white, white. Why you like that?" He didn't say anything, because that's what he loved.

So I said, "Why don't you answer them, Bill?"

"What do you mean?"

"You got a letter from me in Armenian. I've been taking lessons."

Then I turned to Bill's mother and said, in Armenian, "Takoohi, I speak very well. I understand Armenian."

"No, Carol."

"Yes, I do. I'm sorry you feel that way about me. And I'm sorry I didn't reveal this to you before, because now I'm sorry I know." All in the right tense and the right accent.

"You are very sneaky girl."

"No. I never dreamed that while I was sitting in front of you, trying to help and trying to make things nice, you would say such terrible things about me. That you thought of me as nothing because I'm not a house cleaner. Well, I can clean a house better than anyone in the world (which happens to be true). You know I love your son, and you are saying these things about me to him. Even if you think them, you shouldn't say them."

"You hear what she says? She want me to lie."

"Ma," Bill said. "She's right." He apologized to me, and not only did they never do it again, but they began to like me. And when his mother died in 1950, Bill told me that her dying words to him were, "Take care of Carol. She is a very good girl." But by then it was too late.

. . . .

Truman in San Francisco

. . . .

One night in the Taraval Street house, Bill, who often read in bed, began laughing. He seemed utterly delighted and laughed even more. As he closed the copy of *Story* magazine, he said, "This kid is a marvelous writer."

"Who?"

He opened the magazine back to the story, which was called "My Side of the Matter," and said, "Truman Kaput—I don't know—Truman Cappott."

"Do you mean Truman Cap*o*-tee?"

"Oh, God, Carol. You always try to make everyone's name sound so fancy. It's Cup-oat."

"No, that is not his name. I happen to know him very well. He is a dear and close friend. In fact, he has seen me naked."

"What's the matter with you, kid?" He looked at me long and hard. "You don't have to know the person just because I like his writing. What makes you think you have to know this person? That's crazy."

"I don't think any of that at all. I just know him. I can't help it."

"Oh, God, you are a congenital liar. You do nothing but tell lies. It's a disease."

Bill wasn't interested in my life and certainly not in my friends.

"Bill, I am not lying. He's a very good friend. I swear to you he is."

"You are so nuts I don't know what to do."

I felt terrible, so I just pulled out of it all and went into the living room. Bill, as always, stayed mad for quite a few days. I knew he would, so I arranged to pass the time by watching the water go up and down through the glass in the washing machine. Did you ever tell your fortune in an airplane, watching the clouds? You see people you know, recognize familiar shapes. I'd do the same thing with the wash. I could make a reading out of the soapsuds.

The dispute was never mentioned again, but by a stroke of incredible luck, less than a month later, the telephone rang and Bill found himself talking to Truman Capote.

"I've taken the liberty of telephoning you," Truman said, "because Carol and I are great friends and I am an admirer of yours. I'm in San Francisco for a few days and hope very much that you will have some time to see me, because I would like to meet the man Carol married."

Bill was very cordial and made a date to see him the following night at the Top of the Mark, the highest floor of the Mark Hopkins Hotel, a place he assumed every tourist would like to go to so as to see all of San Francisco from its windows. It was an interesting idea, but San Francisco is too foggy to be seen.

Anyway, the plans were made and Truman asked to speak to me. I, of course, without Bill's realizing it, had been listening behind the door the entire time.

"Truman Capote would like to speak to you, Carol."

"How wonderful. Is he here?"

"He's calling you from here. I know most of your calls come from the moon."

I got on the telephone and spoke rather stiffly to Truman because Bill did not move an inch and I felt embarrassed for him that I had received this call. I explained all that to Truman much later, though I never mentioned any of it to Bill again.

I've always disliked people who say "I told you so," so I said nothing.

We had a great evening with Truman, going all over San Francisco. Truman was filled with wonderful stories and so was Bill and that was that. At one point in the evening, when Bill was out of earshot, Truman whispered to me, "You had to have two children? You know this won't last. This can't last—he's insane. I don't know what sane is, but I do know what insane is." Some part of me knew that he was right, but I wasn't ready to say so.

Henry Miller

Bill corresponded frequently with Henry Miller. Bill had given me Henry's books to read and I thought they were a little boring and a little dirty. He had invited us to visit him in Big Sur, where he lived on top of a steep mountain. It was an arduous drive, ending on a tiny dirt road. At the end of the road, there was his little log cabin, which had no electricity.

Henry came out to greet us, wearing khaki shorts—nothing else. And he didn't have a drop of hair on his body or his head. Also, he was rather pale. All in all, he looked to me like a giant slug. Our entire conversation was "hello"; he directed the rest of the conversation to Bill alone. There was a young girl there in bare feet, pregnant. He didn't introduce her to Bill. Bill asked who she was.

"Oh, yeah. That's my wife."

No name.

Bill and Henry, of course, got along perfectly. Why wouldn't they? They were both dog-eat-dog-type men and they laughed at the horror of each other's humor.

I tried to help his wife bring us some ice water, which Henry had asked for. This was the extent of their hospitality. It seemed strange to me, because when one went to even the most modest Armenian farmhouse in Fresno, one was instantly offered everything that could possibly be offered. These were very poor people, but they had a strong sense of hospitality.

The log cabin, which Henry had evidently built much of himself, was really just one very big room with a temporary screen in front of the so-called loo. The loo consisted of a hole in the ground. In twelve seconds, I decided against using it. He had quite a few paintings and drawings pasted or nailed to the logs of the cabin.

"Do you like these, Saroyan?" asked Henry. "Like my paintings?"

"Wonderful, wonderful," Bill said, which was his answer to any question of that kind from anybody.

Henry then took out one that he thought was his very best painting and put it on an easel.

"Look, Saroyan, I want you to buy this painting from me. Don't you think it's beautiful?"

It was of an ugly woman and he had painted lots of coarse black hair on her twat. Neither of us had ever seen a painting like that.

"Hell, no. Look at all that hair on that dame."

This drew Henry up to full height.

"What the hell's 'a matter with you, Bill? Women have hair there. Don't you know that? I'm that kind of painter. You got to grow up sometime." He looked at me and then looked back at Bill. "Doesn't your wife have hair there?"

And Bill, to his undying credit, replied, "My wife is like a baby and it is a pale yellow sweetness. It's not black cunt hair like you drew."

Henry could not believe this.

His wife was by now behind the screen.

"I don't believe that for one second. Show it to me," Henry hollered.

Bill was livid. "You know, I think you're nuts. I think you're crazy. How dare you suggest a thing like that."

"Well, you just made quite a statement there and I want you to prove it."

Bill did not answer and Henry saw he was not going to answer this and I just stood there and his wife was even farther behind the temporary screen. Henry decided to let it go.

"Anyway, Saroyan, you've got a lot of money and I want you to buy the painting. I don't have any dough."

"You are a very offensive man. I am still a writer too, remember? I am not a Wall Street broker. I don't like that painting. It doesn't resemble anything that is dear to me and I need every penny I've earned. So you better call a businessman in." He looked at me. "C'mon, kid, let's go."

I might add that Henry had that entire conversation without ever looking at me except for that one moment.

On the drive home, Bill looked at me and smiled.

"What? What is it?" I asked him.

"You see? You see what other writers are like? And you think I'm difficult."

And for the rest of the day, by virtue of the horror of Henry Miller, I thought Saroyan a hero.

. . . .
Never Say No
. . . .

In the winter of 1947, we rented a furnished house in Oyster Bay, Long Island.

Bill thought a change of scene would be good for his writing, and we both missed seeing snow. Also, he wondered what it would be like to live in the country in the East, near enough to New York City to go in for dinner and be close to the theater. James Cagney had recently fallen in love with *The Time of Your Life*. Bill was smart enough not to sell it to him, which was the custom before then, but to "rent" it—never relinquishing ownership rights.

After writing to some real estate people and asking for brochures, he had found a house. Maybe it was the strain of moving, maybe just fate, but I had a terrible miscarriage soon after the move. Bill, naturally, insisted I'd had an abortion. "What are you talking about?" I said. "Someone came in our room last night and did it?" He was such a maniac. He wouldn't speak to me for almost a month after that.

About two months later, in April, the Chaplins were in New York for the opening of *Monsieur Verdoux* and we went in to see them. We went first to the Stork Club and then to El Morocco, where we had supper in the Champagne Room.

Bill and Charlie were really talking and talking and talking about everyone they ever met and knew in common. Charlie was always so considerate and nice to Bill.

I could see that Oona had one ear wrapped to their conversation. We were so happy to have a small chance to catch up—it was hard on the telephone, as both Bill and Charlie hated us to be talking.

At one point, as we were all eating and drinking, I got kicked in the shin. It was such a hard kick that I could not believe it. It just was too much to bear. I stifled the pain because I didn't want to scream. Everyone seemed to be happy and I didn't really know what had happened.

At that point, Oona said, "Let's go to the loo."

"Oona, I'm not sure I can get up."

"What do you mean?"

"I don't know."

But somehow I got up and hobbled off with Oona.

"Oh, my God," I said, after sitting down and picking up my long dress to examine what had happened. There it was—a bleeding bruise that had discolored the skin right under my knee.

"Oh, no," Oona said. "I thought it was Charlie I was kicking."

"What do you mean? Do you have knives in your shoe? What is it?"

"Oh, God, I was so mad at him."

"Why?"

"Didn't you hear what they were talking about?"

"I did a little, but not all of it."

"They were talking about Rebecca West, the writer. She'd been H. G. Wells's mistress, and Charlie was very impressed. Can you imagine, Charlie was telling Bill how easily he'd made it with her. Charlie kept saying, 'Bill, she was a piece of cake,' and Bill said, 'Goddamn you, Charlie. I chased her around the bed for at least four hours.' Poor Bill, he got nowhere. 'She was well past her prime, believe me, and she still wouldn't let me get near her. So I finally told her to go fuck herself and left.'

" 'Dear Boy,' Charlie said, 'that is not how it is done. You do not chase anyone around the bed. You do it from the moment you say "How do you do?" ' "

" 'Well, you sure know something I don't know,' Bill said finally. 'And I'll probably never know it.' "

Oona sighed and continued, "Carol, I couldn't stand it. That's when I tried to kick him. How dare he tell of his former conquests while I'm sitting at the table?"

"Well, it was years and years and years ago. Before you were born, even. And I think it's wonderful that you're so jealous."

"Jealous? You think I'm jealous? You should see Charlie. He's the most jealous man who ever lived. I swear to you I have never known anyone as jealous as Charlie."

"Oona," I told her, "go in and kiss him. He didn't get the kick. I did. He doesn't even know you're mad."

"All those old bags he slept with! Jesus Christ, I'm sick of hearing it. And you'd think maybe by now he'd be sick of even thinking about them. What am I supposed to do when he's talking like that? Sit there and smile and simper?"

"Well, in this case, what difference could it make?"

"I guess," she said.

I suppose I always understood that men have a feeling about conquest that makes them feel that there's more man than there is. Charlie would have to brag about it to other men. After all, he was very short.

From El Morocco, we went down to an Armenian place on Allen Street where a big sweaty woman in an old black dress did an Armenian dance. We were back at the Pierre Hotel, where we'd taken a suite for the weekend, at about 6 A.M.

I threw myself in the tub, put on a nightie, and got into bed. Bill started to make love to me. I was always happy to go to bed with him because it was the only time he was civil to me. But this one night I was too exhausted.

"Oh, darling, I'm too tired," I said. "Let's wait till morning. I'm so sorry. I'm just about to die from exhaustion."

Bill went right through the ceiling.

"What are you talking about? Until this very moment, you were the belle of the ball. The prettiest, the sweetest, the gayest girl, all night long. You're all luminous beauty when you're with the Chaplins, but now that you're alone with me, you're tired. There's no wit now. There's no effervescence. I don't see any silver sparklers anymore. You're just too tired. Well, so am I. I'm tired of you."

He jumped out of bed, put all his clothes on, took his tiny overnight case, filled it with his things and left.

I think he went to New Orleans, leaving me with the bill.

I didn't see him for a week. In our marriage, that was like ten years.

I have never said no to a man again. I don't mean the man next door, but someone I was already sleeping with. If I was naked with my hair on fire, I'd do it.

With Bill, as I said, I was happy to go to bed with him, simply because it was the only time he was civil to me. When he was overseas and I got a lot of dirty books to read, I found out that girls came. One day, I picked up one of them and it told about this girl having a swell time—over and over again. It was the swellest time you ever heard of. I couldn't understand. I knew girls never came. I never questioned it. I loved the intimacy, but coming—that was just for men. I kept rereading these paragraphs and, after a while, I got very upset. So I called Gloria. Orlando, her butler, answered the phone.

"Orlando," I said, "I'm sure that they're having dinner now, but this is a very urgent matter. She must come to the telephone right away. It'll only take a minute or two. I need her. I'm in a terrible state of confusion."

She came to the phone immediately.

"Darling, what is it? What's happened?"

"Well, you know those books I bought the other day?"

"Yes?"

"Just let me read you this one paragraph." I read her the paragraph.

"Yes," she said. "So?"

"What do you mean 'Yes. So?' You know that girls don't come."

Whereupon, she began to sputter.

"I don't believe this! It's impossible. Are you telling me that you have never come?"

"Have you?" I said incredulously.

"What are you talking about? Of course I've come. I've never not come. You are crazy. Of course girls come. Every girl comes. Except you." I sincerely hoped Orlando, the butler, wasn't in the room. She was really mad. "Why did you tell me all those lies about how wonderful Bill was and what a great time you always had?"

"I did, but I didn't come."

"Well, girls come. And please don't ever forget it. I'm going back to dinner. I'll be over in the morning."

We hung up and I began to think about it. I wondered what it felt like. But I stopped thinking about it after a while, or at least for the remainder of my relationship with Bill. Naturally, I never told him I didn't come. I don't think it would have mattered all that much to him, but I instinctively knew that was not a conversation to have with anyone, much less Bill, and that was the end of the matter.

. . . .

Nothing Left

. . . .

I have been married three times, each time to a gambler. The first two times were to the same gambler, Bill Saroyan. But I didn't know that Bill gambled until the war was over and he was out of the army. It wouldn't have made any difference—it's just a fact.

When Bill came home from the army, he had a lot of money. He was, at that time, one of the richest writers in the world, receiving almost $75,000 a year in book and play royalties worldwide. Even so, while he was overseas, my mother and father supported Aram and me because my father felt that it should all be saved for Bill because he was, in Daddy's words, "a man fighting for his country." Daddy paid for our apartment on Sutton Place and a nurse for our baby and a cook and housekeeper for me. He bought our clothes and everything else that we may have needed or wanted. Plus, he kept the house filled with fresh flowers because he knew I loved that. He was not a meat-and-potatoes man.

Daddy, obviously, had forgiven me for a marriage of which he didn't approve. He never accepted Bill, but our close relationship resumed and I was breathing easier again.

This allowed Bill's money to accrue into a really huge sum, especially for that time. Works that he had finished before going overseas were published with great success—one as a Book-of-the-Month-Club main selection, which meant it made a lot of money immediately. The money kept coming in and going to savings.

When he came home and we moved to San Francisco, Bill realized that he had more money than he had ever had before.

"You know, kid," he said to me one day not too long after we returned from our year in Oyster Bay. "I'm a writer who needs to be behind the eight ball. I've never done any writing when I've had money."

Oh, my God, I thought. If he can't write with me, he won't keep loving me.

"What do you think you should do?" I said.

"What I've always done. I'm going to gamble for a while. Then I'll be able to write again."

What he was saying had no reality for me. But even if it had, I still wouldn't have said anything.

We then embarked on a whole new kind of life. We left the house every night at about 9:30 and went for dinner, and then to a place called Russian Mike's, a small, clandestine gambling casino. It had a roulette wheel and a few tables of different kinds, and tons of the best vodka and caviar.

Bill proceeded to lose and lose, night after night.

He then added to this loss by betting over the telephone—$5,000 a horse race on six races a day. We were now losing $30,000 most days, on top of $10,000 or $20,000 or, one night, $65,000.

In less than a month, all the money that had been saved disappeared. Finally it was all gone. And so was the cleaning woman.

"Well," he then said, "I guess I better get to work."

"Oh, good," I said.

He went up to his studio. I would hear him pacing the floor, even pounding the keys on the typewriter, and throwing a few things around. And the sounds were the sounds of rage. He came out of his room on the second or third day, came downstairs, and began to yell at me.

"No man could possibly write behind an eight ball like this."

I then said something very stupid.

"But Bill, you said you had to have this eight ball in order to write."

"You are insane. You are not a woman. You are not even a person. There's something wrong with you. Any other wife would have protected her husband, would have cared about what he was doing, would have stopped it immediately. She would not have allowed a husband to get in a situation like that. You are not a real woman. Women protect their men. What are you?"

He kept saying it over, again and again. "Who are you? Who are you?"

"You're the king and I'm nothing," I said. And then, after a pause, I added, "Happy, darling?"

"Bill," I continued, "you said that there was no way that you could write with all that money and that you had to lose it so you could work."

"You fucking idiot. What does it matter what I said? You should have stopped me. You must know what it is not to have any money. You should have stopped me. Surely you must know. You should have stopped me," he kept repeating.

The situation was just about as impossible as any situation could have been. I was now to blame for all of it.

He then proceeded to borrow money from everyone he knew. He lost all of that. I never went with him again to Russian Mike's.

Soon after that, he went out very early one morning and came back around noon.

"I've sold this house and everything in it," he said. "We are taking the train to New York tomorrow and can take nothing with us except our toothbrushes and toilet articles and a coat and a few things to wear. One suitcase each—one for each child, one for you, one for me—and then we leave. Don't ask me about anything."

We had talked about going back to New York. But not like this.

"Bill, some of the little paintings that were given to me by my father are very valuable. There is a tiny oil Renoir. There is a Marie

Laurencin watercolor. And a black-and-white Matisse lithograph. You can't just give them away with the house. And some of the books have great value and are beautifully bound—the people you owe don't understand this kind of value. The silver, the crystal—all these things are worth a lot of money."

"Shut your goddamn mouth and just pack the four suitcases. I don't want to hear about what's valuable and all that crap you're telling me. You don't give a damn anyway. You are not going to get us out of this spot. I am going to get us out of this spot. If you had been a real woman, this would never have happened. You should have thrown every book in the house at me, everything you could have found you should have thrown at me."

"You're quite right. I'm not a real woman like the wonderfully real women you have known from whorehouses and housecleaning. I'm not a real anything. Take your house, take your things, I'm not traveling with you anyway."

Of course, we all got on the train and came to New York. He did stop gambling for a while and went back to work. During this respite, we went to the theater and saw all the plays. We had a small apartment with just enough room for the children. He insisted we paint all the walls black. I used a very white, shiny lacquer for the woodwork to take some of the oppressiveness away from the black.

Bill stayed in bed a lot of the time, and every so often he would stay there for three or four days running. He'd say, "Oh, my back hurts," and I would wait on him hand and foot. I would bring him his fresh things, run his bath, change the sheets twice a day, run out and buy new books and new colognes for him, massage his feet, give him a pedicure and a manicure, and brush his hair. I was the best wife I've ever known.

Every now and then he'd get up to write a few letters complaining about his back and his life. He was obsessed with self-pity and his own bad luck. You see, he was an anti-intellectual, and the time for that was over. The world had become far more complex than he'd ever dreamed.

But Bill had the mentality of a matinee idol. He was like an actor who'd made a great success in a certain role in his youth and, when he goes on to summer stock in his later years, still relies on what worked for him in the past. He plays the part they all loved him as in every play he's in, no matter what the play is, and when the old ladies come backstage, he's got the robe and ascot on. But he's ruined the entire play because he's not an ensemble player, he's a star.

That's what Bill did in his writing. He always gave himself the same star part, used the same words, had the same problems. It was the world against the poet. The poet against the politician. And because he had gone on record as loving humanity, he didn't have to be nice to the people in his life. "You're not that kind of writer," I used to tell him. "You're the American Céline."

What I came to realize was that I did not exist for Bill in any way. I had nothing to do with his moods; he was his own world—his own universe. If Bill was discomfitted physically, he'd just as soon kill you as look at you. If he had indigestion, he'd just as soon take a knife and cut off your head.

To him I was a mosquito: I wasn't there unless he had to scratch. It's a terrible feeling when you put your heart and soul and your entire physical being into someone, when you have no secrets and keep nothing hidden, and that happens. Yet I knew he was in love with me in a way that no other man ever loved. It's like saying, "Jack the Ripper was nuts about me." Do you know what it means to me when people say, "My God, what a great love"? I feel as if the SS is coming after me. Bill was not a civilized man. Like many writers, he was an emotional miser. He believed that by giving himself to others, his talent, his creative juices, were somehow being drained.

After a while, I didn't care whether he was angry at me or not. I finally found myself in the awful position of knowing every single thing he was going to say about any subject. He hadn't learned anything new in years, hadn't changed any of his views on anything. His vocabulary was exactly the same as the day we met.

Bill came home one day and told me he was getting a divorce. I wished him luck.

"You better get yourself a lawyer," he said.

"What for?"

"Well, because you need one when you're getting a divorce."

"I don't need one. Just send me whatever papers you want me to sign."

"Are you telling me that you don't care enough about our getting a divorce to even get a lawyer? It doesn't mean a thing to you. You definitely don't want to be bothered with a divorce."

"No, I don't. I don't care what you do. Are you worried about how you're going to divide up your thirty cents? I know you too well, Bill—I'll keep the children, but the thirty cents is all yours. Just send the papers."

The thought that any man would pay money to get rid of me stunned me.

It still does.

Positive Love

Bill and I had stayed married for six years, and now it was over. It was 1949. I stayed, for a time, in the black apartment, very upset at having failed at my marriage. I was inconsolable. Gloria tried to help me, just as she had when Bill was overseas. She came every day. When you were troubled, in trouble, unhappy, Gloria was there. She did all one person can try to do to help another. This, to someone in trouble a lot, had a great deal of meaning, and I knew that it was genuine. That was my favorite garden path of Gloria's.

"You know," she'd say to me, "the saddest thing in the world to me is that your love for him was wasted. I never saw love like that. It kills me."

The other person who tried to help was someone my mother found for me. Ray. My mother had met Ray through friends and told her that I was a young girl with two children and that I was sick at the moment, running a fever, and going through an extreme crisis because I was getting divorced. She asked Ray if she would take care of everything. Ray said she would.

I had just brought the babies home from having their tonsils out. I had just gotten them settled into their cribs when the doorbell rang. I opened the door to see one of the most beautiful faces I have ever seen in my life—Ray's. She had beautiful, smooth café-au-lait skin, and she was sweetly dressed. As I held the door open for her, I tried to help her bring her suitcase in and I slipped and fell to the ground. She bent down and felt my head.

She closed the door, left the suitcase there, and took off her hat and coat.

"Are you Mrs. Saroyan?"

"Yes. And you're Ray."

"Where are the children?"

I took her to their rooms and she saw that they were both sleeping peacefully.

"I think you ought to go to bed. I think you have a high fever. Please let me help you into your bed."

"I want to explain everything about the children."

She looked at me. "I promise that you don't have to. The best thing you can do for the children right now is to get into bed."

So we went into my room. She found some alcohol and rubbed it over me. She gave me a fresh nightgown. I took a bath and brushed my hair and teeth, and when I came back into the bedroom, the bed linen had been changed. Next to the bed was a big pitcher of freshly squeezed orange juice, a glass, and a napkin on a tray. Ray had drawn the curtains and I noticed that she had shut the telephone off. I was feeling weaker and weaker. I got into the bed, and I think I was asleep before she left the room. I must have slept for twenty-four hours at least.

When I woke up, I found Ray wearing a uniform and sitting with the children and talking to them as they ate their lunch. I went back to bed and slept some more. I don't know how much time went by, but pretty soon I was back in one piece and went to play with the children. I noticed how pretty and bright the apartment looked. It was filled with flowers. And how nicely the children had been dressed and how happy they seemed.

She was quite right. There was nothing for me to tell her.

This was the beginning of my life with Ray, which has never ended. She is in the house as I write this.

A Visit to the Psychiatrist

Clifford Odets suggested I see a psychiatrist. He gave me a name and I telephoned him. In a rather low voice, the psychiatrist said that he would see me at 6:30 in the morning, as his schedule of regular appointments began at 7:30.

"Oh, but what about after?" I asked.

"No," he said. "I'm only human."

"Are you sure?"

"I'm simply too tired later in the day."

So I said, "Well, whatever you say then."

"If you like, I'll see you at six-thirty tomorrow morning."

"All right."

I got out of bed at 4:30 the next day. Actually, I was up, so it didn't matter. I didn't know how to dress for the occasion, what expression to put on my face—to be happy or sad. I really had no idea.

I left the apartment wearing a black silk dress, very sheer black stockings, very soft black pumps, a string of real pearls, and a sable coat. Daddy bought all that finery for me when my marriage ended. I could have gone to visit the queen at Buckingham Palace.

I just kept thinking to myself, if this marriage didn't work out, how could any? With all that love, how could any marriage have failed?

I arrived on time.

A very ugly man opened the door and said he was the doctor. I looked at him coldly and said, "I'm the patient."

"I can see that," he said.

"By my clothes?"

"Of course not." He then paused. "You are very beautifully dressed—that is, if you are going tea dancing."

"Yes, I'm aware of that. But I felt like wearing these clothes."

"It most certainly doesn't matter."

"Are you telling me that it doesn't matter what I wear?" I felt as if I'd been stabbed in the heart.

"Well," he said, "in any case, let's get started."

It meant that I was supposed to actually lie down on his disgusting leather sofa, which I was sure was filled with other people's tears.

But I knew it would not get one tear of mine because I immediately hated this man too much. I must have gone there to fall in love and this awful little creep had opened the door.

"Would it matter very much to you if I sat up—at least just to start—to talk to you?"

"Yes, it would," he said evenly.

"I thought so."

So I put my head all the way back and laid on that dirty leather thing. All of a sudden, my mind went blank. I could not remember a single trouble, a single problem. I simply couldn't remember anything. It was incredible.

He said nothing.

I realized I was expected to say something.

"I can't think of a single thing to say to you," I said.

He didn't answer, which was very unnerving.

Also, I knew my hair was getting messed up on his rotten sofa, and the whole atmosphere was so barren and bleak, it seemed as if the Depression had come back.

This man simply would not speak to me.

I said, "You see, I've never been to a doctor before, and I don't know what would be the most helpful way of beginning. I just don't know enough about it."

Still no word from him.

So I tried to tell him very clearly that I was upset because my marriage had failed and I felt it only natural that I was upset under such circumstances. This was probably one of the very worst times of my life and yet I couldn't quite call it neurotic.

"What I do find neurotic," I continued, "is to be on this sofa, trying to talk to someone who won't talk to me. I find that much more neurotic than being upset because my marriage has broken up. Don't you?"

He didn't answer.

"The reason we broke up was because one night, while taking a walk, he said, 'There's a marvelous movie playing at the R.K.O. on 86th Street.' I'd had a thought of my own, so I excitedly said, 'And you'll never guess what's playing at the Loew's 79th Street!' It was the end of everything.

"I have a fever," I then added. (And I had.) "And because of my fever, I've fallen down in the street a few times. I probably shouldn't be out with such a fever. On the other hand, it doesn't matter that much. I feel brokenhearted, living without my husband. I can't stop crying. I still love him. I don't know what to do. I don't want to cry in front of my children. Do you have any ideas of something I could try to do?"

No answer.

The unfortunate thing was that I had not been warned about this as a procedure. I might have been better at it if I had known a little something about the process.

I sat up and took a long look at him and said, "You know, I think you are a creep. I can't talk to anyone who won't talk to me, no matter what their position may be. I'm very lonely. I need someone to talk to. I need to talk to you. I'm not seeing anybody since this happened, because I'm too upset. I don't know if this is the sort of thing I'm supposed to tell you. What sort of thing do other people tell you?"

Silence.

And then I think I fell asleep for a few minutes, which was very nice. It was the loveliest little sleep I had ever had. To have him there at the desk—alert and watchful—made it a perfectly darling little sleep. I felt protected by his presence, which under any other circumstances would have been disgusting.

When I woke up, he was standing.

"Oh," I said, "have I done all my time?"

"Yes."

"Thank you very much for making time for me."

"You're welcome."

And I left, thinking to myself, My God—is that what going to an analyst is like? Is that what it is?

As I started to walk home, tears were streaming down my face.

I thought, I must find a way of helping myself. I must make peace with what has happened, but I don't know how.

When I told the psychiatrist I hadn't been seeing anyone, I had told him the truth. I couldn't see anyone. There was a cannonball in my stomach and an iron key in my throat that kept the sobs locked in.

I decided not to go directly home. Instead, I walked around for a long time, looking in the store windows but not really seeing anything.

When I finally got home, I began to read *Lucy Gayheart* by Willa Cather. I read her all the time; both Oona and I adored her. I came to a scene in a snowstorm, a part that had always meant so much to me. A phrase from it, "That old sweetheart, life itself," kept going around in my head like an old story. Somehow, that stuck in my mind. That's what it is, I realized. One has to learn how to really live one's life.

I had a few thoughts on the subject—nothing very profound, but they stopped me from crying. I quickly calmed down and was then able to begin doing the ordinary, pedestrian chores that one does each day.

I did not feel life near me. The divorce had been a kind of death for me. But the pain was so deep, so constant, and so unending that I suddenly passed a threshold and felt nothing. *Nothing* was a relief. And I slowly got back into the business of life.

Defenestration

One night, at a girlfriend's house, I met an artist with whom I became very involved. He was very famous and successful, and another plus was that he was married. He seemed to fall in love with me, and little by little, I began to forget all about Bill. We had a wonderful time together.

I told my artist friend that I would not sleep with him, but I would like it if we could sleep in the same bed together, as I had not slept alone in the nearly eight years since I'd met Bill. Maybe I should have gotten a dog instead.

My friend agreed, but it seemed difficult for him. He had often been unfaithful to his wife, but this was new to him—to fall in love and not be able to consummate the love. I thought it was so nice of him to stay in that bed with me all night just so I wouldn't be alone. A new feeling was added to my feeling of friendship, and one night, when we were in bed, I slipped my leg across the bed and put my foot on his.

All hell broke loose—I guess I had not realized how inexperienced I was, even though I had every reason to know I was.

We began a fantastic love affair. I adored being with him. I could sense the feeling he had for me, and I felt wonderful when I was with him.

One day we had to go up to his studio in Boston. It took us four days to drive there. Every heated cabin on the way was ours. Once I had him in bed, I never let him out of it again.

We always had a wonderful time together, as one can when one is taking it off the top. By that I mean that I left my problems, no matter how pressing, where I lived, as he left his problems at home with his wife. So I felt light and happy and loved. Which made me feel that I had to get him into the bed at every possible moment. We used to make plans for going to the theater or having dinner with friends or doing various things, but none of that mattered compared to being with him in bed. I suppose he was the beginning of my becoming passionate about sex.

Now I was getting all sorts of fluttery feelings with my absolutely wonderful new beau. And I call him my beau, even though we were together for two years, because I never meant it to go anywhere. I definitely did not want to get married. I was honest with him about that. He was married, but he wanted a divorce. I insisted that marriage was not the way I wanted to live. I thought I was bad at it.

Our liaison continued and it was a very happy time for me. Feeling free and feeling loved at the same time is quite special.

Once, we arrived at his studio in Boston at about 5:30 in the morning and after getting into bed, we made love and fell asleep. Later, we woke up and began to fool around, and I thought I heard something. He suddenly sat up in bed.

"My God," he whispered. "That's my wife."

I heard her calling his name and coming up the stairs.

He turned green but did not make a move. I could hear those rather heavy footsteps coming closer and closer. I panicked.

I had put my clothes and purse on a little chair beside the bed. I took everything and threw it out the window.

And then I jumped out.

It was a one-and-a-half-story drop, almost two. It didn't matter to me, though. I would rather have jumped one hundred stories than be found by his wife in their bed. But on the way down, I remember having this horrible feeling of how far down I was falling and wondering if I was going to land on cement. The window faced the street.

As I fell, my nightgown went all the way up and I saw two or three people watching me from across the street. I waved to them.

I hit the cement on my two feet. I took my skirt, which had already landed, and put it on, and I pulled up the nightgown and tucked it into the skirt. Then I put my jacket on. The nightie was now safely covered. I didn't put anything else on except my shoes.

I hailed a cab and went to the airport.

When I got home, I heard Ray on the telephone with my friend. I was dumbstruck to hear her trying to comfort him. He evidently was telling Ray that I would rather kill myself than put him in a position to be free to marry me.

Ray handed me the telephone, and I said what one always says in these situations: "Hi."

He was totally unconcerned about whether or not I had hurt myself.

"Why did you do that?" he said. "You knew that if you had just stayed put in the bed, she would give me a divorce and we could be married."

"Maybe I did know that. But I wasn't really thinking about you or your divorce. Getting a divorce is your business with your wife. It is not my business, and I wouldn't do that to any woman in the world. Yes, I would rather be dead. You may have mistaken my bitchiness about other women and so on for something it is not. You and your wife have to work it out yourselves. And please don't work it out for me because I don't want to get married and you know that."

As mad as he was, the flowers never stopped coming. They were so beautiful that I decided just to stay mad at him forever so they would keep coming forever.

But then, of course, we did make up.

He brought up the whole matter quite a few times—sometimes jokingly, sometimes seriously.

"You'd rather be dead than marry me. It's a terrible thing to realize that."

"That's a very glib way of putting it. It's not quite like that."

"Well, put it another way."

I couldn't.

The Last Fall

Almost two years had passed, yet Bill had been pressuring me to go back to him. He had found out I was having an affair and it drove him wild. He even had me followed. He was relentless. At Thanksgiving, 1950, he called for Aram right in the middle of a big dinner, and when I looked up at my seven-year-old, he was crying and I died. I'm not going to say for one minute that I went back to him for my children. I'm not that kind of liar. But I was always aware of what they were going through.

My artist friend, who did very well financially, sensed me weakening with each new phone call from Bill. One morning he took me to his lawyer's office and said he wanted to give me two million dollars, plus a million for each of my children.

"Is that what two years is worth to you?" I said.

"No. This is just a gift for the happiest two years of my life. I know you'll do whatever you have to do, but I don't want you to do it because you're feeling financially wobbly about the kids."

Of course I didn't take his money. And on some level I was offended by his offer. He should have known that once he was my lover there would never be a chance that I would take any money.

Charlie Chaplin took a different tack. He and Oona were in New York visiting, and one morning Oona called and asked if I would mind having lunch with both of them in their suite at the Plaza, instead of being alone with her at the Palm Court, where we usually went when she was in the city.

"No, of course not," I said.

When I arrived, Charlie had ordered lunch for both of us. Oona left, saying she had had a large breakfast and she needed to do a few chores in the other room.

Charlie looked at me intensely and then said, "Dear Carol. You are so mixed up and I understand it. I truly do. But my darling girl, you are turning your back on the great love of one of our greatest artists and I cannot bear to see you do this. I know Bill was difficult. He himself told me that, but you cannot go by that. Great love is passionate. It has rage. You're not two people who live in the suburbs and cheat on one another. You've had difficulties but you've had love—deep, deep, beautiful love and that is how you must think about it, particularly when you think about giving it up. You can't. It's bigger than you are. He is an artist. Life is different with an artist. He is a poet. And when a poet loves you, it is like no other love. You will never again be loved like that."

Thank God, I thought to myself.

Meanwhile, Oona had quietly come back into the room and was standing behind Charlie. It was very distracting. While Charlie was going on and on, Oona was mouthing, "No, never! No, no, *no*! Don't listen to that! *No!*" She was as vehement in her silence as he was vocally.

Charlie was such a sweet man. He loved women, but in an old-fashioned way. He wanted them to be protected by money. He loved to see a woman do well, get jewels and diamonds and things. He adored women who married rich men. He loved Merle Oberon when she was married to Alexander Korda, a very successful producer, but when she married a cameraman, he didn't want her to visit him. "No," he said, "It's not the same girl." I think it all came about because his mother had been very poor and always had to worry about the landlady knocking at the door. And don't forget that Bill at the time was still one of the richest of writers as his royalties and foreign sales marched on.

"I know you've had enough of my advice," Charlie continued, "but it is only in your interest, darling. I've seen you together. I've seen the love. I've felt the love. I love the way you talk to each other. Promise me you'll be a good girl and think hard about all I've said. After all, my interest is in you. You are Oona's closest friend and we care about you. I care about Bill in the abstract, of course, but in this particular case, to see a great playwright and poet weep unashamedly in front of me and Oona—it broke my heart, Carol. You must do the right thing and there is only one right thing. Go back."

I didn't say much. I told Charlie how much his interest meant to me and how lovely it was to know that he cared.

He said, "You are avoiding an answer. But it's all right. Take all the time you need."

I saw Bill that night. He telephoned and asked me to have dinner with him in such a really special way—something about what the pleasures of a few hours can do for a lifetime. Despite everything, I found it very moving and said I would love to see him.

We went to a little French restaurant that he seemed to know rather well. We sat there for hours, long after we finished dinner. We talked about everything, which is something we both enjoyed doing—as long as our marriage was not the topic of conversation, because that is when we got into trouble. But Bill made sure it didn't go in this direction, until the end of the evening, when he said, "You have no reason to love me. But you will. You really will again. You are my life."

He said it as though it was the absolute truth, and I think it was.

This opened up a different side of him—a side I thought I had long ago forgotten. It was how he was during our courtship, before we married. It made me remember what I always knew was true: Despite all his insanities and wildness, there was a very loving and romantic part of Bill's passion. There was depth to his unhappiness and to his rage.

He was such a victim of his own personality and tried so valiantly to break out of it that he moved me enough to try to make him happier if I could. I knew better, but I kept playing Charlie's words back in my head: Was I turning my back on a great love? Would no one else ever be able to love me as much?

Yet I was plagued by memories of the deep unhappiness in which Bill so often kept us mired.

People change, people grow, people become different, I said to myself. I went to him. He was still a man who could quietly tell you the world.

Dinner at Eight

It was a very strange thing to marry Bill for the second time, which I did early in 1951. I moved the children back to Los Angeles, to 708 North Rodeo where Bill had rented a house.

I remember feeling somewhat like a combination of a martyred Mother Superior and the greatest femme fatale of all time. So in the end, of course, remarrying him makes as much sense as everything else I did—I did it to feel better about myself.

He does seem to love me, I thought, and I do love him. Maybe one day I'll love him again the way I did before. Or perhaps my early love for him was too much a child's love. This time, I might love him like a woman.

But by the night of the wedding, I knew how doomed our marriage was. There was just no way to escape it. I was doomed and so was he, as far as I was concerned, and he knew it, too.

He began raging almost immediately. But this time there was one difference: I raged right back. He hated that.

"Bill," I said, "isn't this what you wanted?"

"Yes, this is what I wanted. You. You again. I wanted your blondeness and the sound of your voice and the scent of you and the touch of you. But I wanted it without a brain."

"That's how you got it. No one with a brain would have married you. All your wishes have come true."

Oona and Charlie gave us such a beautiful party in Los Angeles for our second marriage. They had at least two hundred people to a great dinner and there were flowers and music everywhere. All the movie stars and celebrities of that time had come, for it was rare for Charlie to give a party. Everyone was in top form and in the air was a gaiety I had not seen or heard in a while.

Of course, Bill acted the role of the winner amazingly well. I did my best to look happy, and having made up my mind to be happy, I somehow did feel happy during the evening. It was like acting. If you can't get it from the inside out, you get it from the outside in.

Charlie made a beautiful speech to us about love, at which point Bill's theatrical sense was awakened and he gave me a long and romantic kiss for all the guests to see. It delighted Charlie.

It was very lavish, and not since have I been to a party quite like that. Everything was the essence of "party"—the party lighting, the party noises, the party music, the party conversation, the party dresses. There was a lovely moment when Oona and Charlie's young children came down and were like little angels.

All the romance of life was right there in that house that night. But Oona—she knew exactly how I felt and she winked at me.

One afternoon, I telephoned Charlie to say that we would love to have a special evening for him—something he would like, though needless to say, not in any way comparable to the party he gave us.

Charlie interrupted and said, "I know exactly what I would like."

"What?"

"I want you to cook an Armenian dinner for us because Oona says you are great at it and I love the food."

As I was cooking for the four of us, the telephone rang. It was Jane Gunther, a friend from New York. She and her husband, John, the writer, were leaving for Japan in the morning. Not wanting to miss them, I invited them to join us. She said, "Wonderful. May I bring Miss G?" I said of course. Miss G was Greta Garbo, who spent much of her time traveling with the Gunthers.

Later the telephone rang again. This time it was S. J. (Sid) Perelman, the humorist, who was also on his way somewhere and in town only for the night. I was thrilled to hear from him and invited him over for the Armenian dinner. "Jesus Christ," he said,

"Can't I just have a hot dog?" I told him I'd do anything to see him.

The dinner went very well, and afterward we went back to the living room, where I served baklava and Turkish coffee. Everyone there knew one another but had not seen one another in a long while. That reassuring murmur of conversation—one of the best sounds to hear when you are giving a party—kept up throughout the evening. The dessert table was full of fruits and sweets. We had a fire roaring in the fireplace.

Even though I had turned off quite a few lights, I could not help but notice how all the men's eyes were riveted on Greta Garbo. She was sitting in the corner of the sofa, hugging her knees to her chest, laughing and talking. She was dressed strangely—in a black silk Valentina dress and a pair of sneakers—and I suddenly realized she had no panties on.

As that dawned on me, I kept standing in front of her to shield her. I didn't have the nerve to tell her, but at the same time, I didn't want her to find out later and be embarrassed. But evidently she would not have been embarrassed. I later learned that she often went to parties like that. It somehow seemed less strange that she did it than it would have if any other female in the room had done it.

She was very giggly and kept calling Charlie "Charlie Chaplin." "How are you, Charlie Chaplin?" she asked. "What is your next project, Charlie Chaplin? I think your wife is beautiful, Charlie Chaplin," and so on.

It must have been quite a nice evening, because no one seemed in a rush to leave. But finally they did. Even "Charlie Chaplin."

Calculating

Bill distrusted his love for me. He despised his desire for me. He had always been this way, but now I was growing older. Twenty-five. He had not changed, but I was changing. I think I was growing, and most of all, Bill and I were no longer the same pair of scissors.

We had been remarried a short time, and then it all came to me like a beautiful field of wildflowers. I knew exactly how I was going to kill him for the rest of his life. And that made my spirits soar, and made it possible to endure these bleak, black days.

I would not be his prisoner. He would be mine. I wouldn't be alone, he would be. I wasn't stupid, he was. I wasn't crazy, he was.

I embarked on the one calculatedly evil act of my life. I decided that having and being nothing, it was wonderful to have found a way to kill him.

I decided to become "perfect" overnight. I figured out how to be the most perfect wife/friend/lover/cook/dry cleaner/gardener/shopper / housecleaner / secretary / laundress / housepainter /man's man/you name it.

I was more perfect than I've ever known anyone to be—I mean perfect for him. I knew that no one else would ever or could ever do what I did for him. I spent the days polishing his shoes and kissing his feet and cooking his food—quietly, always quietly. He didn't like to hear anybody talk. I said very little but I did everything for his pleasure, and when he came into bed he fell into what he always called his garden of roses. The thorns were hidden for the future.

He was sly and he was smart but he did not know that something was different. Perhaps he thought I had outgrown some of the silliness of my love for him and was becoming a "real" human being. I don't believe there is a *real* human being.

His physical love for me ran amok. If I was scrubbing the floor, he jumped on top of me. He could not believe that he had made such a magnificent marriage, what great good fortune he had. He himself was so false that he could not see anyone else's falseness.

I was so perfect that when he lost me forever he would never be able to find happiness with anyone else.

That was my revenge.

One day, I simply looked him in the eye and said, "I'm sick of you." And left.

I left because everyone has somewhere—perhaps deeply hidden— a private ambition. Mine has never changed. I would like to become the best person that I can be. I know that that does not mean a perfect person, yet I want to be the best that I can. I want to learn, understand, and develop as much as I can, and understand the true importance of the fun of life.

I am without a specific ambition such as to be a doctor or lawyer or president or politician or great lover or expert on baking cakes. My ambition is private. It is without name. It has words like "See more" and "See it clearly when you look." "Know more." "Feel everything" and "Fight harder." Fight your own shadow—try to translate people closer to their own truths. Dance more. Sing more. Embrace those you love fully, including their insanities. Everywhere you go, put something beautiful—a note, a poem, a flower, a lock of baby's hair. Don't stagnate—be on guard against it always. Make love in a thousand ways. And kill the death in you. Try to be sure. A. A. Milne wrote: "Piglet sidled up to Pooh from behind. 'Pooh,' he whispered. 'Yes, Piglet?' 'Nothing,' said Piglet, taking Pooh's paw, 'I just wanted to be sure of you.' " These are the things that mean the most because they are the essence of life.

I know that when I finally left Bill, it was not because of anything he did to me. It was because I realized what I would have had to become to remain his wife and that created a head-on collision with all that I had always wanted for myself. I knew I would have to put the knife in him before he got it in me. I knew that I would have to be alert and armed with poison. I had to get there first.

But the thought of spending a marriage being ready with my dagger in order to defend against the dagger that was ready for me made me know how much I had to leave him, how quickly and suddenly.

I don't think marriages break up because of what you do to each other. They break up because of what you must become in order to stay in them.

. . . .

Pacific Palisades

. . . .

In 1952, after my second divorce was final, my children and I moved into a tiny house in Pacific Palisades, the westernmost part of Los Angeles. I did not ask Daddy for any help, because I knew how he felt about my remarrying Bill.

A few very nice friends gave me small parts on television shows whenever they could. Between this work and selling some old pieces of silver, I managed to keep going.

Our neighborhood was the kind where a lot of young married couples lived and the children all knew one another and played in the streets.

Gloria, meanwhile, had divorced Pat di Cicco and had married Leopold Stokowski, the famous conductor. She was twenty-one and he was sixty-three when they married. I had met him before she did; he had six different accents and called me Melisande. He sounded like a dead man. I asked Gloria why she married him, and she didn't like that question. "Darling," she said, "he loves me. He wants to marry me."

"Of course he does," I said. "Gloria, why don't you go on the assumption that every man you meet is madly, insanely, totally in love with you, and that they all want to marry you. Then make a pick. Don't marry the first one that asks you. You pick one."

Oona and Charlie were still in Hollywood and Oona would invite me to her parties. "Nobody needs an extra girl out here," I'd always say, and she'd always respond, "You'll never be an extra girl."

Charlie loved to entertain the people he liked, and after dinner, he would get up and do brilliant and wonderful pantomimes. And Oona, who loved Charlie's pantomimes but had seen them over and over again, would clandestinely motion to me.

"What is it?" I asked the first time.

"Let's go."

"Go? Where?"

"Let's go to a drive-in and get a milk shake." We were junk-food addicts, Oona and I. We spent millions at Hamburger Hamlet when we were in New York. She'd put ketchup on the food at Le Pavillon.

"What?" I said.

"Don't worry, I've got it timed. Trust me, I know exactly how long this takes." And off we went in her car to Dolores's Drive-In. And sure enough, we were right there in the living room when Charlie finished.

In September of 1952, while on the *Queen Elizabeth*, Oona and Charlie were told that Charlie could not reenter this country without appearing before a government board of inquiry "to answer charges of a political nature and of moral turpitude." It was truly unbelievable that they would do this to the greatest artist in what had become the greatest medium of our time. Charlie was a communist like I am Madame Chiang Kai-shek. Charlie couldn't believe it himself, and though he and Oona ended up in a beautiful house in Switzerland, his exile destroyed him. He would rant on and on for years to come about what he would have said to the House Un-American Activities Committee.

What happened to him was based on gossip columns—Hedda Hopper's to be exact. She despised Charlie Chaplin, and in Hollywood those ladies who wear hats at their desks are not to be trifled with. At that time, they carried a lot of weight. Louella Parsons, at least, was known to be a drunk. But not Hedda Hopper. She managed, somehow, to organize a group of haters and arrange that incredible shipboard act of the U.S. State Department.

That was all taking place during "the time of the toad"—the McCarthy era. I think most Americans agree today, with shame, that it was a truly ignorant and ugly time in our history.

At home Bill kept a very close watch on my life. He came over every day. He knew I didn't have anything and he was much more pleased with this life than the life I'd had in New York after the first divorce—a seemingly very gay and, to him, somewhat chic life and, most important of all, a life independent of him.

I became a total bore with him. Every time I saw Bill, he would want to sleep with me right then and there, no matter what time of day or night. And I'd say, "Stop it, Bill, we're not married, I don't want to sleep with you anymore." And he'd always say, "Look, a man has a need. You can't be like that. A man has a need." When he said that, my heart would sink. A lot of men have a need, but I'm not going around sleeping with them.

But whenever he insisted I sleep with him, he gave me something. One time it was a bright red stove, another time it was school clothes for the children, another time it was some blankets for our beds—various things known as necessities. But if you add them all up, it was a lot of sleeping with Bill. He was determined that I be the whore he said I was.

Once settled into the lulling existence of nothingness, I wondered how long I could keep it up.

I amazed myself by keeping it up for over three years—largely because of my suicide plan.

It was a detailed, well-thought-out scenario. I would do it out of town, so there would be no chance of the children finding my body; I had all the bases covered. But, of course, the thought of leaving the children alone, with only their father, kept me from doing it. (That and the fact that I couldn't think of a good note.) I'm not sure how seriously I took it, but my plan was like a little pillow that allowed me to get to sleep at night and helped me get through each day.

I worried about my children. I did the carpool. I did the cleaning and marketing and washing and ironing. I think what I hated most was the ironing, because the iron kept falling on my hand and burning it. I just could not work the iron. But I was trying to be the mother I saw on television: the Harriet of Ozzie and Harriet.

I did everything the other ladies did, but not the PTA. (I explained to my children that I would happily die for them, but I simply could not become a member of the PTA.) I made the children's lunches every morning while they were eating breakfast.

My life got stuck in this routine, which left barely an hour of the day to think about anything, although it was here I first started writing. I can remember hanging the wash out one sunny afternoon and looking at the rows of little houses, all alike. I could not stand another day.

Even though this seemed to be my life, I had to believe that it wouldn't be always. The great thing about life is the question mark that starts with the very next minute and remains in front of you, I believe, even when you die.

· ·

Agee

· ·

In the years that I was alone, I learned a lot and fell in love once. He was the most extraordinary and brilliant man I have ever met to this day, and unbelievably handsome. He probably was the best writer I ever knew. In fact, the book I had begun to write was going to be dedicated to him, but I decided not to do that because I knew that some day it would be as if I had dedicated the book to William Shakespeare—a most self-aggrandizing act.

He was James Agee.

Before we ever met, I admired not only his work—his poetry, his screenplays *The African Queen, The Night of the Hunter,* and *The Quiet One,* his film writing, and his book on the rural South, *Let Us Now Praise Famous Men*—but mostly I admired him. That was because of what he had done during a radio press conference Charlie Chaplin gave after the opening of *Monsieur Verdoux.* The picture was marvelous, but it had been destroyed by the critics, some of whom were there asking questions.

Toward the end of the interview, which I heard over the radio in our house on Long Island, I heard a voice. It was a voice of intelligence, wit, and poetry.

"Yes, sir?" Charlie asked. "What is your question?"

The man identified himself as James Agee, the critic from *Time* magazine. He spoke slowly and clearly and beautifully.

"Mr. Chaplin, how do you feel about a country which has treated you in the manner you have been treated, when indeed you have given it such great artistry?"

There was a long and total silence.

And Charlie then said, "Thank you."

That was the end of the program.

Of course, this man was a hero to me and to those who felt for Charlie. But I was particularly happy for Oona, who I knew had been sitting there the whole time dying. She simply despised the way Charlie was treated. We all felt he was the greatest artist in an industry that he had practically created. Charlie himself would describe how when he'd started out one had to see films in nickelodeons, peering through slots. "I'm the one who's responsible for changing that," he'd say. "I did that." He was the definitive artist of the twentieth century. He helped to create the medium that would change the world.

Naturally, an arrangement was made for Charlie and Oona to meet Agee socially a few days later. They went out for dinner and it was instant love on all sides.

I met Jim myself four years later at the party the Chaplins gave for my remarriage to Bill. I was happy to finally meet James Agee, and at the same time stunned at his handsomeness. He wasn't a dressed-up man—he wore work shirts with khakis and old tweed jackets that really needed the suede elbow patches. But he was six feet four, with black hair and eyes that were navy blue.

He congratulated Bill on the remarriage and said that what Oona had told him about me was so obviously true. I knew that was a great compliment. We talked a bit, but of course Bill and I had to talk to all the other guests, so our conversation was brief.

But Oona had caught the compliment. On the telephone the next day, she said, "Jim really likes you."

"And I really like him," I said.

"I knew it."

"Of course, that's the end of it."

"I know," she said. And then, "But of course, it isn't."

Time went on. I saw him quite a few times at the Chaplins', and after a few months his wife, Mia, came out to Hollywood with their children. He had gotten some kind of assignment in Hollywood and had rented a house so the whole family could be with him. His wife was almost as big as he, but with an incredible face, unusual and beautiful. Most of all, she had a rare intelligence. I could see their bond—anyone could.

We became quite friendly, and in 1952, after Bill and I got our second divorce, the Agees were wonderful to me. They invited me to a house they rented for the summer on the beach every weekend with the children. I dearly loved them both.

A year later Jim came into my life by himself. He telephoned one evening around 7:00. It was the night after Thanksgiving.

"I have taken a place to live close to where you live," he said, "because I would like to see you."

"How wonderful. I can't wait to see you guys."

He very pointedly said, "Carol, I am here alone. This is the time of year Mia has to be in the East for the children's school and her job at *Fortune*."

He asked me if he could come over that night, and I said, "Of course. I can't wait to see you."

He rang the doorbell and came in, looking as only he could look. He had classical good looks combined with a shining quality beyond intelligence. You knew he was a man who had art in his soul and all kinds of knowledge filed in his brain, who knew more about human beings than most human beings would want known about them. He was an extraordinarily brave man about anything he believed in.

The main quality that he had that I had never seen so clearly in anyone else was a complete lack of condescension. If a child asked him a question, he would answer it exactly the way he would have answered Albert Einstein. He based his life on the belief that people were good, decent, and intelligent, until they proved otherwise. I found that conviction more and more rare.

I told him how absolutely thrilled I was to see him. I had given the children their dinner. They said hello and so on and were beginning to get ready for bed.

I had made dinner for us and after we ate we sat there talking for a few more hours. He drank very good brandy but never seemed to get drunk, nor was I ever to see him drunk.

At the time I had been playing one record over and over all day and night for a few months. It was Mozart's Twenty-first Piano Concerto, played by Robert Casadesus. By this time, when I listened to the second movement, it was not really a matter of hearing anymore—it seemed to be part of my breathing. I knew every note. When I was alone anywhere, I heard it. I did not have to have it playing in order to hear it.

I had a phonograph that would replay the record continually until I stopped it. I never stopped it and it played all night long. Jim knew what it was. He said he had always regarded it as one of the best pieces of music he had ever heard.

We talked a lot about the people we knew and, of course, about Oona and Charlie. Jim told me he kept in close contact with Charlie, writing to him often. I'd only seen Oona once since the press conference, when she came back into the country for one night, to get a satchel with all their important financial papers. As long as she was with Charlie, everything was fine as far as Oona was concerned. But during the twenty-four hours she was gone, Charlie went crazy. They'd never been separated for so much as one night before. "I didn't know," he told me later, "how I was going to live through that night."

Finally, there wasn't anything that we didn't talk about. We seemed to have so much to tell each other. But the thing I was truly crazy about was that when it came to be 5:30 in the morning I noticed that it seemed to be the beginning of the evening for Jim, as it had always been for me for so many years.

I have always had terrible insomnia. It didn't matter much to me. I lived with it and I still do. I love those late-night and early-morning hours. The telephone is not ringing. The doorbell is not ringing. The church bells are not ringing. Nobody wants you. No one is looking for you. The heat's off. The whole world is asleep and the night belongs to you alone.

Obviously, that was the way it was with Jim as well.

At 7:00 in the morning, I said, "Jim, I think you better leave now because I want to make breakfast for the children and then I have to wake them up. And while they're having their breakfast I make their lunch for them to take to school. So it's a bit of a busy time."

"Of course," he said. "I'll leave immediately. I had no idea it was so late." He then looked at me. "Does it matter?"

"Of course not."

As he went out the door, he said, "May I come tonight again?"

"Of course."

And he came at 8:00 again and stayed until 7:00 in the morning again. And it was that way the day after and after and after. I never saw anyone else. I didn't need to see anyone else. I didn't want to. He was an entire world.

Every once in a while, I would get very nervous when it was very late at night and I thought I heard something outside. He would go right out and look and say, "No one is there. Why are you so frightened?"

"What if it's Bill?"

"You are afraid of Bill. I am not."

I looked at him and realized he really wasn't afraid of anything, much less Bill. I thought there was something wonderful about that. I wondered aloud why I wasn't like that.

"Because that son of a bitch made it his business to scare you. And he succeeded."

It became so natural to be with Jim every night. It was absolutely natural when we finally kissed about a week after the first visit. And a week after the first kiss, it seemed only natural that we would go to bed together. But I couldn't. I just could not. I knew Mia too well. I knew his children. But far more important, I knew that he had had a heart attack. I didn't know exactly what a heart attack was in those days (what happy days those must have been, not knowing about heart attacks), but I was afraid that if we actually had an affair, he would die. That's how ignorant I was.

"Jim, I can't sleep with you because even though I want to more than anything, I know you've had a heart attack and I'm afraid you'll die."

He smiled at me.

"That's all right, darling," he said. "You will. But if that's the way you feel now, we won't. I just love being with you no matter what we're doing."

Sometimes we would lie side by side on the sofa looking up toward the ceiling and listening to Mozart. We told each other how much we meant to each other.

And I agreed with him—I was sure I would sleep with him one day.

He always brought a manuscript with him in the evenings. It was a story that he was working on. It had to do with his first marriage and falling in love with Mia. He would read it to me. It was fascinating, and he always wanted to know if he was correct about how women felt in this or that situation, depending on what was happening in the story.

Of course, the reactions that he had written were the reactions he himself would have had, which made the story quite wonderful. Because men and women are not that different. They're only a little different. We talked about that, and every night he read a little something from the book. I was so flattered that he was interested in my opinion.

I also loved the way he read—I loved watching him and hearing him. One time, while he was reading, I fell asleep. When I woke up, I was ready to kill myself, except that when I saw his face I realized that he had fallen in love with me and the naturalness of my going to sleep while he was reading his work somehow clinched that. I could feel it. I don't know any other writer like that.

As time went on, I wondered about letting him read the very small portion of the novel I had started writing. One night, I simply left the few pages I had written out that summer on the coffee table. I was busy in the kitchen and I looked out every once in a while to see if he had found them, and when he did, I went quite crazy watching his face. When he finished, he took the pages and brought them into the kitchen.

"I just read this. I didn't know you had written anything."

"And now you're sure I haven't written anything."

"No, Carol, you are a very good writer. I can tell that from these few pages. There is no way you should not be writing."

Because it was Jim saying this, there was no way I could doubt it or say what I would say to anyone else: "You're so sweet to say that." You couldn't say that to him because he didn't do things like that. When he said it, I knew I was a writer. It was as simple as that.

One afternoon, he telephoned to say that he would be arriving at 8:00, his usual hour, and that he had a present for me.

Well, I couldn't contain myself. I was so thrilled. It was getting close to Christmas and I thought, How wonderful—I know that Jim doesn't have any money, but still he is bringing me a present. What could it be?

I opened the door wearing my most beautiful dress, which did not escape him.

"What a beautiful dress."

As he said that, I was looking all over him to see the present. But there was no package. He was so smart—he was smiling at me in an amused way because he knew exactly what I was looking for.

"Shall I give you your present now or shall we have dinner first?"

I began to stammer politely that he might be hungry or something, but it didn't quite come off. He knew I would die if he didn't give me the present right away.

He turned the phonograph off and sat down at the piano and played the second movement of Mozart's Twenty-first Piano Concerto.

I thought I would die. It was so beautiful to watch and to hear him play it, to know that he had just learned it, and that he had just learned it to play for me. I was stunned. It was the gift of my lifetime. And I loathed myself for being so ordinary and terrible as to look for a package, when this man filled the house with Mozart. I couldn't stop hating myself.

When he finished, he said, "I rented a piano and learned it. I know how much you love it so you don't have to say anything."

"There'll never be a gift as wonderful as that for me to give you, no matter what."

"Oh, you don't know about gifts. You've been giving them to me every night."

Then we had dinner.

"Shall I play the record?" he asked.

"No, of course not. I want your sound in my ears."

Later, as we were lying on the sofa, he said, "If I had brought you something that could have been in a package, what might you have liked?"

"Well, a beautiful tulle peignoir."

"What else?"

"A string of pearls."

"What else?"

"A beautiful ice-blue nightgown."

"What else?"

"All the works of James Agee bound in solid gold."

He laughed.

"What else?"

"One pink rose."

"What else?"

"A clock that never goes beyond this hour right now."

"I would like that, too."

They were among the most wondrous nights of my life, those nights with Jim. Christmas was coming so soon and I knew that he would have to go back to New York. It made me so sad to think that, much too soon, the doorbell was going to stop ringing every night at 8:00. Of course, it would have been much too soon even if it had been a hundred years from then.

You see, those nights also filled my days, making them beautiful and filled with expectation.

The time came for him to leave.

"I'll write to you every day," he promised.

"I can't write to you, Jim. I don't want to. I'm worried about Mia."

"I know. But I'll write to you."

The night he was leaving, he came earlier than usual and we had dinner with an old friend, Jeannie Widmark. Jim adored her and so did I, and I still do. But she told me later that our visit made her cry. She said she never saw anything like it in her life—we were both so in love and so sad.

We left after dinner and I drove him to the airport. As we passed Sepulveda and Sunset boulevards, there was a huge lot of Christmas trees for sale. And in the middle of the lot, I saw a tiny pink tree.

"Jim!" I couldn't help exclaiming. "Look! Look at the baby tree. The little pink tree in the middle of the lot. Look. Isn't it sweet?" I just loved it.

"Yes, I see it. And you must have it. Stop the car. I must get it for you."

"Oh, no, Jim. Don't be silly. I just think it's pretty, that's all. And besides, you'll miss your plane."

"Yes. I was thinking of that. Wouldn't it be terrible if I did?"

"Oh, yes, it would be terrible."

I didn't stop. We continued on to the airport. When we got close to where we would be stopping, he said, "Darling, do me a favor. I won't be able to take this good-bye. I want to get out here and I want you to drive back to your house right away. Don't look back. Don't wait for my plane to disappear into the sky. Don't think about this. Don't think about anything. I'll telephone you tomorrow night and I'll write you every day."

We kissed good-bye in the car, our tears mingling. Then he very quickly got out of the car and disappeared.

I started to drive home. It was raining. And between the rain and my own tears, I had to pull over to the side of the road for a minute or two before I could go on.

When I got home, I paid the baby-sitter and gave her a Christmas present. I checked the children one more time and put some of the lights out. I found a note on my pillow.

It said, "I love you." No name. It didn't need the name.

How will these days and nights be without him, I asked myself. How will I live through them?

And I began to really sob. The doorbell rang.

My God, I thought, who could that be?

I knew that Bill, of course, had a key. And no matter how many times I changed the lock, he still had a key. And he never had the manners to tell me he was coming over. He just unlocked the door and showed up. So I knew that it wasn't Bill.

But who was it? I became afraid.

"Who is it?" I said as I went near the door.

And that most beautiful of all voices said, "Guess."

I knew immediately. I opened the door, and Jim was standing there with the tiny pink Christmas tree.

I couldn't get over it. It will always be one of the happiest moments of my life.

He stayed through Christmas, through New Year's, through Valentine's Day. But then he really had to go, and he did.

Jim died in the late spring.

. . . .

Kay and Rex

. . . .

The Palisades routine was taking its toll on me. I was in the little house and I had painted the furniture over and over again.

How, I thought, can I get out of this?

I was almost thirty, had no money, and knew that pretty soon I'd be reduced to taking in other people's wash.

It was 1954 and almost summer, and it had been established in our divorce settlement that Bill would take the children each summer. I sold the last piece of my former finery. All together I had just under three thousand dollars, and I performed what was probably the first brave, independent act of my life. I made a plan of my own and executed it—made all the arrangements. It could have been anything. In my case I decided, for no reason at all, that since I was not married to anybody I was going to get on a plane and go to Europe.

I told the children that I was going to visit my sister in Geneva, where she lived with her husband, the Baron Henri de la Bouill-erie.

"You're going to visit the Baron de la Bouillerie?" they asked, very impressed, as only children can be.

"Yes," I said. "He's your uncle."

"Do you think the Baron de la Bouillerie is going to be glad to see you, Mama?"

"I hope so. Maybe not, though." I was worried that he would still remember that I came to their wedding dressed as a bride, because I was mad at my sister. Maybe not exactly a bride, but I did wear white, which really isn't correct. And I had good reason to be mad. My sister is a great interior decorator. Really one of the best. But when I had lent her a mink coat and she'd turned it into a little mink doormat, a bathmat, and two little pillows on her sofa, I was mad.

I planned the trip very carefully, and when I told Bill that I was going to Europe, he said, "Tough, kiddo. Tough. You're not going anywhere."

"What do you mean?"

"I'm not taking the children this summer. I can't. I'm going to be doing other things."

"Oh, aren't you cunning? It's really interesting how you've made such elaborate plans with the children, and now you're not taking them."

"That's right. So you better revise your summer plans."

"I will. I'll take them with me."

"You can't. They need to be available to me to see when I want."

"Then you have to take them, because I am definitely going to Europe."

He raged on as I left for Europe with the children. First we went to Switzerland to visit my sister, who was glad to see me, and then to spend more time with Oona and Charlie, who had moved into a house at Vevey. I took a few days off by myself to go to London, where I ran into Sydney Chaplin, Charlie's son, and his girlfriend, Kay Kendall, a very fast-rising English movie star who'd just made a hit in a movie called Genevieve.

Kay and I fell in love with each other almost at once, and she insisted I leave my room at the Savoy and stay with them. Though she liked to joke that she looked like "two profiles pasted together," she was elegant, truly beautiful, and much more alive than anyone else. She took to calling me "Wifey," like I was her little wife and she was going to take care of me.

"Sydney," I said one night when Kay was out of the room, "you finally found a real girl. She is everything and more. I've never met anyone like her."

Sydney looked at me. He was exhausted. He said, "Listen, you are about to save my life. As much as I love Kay, I can't help it—I'm sleeping with another girl."

"That can't be true. Who is it? *Who?*"

"Joan Collins," he said. "She's an actress. And that's where you come in. You're saving my life by being here, because I'm going to skip."

I couldn't understand how Sydney could ever want to leave this lithe, luscious, and laughing girl, but he did. One morning he appeared at the front door with a suitcase on each arm, like in *Death of a Salesman*. "Sydney," I said, as loudly and as softly as I could, "Don't do this. Stop it."

"Shhh," he said, and off he went. Then Kay appeared and burst into tears. "I don't know what I'm doing with him," she said. "He's such a liar, and he gets more pimples by the day." She sighed and suddenly said, "Let's open a bottle of wine, Wifey." When it was finished, she had an idea.

"Sydney's sure to call," she said, "and when he does I want you to tell him that about an hour after he left, I died of a heart attack. Tell him you are in a terrible state and you need him to come right away and help with the body. Do you understand?"

"Oh, yes," I said, "of course."

"Do you think I ought to get dressed?" Kay asked. "What looks best when you're dead?"

"Put on something soft and sexy," I suggested.

"Yes, that's it. To be dead and sexy at the same time would be quite a feat."

She got all ready, and we telephoned the florist across the street and ordered quite a few bouquets of wildflowers, roses, and freesia. And forget-me-nots, of course.

Then we sat there. Kay opened another bottle of wine. We sat there. We didn't get the tiniest ring from the telephone. At 11:00

that night, Kay ordered enough Chinese food for six people. We ate every drop and opened up another bottle of wine.

At about 2:00 in the morning, Kay was completely out. I was asleep, too, so I don't know how long the telephone had been ringing, but I finally got up and answered it. It was Sydney. At last.

"How's everything?" he said.

"Sydney, I'm going to kill you. Kay has died."

"Come on, you stop that. She says that all the time."

"No, she really died."

"When?"

"A little while after you left."

"Did you call the undertaker?"

"No, you're the undertaker."

Kay must have heard something. Suddenly she was beside me. "Is that the son of a bitch?" she said. "I want to talk to him." She grabbed the telephone and said, "I hope you are having a good time because I am not. I loved you with all my heart, and this is how you thank me. But that's all right, Sydney, have a good time. I have two hired killers looking for you at this very moment. All those lies you told me about how much you loved me, how much I meant to you—I guess you just tell those lies to everyone."

He must have said something about having only told her the truth.

"The truth?" she screamed. "You never told me the truth and you know it. You are just a liar and that's why you have all those pimples." Then Kay passed out on the sofa and Sydney must have hung up.

When I returned to Switzerland, Kay came with me. We agreed a change would do her good. "Oh, you're Wifey's older sister," she said to my sister when we arrived.

Whereupon Elinor looked at Kay and said, "I am Baby Sister."

"Of course you are," Kay replied. "You just look older."

At a dinner party a few nights later, someone told Kay that Rex Harrison was seriously interested in her. Kay and Rex had just finished a movie together, *The Constant Husband,* but nothing had happened between them—Rex was seriously married to actress Lilli Palmer.

"It's funny," Kay told me later that night, "because I had a little sneaker for him, too."

"Really?"

"Oh, yes, he's quite wonderful." I knew that Kay's instincts were flawless. She had to have a fascinating man immediately to pull up what might become slack and to ease the pain of loss. "I just knew that Lilli would make anything between us impossible."

"Where is he now?"

"They're probably in their house in Portofino."

"Kay," I said, "let's go to Portofino. I've never been there, and the kids would love it."

"Well, Wifey, let's get the show on the road."

By this time, it was 5:30 in the morning, and we decided not to go to sleep. Instead we bathed, had some breakfast, and had a taxi take us to a travel agent. Kay did all the talking, saying that we were not nouveau riche—which meant we could only afford second class. Also, she told them, we had babies with us.

Well, they were not exactly babies. Lucy was eight and Aram nearly eleven. In fact, my son told me many years later that he had had a tremendous crush on Kay.

"Don't worry about a thing, Wifey. I will make the children look little and get them on that train."

And that is exactly what happened.

The train ride through Switzerland to Italy was actually quite beautiful. I looked out the window at tiny villages and got out at some of the stops to buy chocolate.

When *finally* we reached Portofino, Kay pointed out the place where she had arranged for us to stay. It was directly in the middle of the piazza. The water was blue, the sky was blue, and the piazza was filled with flirtations, gaiety, and business. I had never seen anything like it.

The next day, Kay insisted on ordering lunch and we had an eighteen-course meal of the worst food I have ever eaten in my life, a very difficult thing to do in Italy.

"Wifey, what's the matter with you? This is delicious. It's squid."

I looked down at it and at the eels and eggplant that were also on my plate.

"Don't be defeated," Kay said. "This is just the appetizer."

My children and I only wanted pasta, but Kay ate all the rarities and specialities of Portofino, and of course, had a few bottles of wine to go with it all and fell sound asleep in her chair. My children went up to their rooms. I watched Kay, beautifully asleep, having gorged herself with many disgusting things. But then she opened her eyes and smiled at me.

"Wifey, stay where you are. I have just seen someone."

I watched the activity in the plaza for quite some time before she returned—with Rex Harrison on her arm. He was charming and said how wonderful it was that we were there and that he wanted to invite us to spend the day on his boat some day soon. He told us the very wealthy earl of Warwick was his houseguest.

"I'm sure you've met Foulke," he said.

"No, no, I never have," I said.

"And I think Binky Beaumont, the theatrical producer, and one or two others will join us for the trip, too. But in any case, you must come and have dinner at the house. How about tonight?" he said in his best light-comedy voice, which is the best light-comedy voice in the world.

I arranged for the children to have dinner downstairs at the hotel. Kay and I hogged the bathtub, and although we really didn't have any marvelous clothes to wear, we managed to look terrific, at least according to Kay.

There were about eight people for dinner, and the only bore there was Foulke, the earl of Warwick. Lilli was very tense, but she tried to be gracious. Kay was on another planet, and Binky and his friend argued over a play they were producing. Rex was very watchful of the Lilli and Kay situation.

Lilli showed me her bedroom, and as she did, she said, "How long have you known Kay?"

"Oh, not for very long, but I feel I know her rather well anyway," I said.

"What makes you feel that way?"

"She's so open and we liked each other immediately."

"How did you meet?"

When she asked that, all the little wires in my head stood up with a little bit of electricity.

"I met her with her beau, a very dear friend of mine, Sydney Chaplin."

She wanted to really delve into who I was, and why I had this friendship, even though it seemed as if I had already told her. I explained who Oona was and told her that was how I knew Sydney and that by knowing Sydney, I met Kay.

"Oh, then you just met?"

"Yes, you could say that."

"Oh, what do you think of her?"

"I think she's extraordinary," I said. "Don't you?"

"You could say that," she said coldly. "But you seem very different from her. Are you sure you're going to remain friends?"

"I find it difficult to talk in circles," I said. "I think I understand you and I would like you to understand me. I haven't known her all my life, but I somehow feel that I know her. I love being with her."

"You were married to William Saroyan. That's right, isn't it?"

"It's half right. I was married to him twice."

"Oh my, oh dear. That must have been very difficult for you—marrying, divorcing, marrying, divorcing."

"Those were the easy parts. It was living together that was impossible."

"Oh, yes, of course," she said. "Well, you know, no marriage is perfect. But I wanted to have a little talk with you, if only to tell you that I love my husband very much."

"I know that you do."

"And I find myself in a very vulnerable position. You see, my marriage is my life."

"Of course it is. And you have a beautiful life, and I'm sure that you will continue to have it always."

She looked thoughtful, and changed the subject, saying that if I needed clothes or anything while I was traveling, I should call her.

I felt deeply embarrassed for both of us. I knew that something ugly had just transpired between us, and yet it was so subtle—even natural—that I was not able to say anything at all.

Rex was yelling up the stairs for us to come down.

"This is the most beautiful house," I said to Rex when we reached the bottom of the stairs. "Lilli has been kind enough to show it all to me, and I have loved seeing it."

And then, like the Professor Higgins he would eventually become, he said, "Oh, yes, yes, yes, very good."

We walked into the living room, where Kay said, "Foulke wants you to come and spend tomorrow on the boat."

"Well, I don't know," I said.

"Oh, yes, Wifey, we are definitely going. The children are invited."

We said our good nights. But not to Rex, because he said he would see us home. He told Lilli he would be right back.

I didn't talk during the car ride. When we pulled up to our piazza, Rex came out and followed Kay upstairs to our room. As I saw it happening, I went into the children's room, but before I could settle in, Kay arrived.

"He's gone, darling," she said.

"What's happening?"

"He's in love with me and he wants a divorce and he wants to marry me."

"My God, Kay, but what are you going to do about Lilli?"

"I'm not going to do anything about Lilli. He says he hates her."

"Oh, you know that couldn't possibly be true. Maybe he's out of love with her."

"Well, he loves me and I love him and he wants to marry me and I want to marry him and that's the way it's going to be."

"Kay, you don't really know him. You haven't even slept with him."

"Carol, we did sleep together. Yesterday at lunch. In fact, I got a briar stuck up my ass. The briar was terrible and I'm very happy."

And I did remember that she had looked very uncomfortable for a few hours after she returned from her disappearance at lunch.

"He's had many, many affairs since he's been married to Lilli and he says that she knows it and wants him at any cost."

"Kay, you're in trouble."

"I know. But there's nothing I can do about it. That's the way it is. He told me he's been in love with me since the first time he saw me."

The next morning, at 10:30, Kay, the children, and I all piled onto the boat. We were joined by everyone from the previous evening. The trip at first was rather silent and sleepy, for many had gulped down quite a few Bloody Marys in the hopes of getting rid of hangovers. It was also rather strained. The silent drama occurring on that boat was enough to sink it.

After a few hours, Lilli began a conversation with Kay. She said words to the effect of "Why are you doing this to my husband and to my marriage and to me? Why?"

Kay said, "I have done nothing. I have never done anything with your husband. We have never had an affair. I happen to be in love with someone else and you're quite wrong."

At which point, Rex, who had been listening from somewhere nearby, said, "Kay, don't tell that to Lilli. We have been together and we're in love and I want to marry you and I want Lilli to know the truth, so stop lying to her."

Kay went into total shock. She just stood there and did nothing. Lilli became hysterical and said she had to leave the boat immediately. I think Rex said, "Jump overboard." The strain of the years of lying was too much for him. There was a small dinghy on the side of the boat, and Lilli went into it with a member of the crew. She left in tears.

Kay began to cry. I saw a tear or two in Rex's eyes. My children were thrilled at the excitement. Binky and his friend said, "Good God," which is more or less what Foulke also said.

We went out for dinner, but left early because my daughter, Lucy, did not feel well. Rex was waiting for us when we returned. Lucy had a slight fever and seemed a bit disoriented, so an Italian doctor was called. After examining Lucy he said, "She has appendicitis. Her appendix must be removed right away."

I couldn't imagine this. She didn't really seem sick, and yet she was uncomfortable and had a fever. I wanted to get a second opinion.

"You don't have time, signora," the doctor said. "You must have this appendix removed right away. Your child's life is in danger."

Meanwhile, Rex and Kay had gotten a French surgeon off a boat that was docked in Portofino and brought him up to see Lucy.

They spoke in French and Italian and a little English. The French doctor said, "Madam, he is right. Go as quickly as possible. If I had any way of doing it here, I would. But I can't operate here. The Italian doctor makes a great deal of sense and you can trust him."

I bundled Lucy up. We were driven at an unbelievable speed north to the clinic, which was about twenty-five miles away. I didn't know how I was going to pay for everything, but there would be time to worry about that later.

When Lucy was in the operating room, I saw nobody except one or two nuns passing through the halls before the doctor, who knew of my doubts, came out and told me Lucy was fine and resting. He also showed me the appendix, which he had in a bottle. He wanted me to see the infection and what a close call it had been.

I then went into the room where they had put a bed for me next to Lucy's. And I watched her sleeping peacefully until morning.

Each day she got better and better, and pretty soon she knew every nun at the clinic. Our room was directly across from the elevator and one afternoon I heard, through our open door, a voice shrieking from the elevator. "Wifey! Wifey! I've got the money!"

She had gotten the money to cover our hospital bills from Rex. I was so touched, and sorry that she had gone to so much trouble. So many people offered to help me, knowing that a woman abroad usually doesn't have money for such an emergency. But I telephoned Bill, because legally I had to, and told him. He cabled me money—the one time he did so for anything since we had split.

"You are a fucking fool," Kay said. "You should have taken money from everyone. You could have had a capital gains deal out of this. You're always going to be poor, darling. I don't know what would happen to you if it wasn't for me."

She then brought me up to date on her situation with Rex.

"Oh, darling, everything is all settled. Lilli is gone, and he and I are going to London tomorrow. We are taking you with us, and all the plans are made. Don't think of a thing."

I told her that I couldn't go, that I had to go back to my sister's in Geneva but that I would see her in London on my way home.

Home—all misted over in sadness and loss and failure. I never wanted to go there again.

When the children and I arrived in London, Kay had two cars waiting for us at the airport and two maids waiting for us in her flat, which was filled with flowers. There was a note saying that all the publicity had been too much for them and they had had to leave London for the country. However, both she and Rex came in the next day for a few hours to see me. They were both drinking and talking of love and seemed very, very happy, until Kay suddenly showed the stress by throwing her drink in Rex's face.

He barely moved, but he threw his drink in her face.

"Carol, dear," he then said, unfazed. "I think we'll be getting on and we will see you back in America—I just know it."

I came to learn this was normal behavior for these two so desperately in love.

One day two years later, when I was living in New York, suddenly there was Kay on the other end of the telephone. She, too, was in New York—just a few streets away from me. Rex, she told me, was about to open in *My Fair Lady*.

Kay and I got together as much as we possibly could. Rex and Kay were ensconced in a beautiful apartment but were looking for a place to spend the weekends during the hot summer.

Then came the incredible excitement of the opening of *My Fair Lady*. Kay invited me to join them at the party afterward. Even Rex, sophisticated as he was, became as thrilled as a child over being reviewed as he was. All those involved in the show knew what they had, but it didn't lessen the euphoria of the reviews. It was one of the great Broadway events of all time, and everyone felt it. Babe and Bill Paley, Slim Keith, Truman—all the so-called upper-crust New York was there to applaud this brilliant actor finally.

One night, Kay rang the doorbell of my apartment and tearfully yelled, "It's me. It's Kay. Let me in," which of course I did. She was crying her eyes out. She and Rex had had a terrible fight.

"Wifey, may I spend the night with you?"

"Of course," I said.

Several times Kay came to spend the night after fighting with Rex. She was a creature of romance.

"Do you think he loves me?" she'd ask. "Do you think he's tired of me? What do you think?"

I would tell her what I thought: No one who ever knew her could stop loving her.

And soon Rex would come to get her. A love scene would be played, and it would be one that should have been painted, or made into a movie or book. It should have been for all the world to see in whatever medium possible. It should have been on the news.

They were deeply in love. They fought. They made up. They stayed in love. This happened on a more or less regular basis.

The telephone rang late one night, about 2:00 in the morning in fact, and it was Kay on the other end, whispering happily.

"Darling, we were married this afternoon. It was all very sudden; Lilli gave Rex a divorce, but I wanted you to know it and to know how happy I am. This is really a happy ending."

"Kay, darling, it's the beginning of that elusive happiness you always almost had—and now it's here for you. I can't even try to tell you how happy I am for you both."

Rex got on for a minute and I said, "By God, you did it."

Many weeks later, after Kay went to California to make *Les Girls,* a movie with Gene Kelly that she had committed to before her marriage, Rex called.

"Carol, I would like to talk to you. I need to see you. There's something I think you should know. Could you meet me tonight after the theater and have supper with me in the Oak Room?"

There was something different about the way he sounded, something in his voice I had never heard before—and yet I wasn't sure whether I was just imagining it.

In the Oak Room, a very English place which, of course, the non-English adore, he ordered what he referred to as "the usual." I didn't know what it was, but I said, "I'll have the same." He then told me something that I had no face for, no words for.

"Carol, Kay is very sick, and has been for quite some time. I know that you don't know it. She has leukemia. She has had it for quite a while. She doesn't know it. If she does, she's trying to give me a gift. But in all honesty, I don't think she has any idea that she is as sick as she is. She doesn't have very long."

"Rex," I said. "Please start again. I don't understand."

I needed a minute to get myself in one piece and be able to stay in one piece long enough for him to be able to talk freely and not feel that I had died as he spoke—which is exactly what had happened.

I had seen Rex and Kay go up and down, down and up, be glad and sad and in all sorts of moods—up moods, down moods, side moods. But then to be hit in the face—beyond emotion, beyond possibility—this was too much because it was a feeling past hope, past everything; it was the ultimate tragedy. It was as though the world had stopped.

That was the look on Rex's face. It was as though life had ended for him.

He went on to tell me that there had been times when Kay felt very weak and sick and had gone into the hospital for a day or two. And then, at some point while they were in London, she was seeing his doctor. The doctor telephoned Rex one day and told him that he had put Kay out and then given her a very-much-needed blood transfusion without her knowledge. They were getting ready to leave for America and the doctor gave Rex a list of American doctors he thought she would be able to get along with. They were brilliant doctors, and their field was her illness. They had, as a group, made a certain amount of progress, but Rex was told not to put much hope in that yet. They came to America and Rex said he used every excuse he could to get her to the doctors, usually saying he himself did not feel well.

"I could always see when she would begin to fail," he told me. "That beautiful gaiety of hers, her charm, her wit, her silkiness—everything about her would be just a tiny smidgen less.

"I knew that no matter what else happened," Rex said, "I wanted to marry her. The only possible gift to give Kay is everything, all of you. I got in touch with Lilli and I told her the absolute truth. I said there were ways in which Lilli could be a friend if she wanted to be and I thought, on hearing this story, she might decide to be my friend. I told her Kay had only a little time left to live, that she had leukemia, and that she didn't know it, that the one thing in the world that Kay did want was for us to be married and that I would give Lilli anything in the world that I could if she would give me my freedom immediately to marry Kay for the little time we had left.

"Lilli was very moved and seemed to be very upset and said, 'Of course.' We made a plan to set things in motion as quickly as we could. She would, of course, get everything that I had, except for the house in Portofino, which for obvious reasons she wanted no part of. All else would be hers. She said that she would go ahead with it, but there was one condition. She had to see the hospital records. That was arranged for immediately."

As Rex told me that she had to see the records in the hospital, I began to shake. He saw it.

"Carol, I know you don't drink, but please take a sip of that." He motioned to what was in front of me, his "usual": a bottle of Lafitte Rothschild. I did take a few sips, and then ordered a Coca-Cola.

"Why I am telling you all this is that I know that you love each other and I know that I can trust you. And I know that Lilli, because of some silly pride, will tell the story and it may get around to Kay and if it does, since you are the one person she would tell it to, I have only you to help me with these last months—if they are months."

I told him he had me for anything at all that should be done, that could be done, that I would be there for him and for her. I would lie, I would do anything.

"I think Lilli will spread it about, and you know practically everyone in New York that we know. If you should hear it, make sure it is denied by you as Kay's very best friend. I have to ask you to do that."

"Of course I'll do it. It is nothing. I wish there was something I could do to make it different."

We left the Oak Room and took a walk back to my apartment. His eyes were dry. Thinking he couldn't see me in the street as well as he could in the restaurant, I let a few tears fall, just for relief.

"Carol, you can cry in front of me. It's all right. No one is altogether strong. I'm not. You're not. No one is."

"I think you're the strongest man I've ever known and the nicest, the very best."

We reached the front of my house.

"Good night, darling," he said. "If she calls you from California, let me know. Keep in touch. I will telephone you every day."

Only a few days had gone by when I found myself at a party and someone rather famous and fat told a story to a group of people about Kay Kendall having cancer. I very quickly said, "How could you possibly know a thing like that?"

Her answer was, "I do."

"Well, you don't. I am her best friend. Not a day goes by that I don't speak to her. She has never gone to a doctor's appointment without me when I am in the same country that she is. I know that that is not true. I know what is wrong with her—she has an ulcer, and it has been cured."

I said this to explain the doctor's visits, and fatso fell in hook, line, and sinker.

"No kidding," she said. "Well, I'm very glad to hear that."

This happened a few other times. I always remembered to write down who was in the room during the telling of this so-called gossip, and I would tell Rex.

Kay came back from California, blooming like a full-blown golden rose. She never looked more alive—like molten gold, and the aura surrounding her was magical. She had bawdiness but with elegance; everything about her was right. If she threw her clothes around her apartment, it looked like a still life.

Typical of her wit was the time she met Bill. He went backstage to congratulate Rex for his performance in *My Fair Lady,* and Rex introduced him to Kay. Bill said, "How do you do?" and she looked at him appraisingly and said, with that wonderful accent, "Saroyan. . . . Oh, yes. Yes. You're a great friend of my wife's." Of course, Bill didn't know what she was talking about.

I saw her nearly every day. We never ever discussed illness. We always talked the way we had before—our little bits of gossip picked up here and there, clothes, fun, and so on. She would sometimes read or write notes or just listen to music when she came by in the afternoons.

I watched her and if she knew—she was as smart as I thought she was—she never let on. Her face, in repose, thinking she was not being watched, was exactly the same as it always was. She was very beautiful in repose as well as in laughter and in anger.

When Rex left *My Fair Lady,* they were to go to Portofino for a holiday—a long, uninterrupted holiday.

I couldn't help the onrush of tears.

"I'll miss you so," I said. "Don't stay away too long. And you know, if you need me, I'll come."

Of course, I didn't know how I would ever do that, but I knew I would if it came to that.

During the next few weeks, Kay wrote every once in a while—short, darling notes. The most she would ever admit to was not feeling well. In one, she wrote that she was back in "the fucking clinic" for an examination and that they were doing nothing and she was never going back there again.

The Saturday after I received that letter, I left the house to go visit a friend. When I returned, I got the message that she had died. I later found that at the end she had asked for Sydney, whom she still cared for, and Rex, a great gentleman, immediately sent for him. They were both with her when she died. She was only thirty-three.

From that very first meeting in London to the last time I saw her in New York, there wasn't a detail about Kay Kendall that was forgettable. To this day there has never been anyone like her— even in small ways. Her uniqueness (aside from the obvious things such as beauty and taste and all that) was in her ability to give a person a feeling of being loved. Many people love people, but it isn't always felt. It's known about, but not felt. Every time I saw Kay, it was like a celebration of friendship, in spite of the very real dramas that were going on in her life.

I kept in touch with Rex and, even when not in touch, always felt for him and was always dazzled with admiration for his continuing excellence as an actor and his constantly improving the style in which he did it. We all know about Hemingway's "grace under fire"—but he never knew Rex. Rex had style under fire. There's a difference. Style was energy.

Rex remarried several times after Kay. He had to be married because he had to be taken care of. He had to have perfect meals, perfect places to sleep in. He was used to that. But Kay was a very hard act to follow.

I used to get Christmas cards from him. They always said the same thing. "Darling Carol, How goes it? As for me, I'm still pressing on. Love, Rex."

Those simple words told a story of such deep unhappiness—he never really got over the loss of Kay. But knowing Kay, how could he have?

. . . .

"Somebody's Mother"

. . . .

Even though I did want the continuity that my life in the Palisades gave the children, I couldn't live in the style of that confinement. Moreover, I couldn't live under Bill's domination anymore. I decided to go back to New York.

I told this to Bill, and he of course went into a rage. Years before, nothing had frightened me as much as Bill being in a rage. But that was all over. He was always in a rage—so finally, I didn't expect him to be any other way.

"Bill," I said, "no matter how mad you get, no matter how much you threaten me, I'm going to New York. I have to."

Bill was always watching my reaction to his rages. And he made the quickest switch I have ever seen.

"Oh, so you're going to New York? Do you think you could play the part of Mary L. in *The Time of Your Life*? They're doing a revival at the City Center in December."

This was truly something out of the blue. Maybe, I thought, he believed my appearance was right for the character. In Europe, for fun, I had dyed my hair and eyebrows and lashes jet black. With my white skin, I could not decide whether I looked like a newspaper or an ax murderer.

"What happened to all your anger, Bill?" I asked. "What happened?"

"Nothing. What are you talking about? It's just that you're the best actress in the world—we know that. Who else can tell a lie like you? And we'll work together before we leave for New York."

It was as if he'd been a little lamb. I thought about how much acting must have been in these rages over the years. I now knew who the best actor in the world was and who had acted through two marriages and two children and two divorces, every minute of every day and night, who could switch it on and off like no one you ever met.

Of course, I knew that this offer of a part in his play was his way of holding something over my head. He would still be the big boss-man and I was still Stepin Fetchit, with the mint julep.

But accepting the offer would get me out of the Palisades, even if it was just for the play's limited run. Bill's sister would come down from Fresno to look after the kids, and I would take it from there. Once I had enough money, I would send for them.

I said, "Great," because even if he was just pretending to be nice, it was okay with me.

I arrived in New York on December 31, 1954, and was met at the airplane by Gloria, who was with Frank Sinatra. She was seeing him at the time, and to this day she feels that he helped her through one of the most difficult times in her life, her divorce from Leopold Stokowski. She was very happy to have a beau who was fun and interesting and took her out every night. It had been hard with Stokowski; she had always had to be in the concert box looking grand in a way she did not conceive of herself. And she wasn't a grand dame or anything like that; she was still in her twenties.

I'm not sure why that marriage didn't work, but I'd gotten a hint of one reason some years earlier when I was visiting and saw a bill on Gloria's desk. It was from the Bon Ton Fish Market and was for something like $4.80. And on it he had written, "G. to pay $2.40, L. to pay $2.40." And he was very rich, too. The age difference probably didn't help, either.

Gloria loaned me her studio for the run of the play. It was between Fifth and Madison on Sixty-fifth Street and it was absolutely beautiful, with books, a nice bath, and a good-sized kitchen—everything one could possibly need. And Frank had supplied it with every delicacy one could possibly eat: pâté de foie gras, caviar, things like that, and some of the best booze in the world. It was filled with flowers and welcoming notes, and the whole thing was very happy. I felt that I had finally made it out of the Palisades, even if only for a while.

Almost immediately the three of us began going to parties—some little, some big. On New Year's Eve we ended up at some very lavish room with a full orchestra as 1955 was about to descend on us. I didn't know who to kiss at midnight, so I kissed everyone. And there was lots of music and fun and dancing and singing, which lasted until about 4:00 in the morning.

When I got home, I thought of who I would like to have kissed that night, and suddenly felt blue. I thought about the year that had passed and wondered what the New Year would bring.

Rehearsals for *The Time of Your Life,* the play that had won Saroyan the Pulitzer Prize, started the next day, with Sanford Meisner directing. Set in a barroom, the play didn't follow a plot so much as it examined the way its eccentric characters tried to make the best of what life had dealt them.

Franchot Tone had the lead, playing a barroom philosopher named Joe, and I played Mary L., a girl who wanders in for just one scene. They have a wonderful dialogue—it could easily have been lifted and turned into a one-act play—during which they both fall in love but never say it. I believe it was the best scene in the play. Gloria, who had also taken an interest in acting, had a brief scene, playing someone named Elsie Mandelspiegel who was in total hysteria from beginning to end.

The play opened a few weeks later to an adoring audience (lots of friends) and some very good reviews. We settled in for the run, and Gloria and I joined one of Sandy Meisner's acting classes. I had been told I owed much of what success I'd had to what was called "stage visibility"—people noticed me, even in the last row—but I wanted a little more than that to go on. I still considered acting a job, but it was a job I could get; people seemed willing to hire me. It brought in more money than selling stockings at Bergdorf did.

My fortunes were growing. I had finished the book I had been writing in the Palisades. It was a novella about my childhood, a sardonic little book. Jim Agee had read every word of it and told me it was perfect for what it was. "Tell me what to change," I had said.

"Please don't touch it," he had responded. "You're going to heckle this thing to death. Leave it alone." He recommended that I send it to David McDowell at Random House. I did, and they accepted it, paying me $1,500. I opened a savings account for Aram and Lucy, and gave $750 to each of them. We were on our way!

Bennett Cerf, who ran the company when he wasn't on "What's My Line?," did want me to change the title, however. The one I had was perfect: *Somebody's Mother*. Needless to say, it was from the song, "Be kind to your web-footed friends, for a duck may be somebody's mother." Bennett didn't like that. He thought that it had too much edge for a book that he felt was poetic and young.

The title that was used was *The Secret in the Daisy*, a ditzy thing that allowed for a sappy cover. I felt that the title was an embarrassment and that, in a strange way, it diminished the book. "There's no such thing as too much edge," I said. But there was no way I could stand up for myself—I was simply too hungry. For anything.

The book was published under the name Carol Grace. That was the name Bill had given me when I appeared in *The Time of Your Life* and it had stuck. I never wanted to do anything under the name Saroyan; it was so uniquely his that I thought it would be terribly unfair.

The book got wonderful reviews. And I must tell you that Bill loved it. He thought I was a good writer, always. "If you really went to work, if you did nothing else, you'd put them all away," he said. "And I include myself in that one."

This praise did not, of course, make it a bestseller. Random House printed only ten thousand copies, but the two bookstores I frequented on Fifth Avenue were sold out in a week. Few of the reviews were like the ones that I'd fantasized about as I was making necklaces of paper clips when the writing wasn't going well. I had never written anything before, and I was far more deeply involved in the reviews I would get than I was in the book.

It reminded me of Al and Dolly Hirschfeld's daughter, Nina. He, of course, is the famous caricaturist, and Nina had decided at one point to draw. So they bought her an easel and all the other supplies she would need and arranged a special room for her to draw in. But every time they went into the room, the only things they could find were huge pieces of white paper totally blank except for the spot at the bottom of the right-hand corner where it always said, "by Nina Hirschfeld." I think that's as far as she got.

Having a book published was a big thing in my life, and it might have been a turning point if I'd kept on writing. But I didn't. I had a lot of beaus and saw a lot of friends and got all dressed up every night after the theater to go dancing. I was having the busiest, biggest, gayest time ever. And within a year I would fall in love again. Being in love to me was not only more important than any book, it was more important than anything. It always has been, and it always will be.

. . . .

Breakfast at Tiffany's

. . . .

At 3:00 every morning that I was in New York, I would meet Truman Capote at a private club called the Gold Key Club on West Fifty-fifth Street. The lights were low and we would sit in big chairs in front of a fireplace and talk and talk. Even when we'd been on different continents, I was never not in touch with him, either by phone or note. But now that we were both in New York, he wanted me to know what the city was like, especially as I really hadn't lived there in such a long time.

He drank and I drank. Actually, I had started drinking each night after work when I left the theater and went out dancing with a date. I drank gin and ginger ale. Truman told me that it was a low-down combination.

"Sweets," he said. "Why not have gin with a beer chaser? It's much better."

So after that, that is what I drank. They were called potboilers or boilermakers or something like that.

But I didn't get drunk or feel drunk. I felt wonderful and I had more energy than ever before.

Truman would describe everybody—Babe Paley, Slim Keith, Phyllis Cerf, Gloria—and everything. He talked about the differences in the various social stratas of that special New York City, where and how people were placed, who were the most elite and the richest, where they stood as hostesses, and how New York was really run. And who was top dog and who wasn't. Babe Paley was always top dog. You know why? She was one of the nicest people who ever lived, and one of the most beautiful—even if she was married to Bill Paley, the head of CBS, who once came up to me and said, "You've always been my fantasy." I wasn't flattered in the least, knowing that he said it to everyone.

Truman's descriptions about the whole New York City hierarchy were so very clear and seemed so accurate, even from the little I had already known about some of the people. After several nights, I realized what he was doing.

"You're writing about this, aren't you?" I said. "If I could draw, I could almost draw it all on a sheet of paper. It's going to be a book."

"You're right. It's going to be my big one." He eventually began to call it *Answered Prayers*. He worked on it for years, but he never got it into a form he was happy with and stopped quite a few times to write other books.

"Do you really think these people are interesting enough?"

"The way I'm going to do it, yes." He was going to go to the heart. He was going to be ruthless, too. "You'll never be a writer if you're afflicted with a lack of ruthlessness," he said. "You have to get over that if you're going to be a writer." And if what he told me had been recorded just as he was saying it—as unfinished as it was—it would still have been a big book.

When daylight came, I would be telling him my various tiny successes and what seemed to be huge failures, and he was indeed a most constructive friend and told me things that helped me greatly.

One night, though, he began talking about something different. "I knew a girl once, she was nothing like you. In fact, she was almost a hooker, but I liked her a lot. She came from the South, I don't know how she ended up, and I've always wanted to write about her. But I'd like to do her as you, I'd like to have the things that I know happened to her happen to you. I want you to stick around with me a little bit, I'm going to do you as Holly Golightly."

And every morning at about 7:00, we left the Gold Key Club and walked to Fifth Avenue, where there was a man with a cart of doughnuts and coffee. We'd buy some and then continue on toward Tiffany's. On the way, we'd look at clothing in the windows of the stores on Fifth Avenue, places like Bergdorf's and La Vieille Russie—all very chic.

"Oh, honey," he'd say. "Take a look at that. You'd look like a knockout in that." He would sigh. "Why don't we have any money? I should get you that dress. Well, maybe we'll think of a way of getting it."

Then we'd see a very tailored coat or hat.

"Oh, it was made for you, darling," he'd go on. "You're so feminine, you should always dress like a dyke. It would be great. I know just what you should wear and it should always be black and white."

Each morning, we'd end up eating the doughnuts and drinking the coffee in front of Tiffany's. The same guard was always there. He was rather friendly and got to know us, so every so often we'd bring a doughnut and some coffee for him, too.

After standing there and just staring at all the diamonds and gold, we would cross back to the other side of Fifth Avenue and go to the Plaza, where we would sit on the steps of the fountain. Then I would go to the loo and wash my face and fuss with my dress and put on fresh makeup and perfume. We were now ready for an early lunch at Romeo Salta's, which was near. We had that early lunch every day, drinking right through it and still feeling wonderful and not drunk.

"Honey," Truman said, "you could drink any man under the table. I didn't know you could do that. That's wonderful."

Afternoons, I would rush back to the studio, check on the children in California, take care of the mail and the telephone, do some small chores, and start picking out a dress to wear after the theater that night. Sometimes I took a nap, but really I didn't sleep very much. I followed the same routine every day.

One afternoon, I got back to the studio and started to do my usual chores when suddenly, wildly, I wanted a drink. I had had some parties there, so all the booze was gone. I looked everywhere and wanted a drink more than I have ever wanted anything.

I'll run down to Madison Avenue and pick something up, I thought to myself. But the very thought of wanting to drink by myself horrified me, as up until then I had only regarded it as a social thing. I knew that if I was to go down and get that drink, it would be something that I could never contain.

Once that thought took hold, I decided definitely not to go to Madison Avenue to buy a bottle of anything. Or ever have another drink again. This was no hardship because the habit had not taken—yet.

Later that night, when I met Truman at the Gold Key Club, I ordered a Coca-Cola.

"Why, honey," he said. "What's come over you?"

I told him about my afternoon.

"You're doing the right thing," he said. "You cannot afford in any way to become addicted to anything but your life. You are very strong and very smart to do what you're doing at this moment instead of trying to do it a few years from now. I can't. I have to have a drink. I could probably have less, but the funny thing is, I don't feel drunk."

And actually, it wasn't until many years later that Truman seemed to get drunk.

"Darling," Truman said that night, "when do you sleep?"

"Hardly ever. I don't like to sleep. When I go back to California, I guess that's all I'll do."

"Carol, don't you know that that's all over? You came here and did every single thing you were going to do. You don't ever have to live under Saroyan's thumb again, either married or divorced.

You have freed yourself. I can see it all now. Your life is just beginning. Now why don't you sleep with some of these rich men who always want to sleep with you? There would be nothing wrong with doing that, and it would solve a lot of your problems."

"I don't have a strong stomach. I can't sleep with anybody I don't care about."

He looked at me.

"That's just plain silly. You think all women want to sleep with their rich beaus and husbands?"

"No, I know they don't. But that's why they are the way they are. And I'm never going to do it. That's the one place I trust myself, the intimate part of me. If I love to sleep with someone, I love that person."

"God, for someone so smart, you are so naive. If you sleep with poor people, you become so attached. I think you should think about changing that as long as you are fixing up the drinking. Well, we'll still go to Tiffany's every morning whether you drink or not or sleep with a rich man or a poor man. But have you ever thought you might become addicted to sleeping with poor people?"

"I will never become addicted to anything. Well, I'm addicted to literature, and that's what makes it so hard for me to write. Today I was reading Jane Austen. She wrote, 'You have delighted us long enough.' Now how could I do anything after reading that?"

Truman laughed. "You only picked out one of her best lines. Wade through all of it and let me know how you feel. It's not all interesting. But she made some great statements for her time, and I want you to make some good ones for now. You know I didn't pick you to be Holly Golightly for nothing. You are Holly. It's just that you don't do those rotten things Holly did."

Breakfast at Tiffany's was published in 1958 but not quite as soon as I'd anticipated it would be. For Truman kept showing me the last page and asking me what I thought. "It's perfect," I'd say, and he'd say, "You think they're all perfect."

What he was doing was punctuating and repunctuating. "You must make the reader read in your cycle," he would tell me, "and you can only do that with punctuation. Always punctuate that way instead of grammatically, and don't let anybody change that. You'll trap your reader into your own breathing, and then the reader is trapped."

I didn't really know what he meant until he called one day and said, "I got it. I'm bringing it over to show it to you. I want you to see this. It's important for you." And this time it was completely different from all the others. It took Truman three months to do that last page, but the minute I read it, I knew he had been right.

. . . .

Who Is Walter Matthau?

. . . .

"Who is Walter Matthau?" I asked George Axelrod.

"Jesus Christ. I've just given you a part in my play and you obviously haven't been near a theater in years. You don't know who Walter Matthau is? He only happens to be the best young actor in America."

"My God, well, when I move to New York for good, I'll get to see all the plays and get around and I'll know who's who."

George was a very talented young writer-director I'd first met while living in California.

"You hate it out here, don't you?" he had said.

"Yes."

"Can you act?"

"Of course. I'm acting right now."

"Good. I'll give you a part in my next play and that will get you out of here."

And, sure enough, while I was in New York for *The Time of Your Life,* George offered me the part of the secretary in his new play, *Will Success Spoil Rock Hunter?* It was the Faust story set in Hollywood, with Walter playing the writer, Jayne Mansfield the big movie star, and Martin Gabel playing the agent, otherwise known as the devil.

I returned to California between plays to get my children and found a wonderful nanny, Janet Law, who said she would be

delighted to take care of them in New York. Rehearsals for the
play were going to start at the end of August 1955, and to get out
of California again I had to duel with Bill until I reached the
border. He claimed I wasn't allowed to take the children out of the
state, but what he really wanted was control over me. But I made
it to the first rehearsal, which took place without Mr. Matthau—he
was stuck in a flood in the Poconos where he had been doing a play
in summer stock.

He arrived for the second day of rehearsal. He was much more
handsome than George had described him—in a marvelous way
that could go in many different directions. In his mid-thirties, he
might have been a politician from the Midwest. He might have
been a writer (I could see it all—the fireplace, the pipe, that act that
a lot of writers like to put on every so often, especially when they
can't write). He easily could have been an English literature professor at Princeton, with a once-pretty wife. He looked like a great
detective. He could have done anything, been anybody—Abraham Lincoln, Carl Sandburg, Robert Frost. He looked strong, and
his good looks were rugged and romantic.

He was very funny and told a lot of jokes, so the second day of
rehearsal was not nearly as stiff as the first. I thought he was trying
to put people at ease, but then he would turn on them and seem
to make them feel simply awful. I didn't understand at first that he
turned only in fun—his idea of fun. One of the first things he ever
said to me was, "Have you ever come?"

I was simply stunned. Not knowing what to say, I responded
with "How could I have? We have never been in bed together."

Walter smiled. He knew a lie when he heard it.

Still, it was a very compelling question that he had asked me. It
made me self-conscious. I kept looking at myself in the mirror,
wondering if I looked like a nun.

The next day I arrived at rehearsal wearing more makeup than
ever and a very clinging black dress. He took a good, long look
at me.

"What are you trying to say?" he said.

"Guess."

I knew he was married. I could tell he wanted to go to bed with
me. I had never had a one-night stand. And I was sick of myself

for falling in love as deeply and totally and insanely as I always had. I calculated, "He's perfect. He's the perfect one-night stand."

So I waited.

He was the most fun to talk to because his mind always ran away from the conversation you had begun to the conversation that he had decided to have, and that conversation was either about what he was going to have for dinner that night or if he had been to the loo that day (and whether or not he was happy about it). I found that interesting, having read Mozart's letters, which are all about that sort of thing. It also turned out that one of the very biggest things in Walter's life was his love for music.

He told me one of the most incredible things I had ever heard in my life.

"I bet you'd like to know what my wife is like," he started out.

"Oh, yes."

"Well, here's what she's like. The other day, I had to go to the loo. There is only one on the floor of our apartment building and we share it with two other tenants. I got home and absolutely could not wait to get to the loo, but someone was in it. I thought I would die. I knew I was a goner, so I yelled for my wife, who came running out of the apartment. 'Get me a brown paper bag as fast as you can,' I said. I stayed there an extra minute in hopes that the occupant would come out. However, no one came out. I ran back to my apartment and had it all in the brown paper bag. My wife took the bag and went out to the alley to leave it in the garbage. A gang of hoodlums came and grabbed the bag from my wife and ran away. Well, you cannot imagine how upset she was."

"Upset?"

"Yes, she was very, very upset. And as she came up the stairs and I came down, she told me what happened and she said, 'Do you think we should call the police?' "

I stared at Walter, immobilized with the wonder of it all. I thought to myself, who is this woman? She must be insane. This story couldn't possibly be true. He is married to a great humorist, a genius, in fact—or he is married to the dumbest person that ever set foot on this earth. I wondered which one it was.

We rehearsed in New York for about four or five weeks and I had lunch with him every day. I learned a lot about his life. Of course, obviously, he was unhappily married. They had had a few separations. I asked him why they kept getting back together again.

"Well, she isn't that much worse than the girls I've been sleeping with."

"You're not exactly an incurable romantic."

"Not yet," he said.

Some nights after rehearsal, he asked if I would have supper with him. It was an Indian summer—the nights were hot and we would walk all the way home to my apartment on Eighty-first Street and Park Avenue. He began to take my hand. And then one night he kissed me. I couldn't invite him in because my children were sleeping upstairs. He understood that, so he didn't make any problems.

I really loved being with him. His conversation was never upsetting. He never dwelled on anything unpleasant. He was very interested in astronomy—the stars, the planets—and being with him was like a whole summer holiday. All the problems of living always seemed suspended. I knew he liked me. I just didn't know how much. I guess this was because of his droll, understated style.

There were nights I didn't go to supper with him, because I had a lot of beaus. He asked me if I liked any of them.

"Not as much as I like you."

"How much is that?"

"It's a lot," I told him. "A whole lot more than I've liked anyone for a very long time. I like your company, I love your looks. And I love to hold your hand."

He said under his breath, "Wow."

And then it got to the point that we would separate and I would be in my apartment and he would go back to his, but before he would go upstairs to his wife he would call me from a phone booth.

"I miss you," he'd say. "I want to be with you."

"I do too."

"Well, we'll work out something. See you tomorrow."

Everything about Walter was so nice that he didn't fall into the category I wanted him to fall into: easy to forget. He was not forgettable. He was quite a person.

I once said to him, "You have so much compassion for the

world that it scares me a little because most people like that are usually not really that nice. They've already set themselves up as good guys so they let it go at that and they tinkle all over the world." I paused. "Why are you staying married to a woman you don't like at all?"

"Because I'm a good guy."

"Oh, my God, that's the worst answer. Don't get the wrong idea. I don't want to marry you or anyone. I don't want to marry anyone as long as I live. I want you to know that."

"Are you sure?"

"Positive."

"Any special reason?"

"Yes. I'm not good at it."

"Is anybody good at it?"

"Well, I don't really know. I just know I'm not."

"Do you still see Saroyan?" He wanted very much to know that. "Yes."

"So you're still scared of him, aren't you?"

"Yes."

Walter was now taking me home every day, even on the nights we would not eat supper together. I thought he lived way uptown, because he would hail a cab for us and I would always get dropped off first at Eighty-first Street.

But a few days before leaving for Philadelphia for the first real tryout, everyone's addresses and telephone numbers were put on the bulletin board. We were in the Belasco Theater, which was on West Forty-fourth Street. Walter's address was 444 West Forty-fourth Street.

Of course, he's madly in love with me, I decided after staring at the bulletin board for quite some time. There's no other explanation. Why else would he go that far out of his way day after day? I had every reason to know that Walter liked me, but now I had the final piece of proof.

I'm going to have an affair with him, I thought, the minute we get out of New York.

. . .

His wife came to the train station to see him off to our tryout in Philadelphia with their baby son and her hair in huge curlers, over which she had put a scarf. I'd pictured her as very pretty, WASPy, sort of long-legged and tan from the summer, and instead she looked like Lola Delaney, the character Shirley Booth played in *Come Back Little Sheba*. It was a very big shock to me. But a man is very revealed by his wife, just as a woman is revealed by her husband. People never marry beneath or above themselves, I assure you.

On the train, I told him a joke: "It is opening night at the Metropolitan Opera and every lady in New York has spent months figuring out how to be the best dressed, most bejeweled, best coiffed, most everything woman there. In one of the boxes, as the overture begins, a woman taps another on the shoulder and whispers in her ear, 'You've got a curler in your hair.' The other lady turns around and says, 'I know, I know. I'm going someplace later.' "

I smiled at Walter.

Walter never laughs out loud, but this time he didn't laugh at all.

Philadelphia, of course, was heavy with activity—dress rehearsals, light rehearsals, rewrites, a few cast changes, panic on every front. I watched it all, as the mechanics of a big pre-Broadway opening were all very new to me, but Walter, of course, was extremely calm. He'd been through it many, many times and was not about to add to the chaos.

A lot of pals of the Axelrods and mine—Irving Lazar, Arlene Francis (Marty Gabel, her husband, was in the play), Adolf Green, and Betty Comden—visited us in Philadelphia, and we would usually have supper with them after the theater. I invited Walter to join us a few times. He said he'd rather not.

"I'd like to have dinner with you alone."

Well, of course, he is an actor, I thought to myself, so he has to be the main event. But I missed spending those evenings with him and was bored to death with all my pals.

We had a sort of testy little fight about it, and I felt terrible. I was staying at the Barclay and he was staying at the Warwick. After the performance that night, I went back to the hotel and turned the television on, had room service, took a bath, and tried to read. I couldn't concentrate. I tried another book. I still couldn't concentrate.

I put on my raincoat over my pajamas and some shoes and walked to the Warwick and knocked at Walter's door.

He opened it.

"Hi," he said.

"I've come to sleep with you."

"Great," he said.

And we went to bed.

Walter has a duality about him. Bill, of course, did too—his was a most frightening phenomenon. He proclaimed loudly how he loved everyone but was filled with a deep hatred for the world around him. Walter's duality is more subtle. To the outside world, he is casual, a man's man, funny, rude, and seeming to accept things as they are. In actuality, he is the most passionate man I have ever known. He is the most tender, the most romantic, the most sensual. Nothing is casual with Walter, especially in bed. His is the ultimate sexuality combined with the most beautiful romanticism.

There went my one-night stand. I knew, although I could not even say it to myself, that I wanted to be with him forever. Worse than that, I couldn't live without him. I had never, ever, experienced being that alive.

We slept together everywhere. This has never waned, even as I write this. Sometimes when we fight, I say to myself, I hate him, I never want to see him again. But all I have to do is think of a bed, any bed we've ever been in, or any floor we've ever been on, trains, boats, cars, getting off the freeway so that we could park on the side of the road somewhere where it was dark because it couldn't wait another minute.

Walter has an instinct for pleasure that is genius. And I have always felt like the girl of the world with him.

That was the year 1955. Today, in 1992, not even the tiniest light has dimmed. He has become far more outrageous a man than he was, and many, many changes have happened in our lives. But I will never tire of the feeling I have when I am in Walter's arms. The deepest and best happiness I have known has been in his arms. I will tire of everything else first.

Of course, we have all been taught that sex is the first thing to go, but I know differently. Money is the first thing to go.

Once *Will Success Spoil Rock Hunter?* opened and was a definite hit, Walter and I started spending even more time together. We'd see each other late in the day before the show. Quite often we'd have an early dinner together. After the show, we would always go out, if not directly from the theater, then after I had gone home first.

Occasionally, I would have to go somewhere—a party or a late supper—but I would only stay long enough to be polite and then rush home, dial Walter's telephone number, let it ring twice, and hang up. That was our signal. As soon as he could, he would telephone and be on his way.

"How can you get out like that?" I once asked.

"I tell her I have to take my constitutional."

"In the middle of the night?"

"She's very dumb and she goes right to sleep. Sometimes she's asleep when I get home from the theater so she doesn't know that I've come in and gone out and come home again."

I couldn't help wondering how she could have felt so secure. She was in complete control of herself the few times I saw her. I've met quite a few people—men and women—who are very thin. I don't mean physically. I mean that these people don't delve, they don't wonder. They seem to be absolutely sure of themselves. Of course, when a woman is sure of herself as a woman, it can be interpreted as a tribute to her husband.

But I have wondered how many times what it would be like to be that sure of oneself. It must be wonderful. I have never been sure about anything, and to see a woman in curlers with total composure is quite a sight. But you see, she was so secure that it never occurred to her that Walter could be even the slightest bit interested in anybody else.

I never look at Walter without wondering if he has a secret, if he's lying (which he's great at, but I'm better). I am, by nature, suspicious of everything. But I do try to keep that all to myself. And sometimes succeed.

Walter and I did great things together and had such a good time. I continued to leave the rest of my life where it belonged—in the closet.

We went to all-night movies on Forty-second Street, where they had double, triple, and quadruple features. Sometimes, very late, there would only be three or four other people in the theater—absolute bums. We would see old movies—good ones and bad ones, whatever was playing—just so we could sit and hold hands.

I learned a great lesson in those movie houses. If there was anything good at all on the screen the theater was silent. Anything that was baloney was received with fierce pounding—of chairs and feet and arms—and language beyond profanity. The audience simply kept screaming until the movie got better.

Onstage Walter and I had an interesting relationship. Our scenes were supposed to be simple, but Walter began to get obstreperous, doing things that only I could see, like crossing his eyes when he spoke to me. Naturally, I was riveted with fear each time I came onstage.

"Walter," I said, "don't do those things. I'm not as experienced as you and I'm having a horrible time."

He wouldn't stop, though, so one night, when he came in and said the line, "Is this Rita Marlowe's office?" I looked at him sweetly and instead of saying yes I said, "No, it's across the hall."

He said, "You know—you're cute."

That was my only victory on the stage.

. . .

That winter, I would go home and take off all the theater makeup and have a quick bath and put on warm clothes—big, bulky sweaters and scarves and boots—and wait in front of the building for Walter to pick me up. And we would walk into the cold night. There's only one better kind of walk and that is when it is snowing hard as the evening lights go on.

We would walk down Park Avenue and pass the same policeman every night. We would be talking, and it always seemed that just as we were passing this policeman, I would be saying a dirty word. That became sort of a game after a while.

A lot of nights, after the performance, Walter would hire a car and we would drive to Coney Island for a Nathan's hot dog and a walk around the boardwalk. We would just talk and look around. It was pretty much the middle of winter, but still, a few places were open.

We walked all over New York. It wasn't that I loved the walking, I just loved to be with Walter under any circumstances, and in those days, we didn't have a place to sleep together. We couldn't sleep in his apartment, obviously, and even though my children had met and liked Walter, we couldn't sleep in mine because of them.

There was a tiny place on Lexington Avenue called Calico Kitchen where we would have a hot bowl of soup before walking back.

Jeannie Widmark, a great pal of mine, was the kind of woman who would show up at your place with a bottle of aspirin if you were sick. When I told her what Walter and I did every night, she said, "That's very silly. Dick and I have an apartment in the city that no one is using. I think you should use it."

Finally we did. I had just started smoking, after having refrained for years because Oona had said to me once, "Oh, you're not going to do that, are you? Your hair is going to smell like smoke and no man will ever love you." And Walter and I lay there in the dark afterward, talking and smoking, which is fun. It sure beats sleeping with a man who falls right to sleep.

But one night I forgot about my cigarette, began to fall asleep, and burned the sofa. That was the night that, for the first time, "it" happened to me. I was thrilled, stunned, and confused. Walter looked at me and said, "Now you don't have to pretend anymore." I tried to get the sofa repaired, but to no avail—it was simply too burned. I tried to make up for it by always keeping the apartment very clean and buying champagne and fresh towels and pretty sheets and soaps and nice little tidbits to eat and Rigaud candles for when they came in from California. But the sofa was still burned. I thought, by some chance, all my efforts would divert their attention, especially the little throw I put on the bottom where it was burned the most.

The strange thing was Jeannie and Richard never mentioned it, until one day I had to—I confessed. I said how sorry I was, and how when I was rich someday I would buy them a new one.

"I don't want a new one," Jeannie said. "I love a romantic sofa."

The few times we tried hotel rooms—no matter how nice the hotel was—there was something not quite right for us. It would have been swell if we'd just been fucking, but Walter and I had really fallen in love.

· ·

Carson McCullers

· ·

Carson McCullers and I became very friendly in 1958 when I was a standby for Anne Baxter in Carson's play *The Square Root of Wonderful,* which I still feel was a very good play that was ruined by a set. It looked as though there was a toilet in the middle of the stage. There wasn't—it was a partition. Yet it managed to ruin the play. No, on second thought, Anne Baxter ruined the play.

Originally from Georgia, Carson was one of the most talented writers of her generation. In *The Heart Is a Lonely Hunter, The Member of the Wedding,* and *The Ballad of the Sad Café,* she wrote about loneliness, isolation, and the awful lack of love in people's lives.

The Square Root of Wonderful is about a very soft, beautiful young girl who dreamed the most romantic dreams. She had married a man, divorced him, and is now very torn because she wants to marry him again and knows it won't work. It won't work because that kind of love—Big Love—never works. Big fat plain old passionate love. It's not good for everyday life. It's good for suicide. It's good for dying and it's romantic and frivolous. It's really out of fashion, too. But I still believe in it, more than anything else.

I don't consider myself an actress, but I could have done that part in my sleep. As the standby, I sat in the audience and took notes from Carson as they were rehearsing, or sometimes from José Quintero, the very gifted man who was trying to direct it. But there was a problem.

"I cannot direct Anne Baxter," he said once, "because I cannot direct 'stars.' "

"Well, she's not a star anymore," I kept telling him.

"Yes, but she has a star's mentality."

"Why did you cast her?" I asked.

"I didn't. Joe Mankiewicz did." Joe was producing the play and ended up directing it after José finally left. And even with all his experience with Anne Baxter (having directed her as the ruthless ingenue in *All About Eve*), he couldn't hold her back, either. She kept running across the stage like Lou Costello. At one point, she decided to bustle across the stage like a buyer from Bergdorf's. Neither would do.

Anne Baxter's success in *All About Eve* had not been that long before, and she looked upon me as a character right out of it—she was sure I was the understudy who was planning to take her part away. I would have loved to have done that, but things don't happen that way and one doesn't try for it that way. I needed a job and understudy is what I had.

On Thanksgiving Day, there was to be an evening performance. I would have to be in the theater by a certain time no matter what, but I got a call from the stage manager in the middle of the afternoon saying, "I think you'd better come in right away, Miss Grace. Miss Baxter has eaten herself silly."

Naturally, I left for the theater immediately and rehearsed quickly with the other actors. Miss Baxter, it turned out, was in back of the theater watching some of it. As the rehearsal broke up, she came up on stage.

"You're never going to play that part," she said.

"Neither are you," I replied. And the reviewers bore me out.

Eventually the play closed. It was terrible to see the play go down as it did, because it was such a good play. And Carson did not take the failure well. She loved the play; it was very personal for her. She had a sweet nature, which is always unexpected in a writer, and the pretty face of an ex-Vassar girl. But she had had quite a few strokes before I met her, and she always held one hand still, with the fingers down.

I spent a little time with Carson after the play closed and got to know her in a different way. "I love your clothes," she said in her very southern way. "Where do you get your clothes? I want all your clothes."

"They're not very expensive because I don't have any money."

I introduced her to a dressmaker I knew, and Carson was very pleased with her. She called a few weeks later to say she would come by for a visit as she would be in town for the day. She came by in the late afternoon, and we began to talk about men.

"Carol," she said, "you must introduce me to some very rich men. I know you know everybody, so you surely must know some very rich men."

"I know a lot of people, Carson, but I don't always know how much money they have."

"Well, let's find out." She started to go through every page of my address book, occasionally writing a name on a piece of paper. She said she would look them all up and see if any panned out.

"Carson, what makes you think money is the answer?"

"You do know that I am brilliant and I have what I need. I simply need a very rich man to take care of me."

"But you must have some money, don't you?"

"Yes, but I think I should save that money. I'm a writer, you know, and it's very hard to know when anything will ever make money. We have just had an example of that."

She left, and I next heard from her after she had gotten together all the information she needed.

"Well, none of them are rich enough to be as dull as they are," she said over the telephone to me. "So let's forget this for now, but if you do run into anybody, let me know."

Truman called one day and asked if Carson had tried to get me to set her up with any rich men yet. "Honey, I'm calling to tell you, don't get too involved with Carson. I know how you are," he said. "She's sort of pretty and a little sick and I know you around pretty, sick people. I don't want that to happen here. She's a terrible pain in the ass and she'll eat up your life if you let her." He added that most of her friends were tired of her. That was sad. She was trying to make some new friends in order not to be alone all the time. There's something about someone in her forties trying to make new friends that tells an awful story.

I don't remember where I was when I heard that Carson was dead at a relatively young age. She always knew that she wasn't going to live to what they call a "ripe" old age. (There are no ripe old ages.) But I remember feeling pangs about her aloneness. You could not know her even a little bit and not feel it surrounding her. I got the feeling she spent a big part of her life, when she wasn't writing, trying to find a friend. Carson became who she wrote about.

· ·

The Cold Wind and the Warm

· ·

The period following *The Square Root of Wonderful* was very difficult for me.

I wasn't up for any parts, and I was in quite a bit of debt. I owed the laundry seven hundred dollars, so I was now washing the sheets in the bathtub. And I owed Mr. Novick, the grocer, thousands of dollars. He was a marvelous man, but because I owed him so much and was on unemployment insurance, I decided to try and cut back by shopping at the A & P for a while.

One afternoon, Mr. Novick called me.

"How are you, dear?" he asked.

"Oh, I'm fine, Mr. Novick. It's just that I haven't been able to get a job and I was trying to save on my expenses until I could start to pay you. It's just terrible. I feel awful about owing you so much money."

"Now, dear," he said, "it's one thing to owe me money. I can handle that. But to lose your business? That would be just terrible."

And the wonderful thing was he was a man who actually felt that way.

"I don't know what to say, Mr. Novick."

"There's nothing to say. This is only right."

So I thanked him. And when I got off the telephone, I had an odd thought. Now that I was back with Mr. Novick, I felt I was back in business.

The telephone rang, and it was a call to read for a part in *The Cold Wind and the Warm,* a new play by S. N. Behrman. It was based on *The Worcester Account,* autobiographical stories by Mr. Behrman that had appeared in *The New Yorker.* I had a very vague, faraway memory of having read them, and what I remembered was that he looked back at his roots without any condescension.

I read for the part that afternoon. The character was based on a girl he had loved as a very young man and fantasized about and could never quite forget. I fell in love with this beautiful play and with the part of the girl. I knew I could do it. I also knew that the director, Harold Clurman, did not want me to have it because his girlfriend at the time said if he did not give her the part she would leave him. Harold did everything he could to sabotage my getting the part. I read for it eight times, which is almost unheard-of.

The last time I read for it, Mr. Behrman came up onto the stage to talk to me. (He was a marvelous man who wrote sophisticated drawing-room comedies and knew a lot about a lot. He had great manners—a rarity in the theater—and was altogether elegant in every way. Someone told me that Fanny Brice used to call him "the silk herring.")

"That was beautiful, Miss Grace," he said.

"Thank you so much, Mr. Behrman. I love your play."

"I understand you have two children."

That lousy rotten Harold, I thought to myself. Here I am trying to get the part of a girl who goes from age seventeen to twenty-seven and then kills herself, but Harold had to tell Mr. Behrman that I am three hundred years old, just because my son is fifteen and my daughter is twelve.

However, I just looked at Mr. Behrman and said simply, "Oh, yes, I do."

"How lovely. And how old are they?"

"Uh . . . two," I said slowly. "And, oh . . . three."

"That's so nice," he said, and then it was time for the next person to come in and read. I left the theater, not knowing what to think.

As it happened, and despite the fact that my children were practically old enough to play it themselves, I got the part in *The Cold Wind and the Warm.*

I was thrilled. I got it probably due to Mr. Behrman and the fact that the play had a producer who was really a prince, Robert Whitehead. He is fair and decent and strong and handsome. He was aware of my unfortunate situation with Harold Clurman, who would never even rehearse a scene I was in until, finally, the other actors who were in my scenes begged him to at least do the staging.

"I'm going to direct it the way I please," Clurman said.

"I know you are," I said. "But no matter how you direct it, your girlfriend's not going to be in it. She's not pretty enough."

"That's where you're wrong. She doesn't have to be pretty. That's not what the part calls for."

"No, that's where I'm exactly right. This girl is the classic high-school flirt. A man can go all his life thinking of that high-school flirt. I know who this girl is, so you're not going to do this to me, Harold."

After that Harold began rehearsing my scenes, and we opened to very good reviews in Philadelphia. Of course, he was still at it with me, but I tried to ignore him.

The play had a wonderful cast. Maureen Stapleton, who is younger than I, was playing my grandmother.

"Just keep moving," she would advise me. "Speak loud and get a lot of sleep."

Truman telephoned while we were in Philadelphia and said,
"Honey, I know you're scared out of your skull, so I'm coming
down to tell you what to do. I hear you're very good, but I know
that I would know whether you're really good or not better than
anyone else. And if you're not good in it, I'll tell you how to be
good in it. I'm coming tomorrow. Book me a suite in your hotel.
I'm not going to tell anyone which performance I'm going to see."

It turned out he was making the telephone call from a suite only
a few doors away from my room, and he was going to that evening's performance.

After the show, I saw him backstage and we both laughed.

"I want to tell you, darling," he began, "that you look so
beautiful that it doesn't matter what you do in the part as long as
you show up because they're only looking at you anyhow. They
never saw anyone who looks like you. But if you really want to
fuck around with all this acting stuff, you're going to have to act
better, honey. You see, you're not a natural-born actress. You're
a writer, but that's a different thing. No good writer can be much
of an actor. He feels too ashamed of himself."

Truman then proceeded to give me advice on how to improve
my performance. He told me to do exactly what I was doing but
ten times more so. He explained to me that even if an actor
happens to have the wrong take on a part, if, since nobody else
really knows how the part should be done, he does it with great
sureness and definition, everyone is fooled. George C. Scott does
that all the time. Truman said that it would be a way of letting
everyone know, "Forget it, kids, I am here forever." And any
excess could be removed before the opening night in New York.

His advice worked very well onstage. It made the part much
easier to do and it also was better for the other actors to play
against. It gave the scenes more clarity. Mr. Behrman was delighted.

"Miss Grace," he said, "I know that's not the direction Mr.
Clurman gave you."

"No, it isn't."

"That's just perfect. It's just what I want."

Truman spent the next three days with us until the play ended
its run in Philadelphia. He came to every performance and made

notes for me each time. And his notes were really doable. Instead of just telling me to flirt, as Harold would have, he said, "You know how gay and darling you are when you come to a party. Just do it like that."

"Okay," I said. "I get it." I really did feel much stronger in the part.

I went back to New York (which I had to leave at 5:30 the next morning for our next stop, New Haven) with Truman, who had hired a car. Maureen came with us. We could see the driver's hair standing on end and his ears turning red as we gossiped and gossiped about anyone any of us ever knew and who they were sleeping with and what special significance each affair had—who liked to do what to whom and why.

By now, I think the chauffeur had had enough of us. I saw him take a flask out and take a long swig. Maureen saw it, too, and since she had finished what she had brought to drink for herself, she spoke up.

"Hey, how about me?"

The driver gave her the flask, which he didn't see for quite a while. But Truman needed a drink and said we should stop and get some champagne. We did.

By the time we reached New York, I asked, as a favor, if they would mind dropping me off first because I had a headache. What I didn't say was that I also could not see myself pushing Maureen up three flights of stairs with Truman in the state he was in.

Truman knew immediately why I was doing this terrible thing to him.

"Don't worry, Maureen honey, fat as you are—I'm going to get you up the stairs. Carol's too delicate."

He knew that by this time I was really so tired I couldn't see.

What was interesting about this ride was that we never stopped laughing. We kept laughing and laughing—not that anything was so funny. It was just that they both enjoyed each other so much. And I enjoyed them. There was almost no state they could be in that I wouldn't prefer them to anyone else. They were two total wrecks that day, but adorable—funny and adorable.

. . .

After New Haven, we went to Boston, where I shared a double room with Suzanne Pleshette. She's the best friend you could ever have, filled with the most beautiful aspirations, and very brave. She replaced Lee Grant (they fired her before the required five days passed so they wouldn't have to pay her a big salary). Those were very big shoes to fill, but Suzanne filled them with grace and charm, and it didn't take long for her fellow actors to love her.

It was snowing while we were in Boston, and that alone made everything wonderful. Snow is my favorite thing in the world. My second favorite thing in the world is smoking. I would like to smoke in the snow every day.

Our room was adjoining Maureen's suite, which she shared with her dresser, Eloise. She is still Maureen's dresser when she does a play. Eloise was impossible. She would only tidy up if her own boyfriend was going to visit. Otherwise, Maureen's suite was a chaotic mess. It was so bad that we all had our meals in our bedroom rather than in Maureen's living room.

Boston was our last out-of-town stop, but even so, there were replacements made in the cast. That makes for instant dislike in a cast where people have become close to one another and have begun to feel like a family, responsible to and for one another. Timmy Everett was one of the replacements, and though he had quite a reputation as an actor, when special rehearsals had to be held rather constantly so he could take over the part, the resentment was really terrible. And very unfair, since he had nothing to do with the firing of the other actor.

So Maureen and Suzanne decided that we would invite him to join us at our hotel for Thanksgiving dinner. Timmy seemed to be delighted. And we made arrangements to have a real old-fashioned Thanksgiving dinner—turkey and stuffing and fresh cranberries and pumpkin pie and all the other things that make up memories of real Thanksgivings. We arranged for it to be ready for the late afternoon, since we had to play that night.

Mario, our waiter, brought a beautiful centerpiece of autumn leaves and fresh cranberries and even a pomegranate. The candles were lit when we arrived. This was, of course, all set up in our bedroom, because although Maureen's suite was clean, Eloise had only cleaned it so she could have a heavy date and she definitely did not want us to mess it up beforehand.

When we sat down and began to pass around the hot rolls, Timmy seemed to be a bit shy. After a while, the conversation opened up and we talked and ate ourselves silly, gossiping a lot about everyone. This seemed to loosen Timmy up.

Suzanne told a few secrets about a love affair she was having with a man we had code-named El Cheapo. We called him this because they went out dutch treat all the time and he, of course, had much more money than she. It didn't really matter though, because Suzanne had beaus from all over the world calling day and night. And when they didn't, she had her own black book to fall back on.

Maureen, of course, talked a lot about David Rayfiel, a first-rate playwright. I still think that both of them love each other more than either of them could love anyone else. And I talked about Walter, who came up to see me whenever he could.

All in all, though, I have to say Eloise was the winner. She had a different friend over every day and night. On the last day of the show, she had her husband come and pick her up. It wasn't easy to have a friendship with Eloise since it depended completely on what one bought her; she simply adored presents.

As we ate, we could hear the sound of Eloise laughing coming from Maureen's room. This seemed to make Timmy really open up. He started to tell us what he had been doing for the last few years.

He was madly in love with Jane Fonda, more than he had ever loved anyone in his whole life. But she had evidently left him for someone else and he had gotten another girlfriend after a period of mourning. He found out by accident that his new girlfriend was cheating on him and he said that it had driven him to the brink of insanity, which I don't think was an exaggeration. He said he had made up his mind that he would have an affair with his girlfriend's boyfriend. And so he seduced him.

Timmy looked at us.

"Would you please pass the salt?" Maureen asked.

"Oh, I'd like more cranberries," Suzanne said.

I went completely to pieces and ate the rest of the turkey. We tried to keep straight faces as though we heard stories like this every day. We knew there was only one thing we could not do and that was let him know that we were shocked. He continued to look at us in silence so we had to acknowledge what we had just heard.

"What a darling idea!" I exclaimed.

"That's what I call smart," said Maureen.

"Oh, Timmy, how wonderful," said Suzanne.

This, of course, drove him farther into madness and so he graphically described every detail of this affair and every physical pleasure it held for him. He recounted the few little doubts that he had concerning whether the girlfriend's boyfriend was being true to him. He figured out a simple way of handling it: He'd go back to the girlfriend and start sleeping with her again, and so he did.

At that, Maureen and Suzanne and I toasted him and sang "For He's a Jolly Good Fellow," and we sang it and sang it and sang it, really to keep him from saying anything more—but of course, he never realized that.

Toward the end of dinner, about five minutes before we were leaving for the theater, Walter called us from New York. He wanted to know what kind of Thanksgiving we were having.

"Well," I said, as I looked straight at Timmy, "we're having one great big old-fashioned Thanksgiving dinner."

We left Boston and went to New York. The reason I had managed to stay with the play this long (against all of Harold's best efforts) had to do with something that had happened earlier, when we were in New Haven, where girls were darting in and out of hallways and doors, simply waiting for me to fall on my face.

On opening night in New Haven, Mr. Behrman, Robert Whitehead, and Harold Clurman invited Thornton Wilder to see the play to get his opinion, which they valued. He came to the play, and when it was over, he said one thing.

"I want to meet Miss Grace. I must see her. I must see her right away."

They reminded him that Maureen Stapleton was waiting to see him.

"Yes, I want to see Maureen, but first, I must see Carol Grace."

Amazed, they brought him to my dressing room, which was in some cellar, and as I opened my door all four started to step in.

"I would like to speak to Miss Grace alone," he declared.

In total confusion, they closed the door. Here was this man demanding to see me when we didn't even know each other.

I was thrilled to see Thornton Wilder, for although we had never met, we had been writing to each other for many years. When my novel was published, he wrote me a very long letter. Rather than sending it care of my publisher, he sent it to a mutual friend, the writer Garson Kanin, to make sure I would receive it. His letter told me all about my book and what he loved in it the most. And he wrote of a few possibilities for my next book. I, of course, wrote him back in a happy delirium and we became pen pals.

"I knew you would be beautiful," he said to me when the door closed.

And we talked and held hands and I told him how much it meant to me that he came all the way down to the basement to see me. Then he kissed me on the cheek and said one last thing.

"Don't forget who you are. When the play is over, go back to work. You will be a great writer someday. I have never been wrong about that."

That was the only time I ever saw Thornton Wilder. I burst into tears as he left.

We continued to exchange letters for many years, and just before he died I wrote to him after rereading *The Skin of Our Teeth,* one of my favorite plays. There were two lines in it that I loved and took to heart, spoken when a son returns home from the war and confronts his mother.

"You never loved me," he says.

And she looks straight at him, very sweetly, and says lightly, "Ah, you were unlovable."

I wrote:

Dear Thornton,
WOW!

Love, Carol

P.S. "You never loved me." "You were unlovable." That exchange is the best of any play or book or poem of this century and cuts through all the most insidious and insane kind of thinking and you make me feel free and wonderful for which there will never be enough thank-yous. You are the only one who has ever said anything like that. You will never know what it means to me. I am going to stop worrying about the different flowers on the different robes I wear when I hold my baby. I've been worrying that if the flowers are not perfect, the son's eyes will rest on the wrong flower and he will be crazy and it will be all my fault.

The point of all this, besides the pleasure of simply remembering Thornton Wilder, is that that night in New Haven, he turned things around for me. The big brass all knew he had never met me and were stunned by the amount of time he spent in my dressing room. They knew nothing about any book I had written and they simply thought he must have fallen in love with the heroine of the play. This made quite an impression, even on Harold Clurman.

All the girls disappeared and the part was mine once and for all.

On closing night, five or six months later, Mr. Behrman and Robert Whitehead invited Maureen and me to have dinner with them several days later at Le Pavillon, which at the time was the very best and most beautiful Park Avenue restaurant in New York.

Dinner was lovely, what with all the pressure being off, and being surrounded by the charm of two men who seemed to share such a cavalier spirit toward people. Everything was going beautifully until Mr. Behrman turned and asked how my children were.

At which point, I sort of smiled and said, "Oh, they're fine, thank you, Mr. Behrman."

"Yes, I understand that your three-year-old is absolutely remarkable," he replied. "He is the only three-year-old with a seat on the stock exchange."

Maureen Stapleton

Maureen Stapleton is an absolute divinity. There's just no one better. There's no one with her clarity of thought. There's no one with her innate sweetness and decency. There's no one I would trust more. There's no one I could love more. She is probably the most talented actress in the world, although she misuses herself. She is the least pretentious person I've ever known. And she is very beautiful—she looks like a shattered old-fashioned valentine.

Since I have known her (we met through theatrical friends in the early 1950s) she has always gotten drunk the minute the curtain goes down. After the final call, Eloise is standing there with the vodka. She is never drunk while performing, but she is always performing with a hangover. She is still the best actress around, so I can only begin to imagine what she might have done had she been able to get the drinking under control.

I had a terrible time about that with one producer who came to see her in *The Cold Wind and the Warm.*

"Jesus, Carol, what a shame," he said just after the curtain call. "I've got such a great part for her, but I wish to Christ she wouldn't drink like that."

"What are you talking about?" I said. "She wasn't drunk tonight. I swear to you, she is never drunk on the stage."

"Carol, you're such a nice friend, but don't waste your time."

"Come on, come on," I said. "We're going to go down to her dressing room."

Well, in the time that it had taken him to come up to see me, have that conversation, and then go back down to Maureen's dressing room, she was drunk. Made a complete liar out of me. He just looked at me and said, "You're sweet."

Maureen thinks of herself now as just a grandmother, which is all she feels like being these days besides doing a few acting jobs. She lives with her guilt about drinking around her children and tries to appease all that with money.

She's destroyed her body and aspects of her talent, but even she can't spoil or use up Maureen herself; her laughter and her grace cannot be destroyed.

Once Maureen and I became close, close friends, I would talk to her for hours.

"I know a lot of men who are really in love with you," Maureen said to me once.

"Of course you do."

"Have you slept with a lot of men?"

"I certainly have."

"How many?"

I had no choice but to tell her the truth.

"Is that all?" she screeched. "You can practically count them on one hand?" She was in shock, and it would have been worse if she'd known I'd counted Bill twice. And Jim Agee once because Jim was love and not going to bed with him was a small detail compared to all there was between us. Ken Tynan, because I wanted to hold my own. It took a few moments for her to settle down. "My God, I've slept with at least one hundred."

"Who?" I couldn't believe it. "Who are they? What do you mean, one hundred? Who?"

"I don't even remember who they are."

"You don't remember who they are?"

"Six. That's nothing," she grumbled to herself.

"You're not taking into account that I was married most of the time and even when I wasn't, I was having big, big romantic affairs."

"I don't understand you at all. You haven't slept with anyone."

I thought she was crazy. "Well, you've slept with people you don't even remember. Do you remember anyone you've slept with?"

She paused and thought for a moment.

"Yeah, I remember six."

Maureen likes to give all her things away, and she has offered me pieces of her pristine, perfect-size-ten wardrobe that she has not fit into for twenty years but is saving to wear when she is at her right weight again.

"What do you think?" she once asked, holding up some miserable dresses.

"Burn them." They were the ugliest dresses I had ever seen in my life.

"I know. I know they're old. But still, don't you want them? They're still pretty."

"No, I do not want any of your great size-ten wardrobe. I must remind you, Maureen, that you are burglarized every summer and the thieves take everything *except* your personal wardrobe. They won't take one pair of your stockings because they're the wrong color. They won't take any of your shoes because they're pointy like the pope's shoes. They won't take your dresses because they're so old and ugly."

She looked at me.

"They've never been worn," she said poignantly.

"Maureen, when *you* wear them, they'll probably look very pretty."

Undaunted, she proceeded to try to give me something else. She insisted that I was going to have a present whether I liked it or not. Eventually she was offering me furniture.

"No."

"I have just the thing for you. I have just the perfect thing. You will see." And she brought out two of the most beautiful petticoats—one hand-embroidered with rosebuds and fraises des boise, and the other hand-embroidered with little angels on beautiful ice-blue silk. "Now, let me hear you say no."

I stared at Maureen and the slips. I could not believe she was doing this and that the history so totally escaped her.

"Maureen, I had those made for you in Paris. How could you

not love them? How could you give them away? How can you not wear them? How can you be so rotten?"

"Oh, my God," she said, but she quickly recovered. "Fuck it, they'd look better on you. Forget about it. I have something else for you." And she brought out a beautiful peignoir with a matching nightie, all done in white lace with pink ribbons. "How about this?"

"I'll take it," I quickly said. "No matter who gave it to you."

"Carol Lawrence gave it to me."

"Fine. I want it. I'll take it."

She has a thing about giving away her possessions. On the opening night of *The Cold Wind and the Warm,* I gave her one of my most prized possessions, an antique pin. I told myself, it's more precious to give away something you love and want than to just go into a store and buy something.

It was blue enamel with white forget-me-nots and a little diamond in it, and it was the dearest piece of jewelry I ever saw. In fact, it was my last piece of jewelry. I had sold the rest. I didn't tell Maureen that it had been a present to me from Oona. The next thing I knew, she gave it to Irene Worth as an opening-night gift for *Toys in the Attic.* It managed to come up in conversation for some reason or another.

"Yeah, I gave Irene this antique pin with blue and white forget-me-nots."

"Maureen, I gave you that pin, and not only that, Oona gave it to me. And Irene Worth is a friend of Oona's, and they have lunches together in London. You get that back, or Oona will feel terrible."

"Forget it. It's done."

And, in fact, Oona didn't feel it was terrible at all. She thought it was funny. That is just the way Oona was.

Another time, I gave Maureen a brand-new black mink wrap. It was beautifully designed and she needed it. She had nothing to wear in the evening (nor in the day, for that matter. She would simply turn her nightgown back to front and be ready for dinner.) She wore it one night to the Tony Awards and I never saw it again. On other evening occasions, she wore her old raincoat.

About a year later, I said, "Maureen, why don't you wear the little black mink fur tonight when we go out—you look so pretty in it."

She looked at me. "You know, I was hoping you would never say that to me."

"Why? What's wrong with saying that?"

"What's wrong is that I gave it away. I gave it to Mildred Brown."

Mildred Brown was the wife of the man who was building us a country house next to Maureen's house in The Town of Day (that's its real name) in Upstate New York. He was doing his country bumpkin act with us city slickers like you never saw. No matter what you'd say, he'd reply, "I'm just a country boy" as he turned into a very rich country boy.

"How could you give her that? She could buy sixty of those with her pin money now! They have all our money. Now they have this too. "Maureen, wake up. Get it back."

"I can't. I'd rather die than ask for it back."

So it goes with gifts and Maureen. Anything to do with Maureen is fun, but the fun now of giving her a gift is to guess who she's going to give it to.

Maureen and David Rayfiel got married in July 1963, in a diner called Red Hots up in Lake Lucerne, New York. I was her bridesmaid.

They had been going together a long time. At certain times, she wanted to get married and he didn't. At other times, he wanted to get married and she didn't. Now, Walter and I were pulling them together. It was only the four of us up in Lake Lucerne and on the day of the wedding, Maureen wouldn't get out of bed and David went out in a boat and stayed in the middle of the lake until the late afternoon.

I finally got Maureen into the bath, and we all drove to Red Hots. After the ceremony, we went back to the house and one or two people dropped by.

One of them was her cousin Red. He knocked at the door, looked at Maureen, said, "Oh, I forgot something. I'll be right back." And we never saw him again.

Maureen told me her whole family was like that.

"I wish mine was," I said.

Finally, it was late and I realized no one else was coming, so Walter and I slowly and discreetly disappeared. While we were in bed, we heard David, loud and clear, saying to Maureen, "Alone at last. Except for you, of course."

We then heard him say something quietly.

Maureen screamed, "Of course I had a bath."

David knew Maureen rarely took baths. But she is never dirty. I definitely think the alcohol disinfects her.

They had a strange marriage. I know David really loved her. He appreciated all that was best about her. But the drinking kept the marriage rocky. She weighed 238 pounds. She drank and laughed and didn't change her clothes.

"You can't do this, Maureen," I said. And I begged David to tell her how unhappy he was about the drinking. The night of the opening of David's play, *Nathan Weinstein's Daughter* (one of the ten best plays of that year), he asked her as a special favor not to drink. Just this one night. She promised, and she drank.

After a few years, it was a matter of his sanity. He had to find someone else and did.

I told David that he should tell Maureen how unhappy he was, but never to cheat. I felt that by telling her, he would give her a chance to know how far gone it all was. He didn't do that, and the newly acquired girlfriend sent notes to the house.

This was the biggest nightmare that Maureen could possibly have. It just was. She went crazy. Truly crazy. Pills were added to the booze and the drinking reached a fevered pitch, beyond anything it had ever been.

Early one summer evening, we were in a limousine and Maureen let out a scream from the bottom of the world. She fell to the floor of the car. I looked out to see what she had seen and it was David walking on Madison Avenue holding hands with his girlfriend. Now she was a witness to her nightmare. There it was, and she had seen it. We drove right home and I sat up with her.

"I can't believe it," she kept saying.

"What? What can't you believe, Maureen?"

"He cheated on me. He has another woman."

I then had to tell her that she was no longer a woman, that she had defeminized herself with her drinking, and was no longer a wife to him in any way. She was too drunk to sleep with him, or to do anything else with him.

Maureen could not drink and could not get drunk that night. I realized then that I was doing something very wrong.

She definitely needed some help and someone had to make the move. All I could keep saying was "I'm not going to hold your hand while you jump out the window."

Finally, I telephoned Robert Whitehead, a true prince of a man. He was very dear to both Maureen and me. I asked him what to do.

"I'll be there at seven o'clock," he said. It was now 5:00. He said I should have her dressed and ready to leave and we would both take her to this place he knew of. He arrived on time, and we went to a small hospital on the East Side.

Secretly I tried to arrange to get the bills from the hospital, only to find that Bob had already tried to make this same arrangement. We both found that somewhere in this mess Maureen had already arranged it for herself.

Finally, Maureen was in her room and in bed. I sat down beside her. I looked at her in her unendurable pain.

"Maureen, I realize when this is over—and it will be over—that there is one thing you must do."

"What?" she murmured weakly, hanging on every word as if I knew something that she didn't. I did and I told her.

"Get a full-time maid."

She never got over that.

"I have a lady who comes in once a week," she said.

"Not the same," I said.

She closed her eyes and fell asleep.

The reason I told her that is quite simple. A maid is the secret of the girl you love, and I wanted to keep reminding Maureen that she was not only a female, but a spectacular one.

I went to Elizabeth Arden to buy her the prettiest, fluffiest lingerie and robes and nighties and soaps and powders and makeup and hairbrushes and all sorts of things like that.

When I came back, she was still asleep. The nurse told me she would sleep most of the day. As Bob Whitehead was leaving, he said, "Don't put too much faith in this, Carol. It doesn't always work."

But something in Maureen turned around in the next few days. She began to take hold. She made arrangements for herself to receive all the care and attention she could get for her problem. She made appointments to meet with Dr. Ruth Fox (who had quite a bit of success working with alcoholics) as soon as she was released. And she made further arrangements so that after a few sessions with Dr. Fox, she was going to take herself up to a place in Roxbury, Connecticut, that was known to provide very good care for people with the same problem.

Maureen stayed at Roxbury for four months, lost a hundred pounds, then lost even more weight and was much too thin for a while.

In the middle of the summer, Bob Whitehead said, "I think I was wrong. I think this is taking."

Maureen did *Plaza Suite* on Broadway with George C. Scott and was back in the world she knew and loved. She was a big success and did not drink again for almost five years.

It made me remember those rare, once-in-a-while happenings: little blades of fresh green grass coming out of broken cement in sidewalks—unexpected, unannounced, uncared for, but it happens anyway.

With all her femininity now regained, she became her confectionlike self and looked incredibly beautiful. She was someone who had shown enormous, breathtaking, dazzling strength. Because no place can do it for you, no doctor can do it for you—they can only help you do it for yourself. So added to the delicious fun of being with Maureen, there was now the knowledge that you were with a person of valor. She had a little tiny flag sticking out from her forehead and it said "valorous." I saw it.

Sadly enough, after five years one of her doctors said that she could have an occasional glass of white wine. And that was the beginning of the end, because alcoholism is a very insidious disease that does not allow its victims even that indulgence. And it marched on and on through many years, even as I write this. Her beautiful gifts are so great that they are still viable. Her timid strength tries to assert itself every once in a while, but it never wins.

A lot of my most loved friends have this kind of problem. They are the most moving people in the world, because they have a wish for life to be beautiful, more beautiful than it could ever be, with an abundance of love for everyone. And the problem arises from the gap between what one thought life could be and what life really is.

Who wouldn't want to escape it?

O'Sullivan in Spain

I first met Kenneth Tynan, the young and brilliant theater critic for *The London Observer,* at a dinner party while I was still in California in 1954. That night, he asked me to come to London and marry him. That drew me to him. I don't like careful, self-protective people.

My affair with Walter was intensifying and my feelings were becoming so deep it began to scare me. I thought maybe I should mess things up a little bit, so when Ken invited me to Spain I accepted, mostly to get Walter out of my head. Ken knew I was in love with Walter and chastised me because Walter was a married man. He forgot that he was, too.

"Tell me about your wife," I said.

"I hate her."

"Everybody does."

"Well, of course, that is why I have stayed with her, really. I do feel sorry for her."

"Does she love you very much?" I asked.

"No, I don't think so."

"I know, but does she think so?"

"Yes, she does."

"That's all it takes. If she thinks so, she does."

"That's ridiculous. Haven't you ever thought you loved someone and laughed about it later?"

"No, I never have. I don't think I ever laughed about love. Love
isn't funny. Hate is funny. Love isn't. Love can kill you. Hate can
keep you alive. At least, the kind of love that I'm talking about,
which is probably not the kind you are talking about."

"What does that mean?"

"That means that I am talking about love that goes beyond all
boundaries, all other feelings. I'm talking about love that lasts
forever. I never want to feel that helpless, that overwhelmed, that
terrible dependency, that awful business—living off someone else's
smile."

We talked for the rest of the evening, and he had me promise
to write him every day, and off he flew to London.

I wrote him quite a few letters that said, "How are you? I am
fine. Love, Carol." Finally, I got a letter saying, "Darling, I am
fine, too, and I know how fine you are from all your letters. Would
you mind writing me a real letter?"

I knew that I didn't really know him yet. It was fun to flirt in
the mail. And his letters were fascinating. Of course, that was very
intimidating. I had no idea how I was going to write him a
fascinating letter about how the new detergent was doing on the
dishes.

Of course, when people are not actually there, I have a strange
way of forgetting about them. It doesn't show much depth on my
part, I know, but it was a relief to be that way after the way I had
felt when Bill was overseas. But I really didn't think about Ken a
lot, except when he wrote or telephoned, and I had only really
seen him once. I believed him when he said he loved me, and I
loved that part of him, that uncareful part. Because the thing with
men in general is that they are afraid to say "I love you" and it is
like committing suicide if they ask you to marry them. So I cannot
help but admire it if one plunges in head-first, as Ken did.

.   .   .

Later in '54, on my trip to Europe, I saw Ken, and he came to the States with a certain amount of regularity after that because of his work.

Ken was one of the most extraordinary critics. He so loved the theater and he loved actors and all the people who got out there and tried. He deferred to them and seemed to be always aware of the problems they had. He knew what failure meant to actors and playwrights and directors. He was one critic who sat there and rooted for them. He made a difference, a big one.

Unlike most critics, who live off the theater, he gave to it. He tried to infuse it with new life. He was aware of the possibilities it held and what a force it could be, what great potential power lay underneath the proscenium. He looked on the theater as something that would change us, help us. It was never just a play.

I remember going with him to see *A Hole in the Head* by Arnold Schulman. Lee Grant gave a magnificent performance. She's a marvelous actress, but there was something about her in this part that was especially moving. It affected Ken deeply. I saw tears in his eyes as he watched her play a Florida widow trying to buy just one lamb chop from the butcher. Her way of doing that thrilled him.

"Do you know her?" he whispered.

"Yes."

"I must meet her."

We went backstage afterward, and as I was introducing them he got down on his knees and kissed her hand and told her how glorious she was on that stage.

Lee was thrilled.

She telephoned me the next day and asked whether I thought he would be writing about it in *The Observer*.

"Of course," I said. "That's why he went to see it."

And he certainly knew how to write about it. There was no holding back—he told what the experience had meant to him, the incredible beauty of Lee's performance, the talent that it took. More than likely, he wrote, she could play anything. As usual, he was right.

.   .   .

I stayed with Ken at the Ritz in Madrid. He knew that I had never seen a bullfight before, and he took a lot of time explaining it all to me beforehand. Every so often he would say, "I see your mind is wandering."

"Well, once I see it, Ken, I'm sure I'll be able to follow you more easily."

"Let's hope so."

Actually, it didn't work out that way, because when we went to the bullfight I was afraid to look—I didn't want to see those things happening. But I did catch on a bit, and I tried to keep up with what he was talking about. It was so boring, though. And the idea of people's excitement because they may see some blood is quite sickening to me. However, I was not going to ruin our rendezvous with talk of being decent. Here we were, a couple of cheats—well, I wasn't as big a cheat as Ken.

We left Madrid and went to Seville, where we ate lunch every day on a beach. I saw nothing but live fish on counters—you were supposed to pick one to be cooked—and was ready to die.

We had separate rooms wherever we went, but we did sleep in the same room, in separate beds pushed together, where all we did was actually sleep.

He had great tenderness and he wanted to sleep with me. But I had come to Spain on the condition that he would not, and he was sensitive with me. He knew I was still in love with Walter.

But finally he said, "A man is just a man. You are expecting me to be some sort of saint and it is very hard on my entire nervous system and that's why I am so cranky."

One night, he became terribly aroused and tried very hard to have an affair with me. I brought up all his promises.

"Oh, but that's so silly. We're together. At any moment the nuclear bomb is going to wipe us all out. If we don't live now, when? If we don't live now, who?"

He began to embrace me, but there was something wrong about it. I don't know what it was, but he seemed quite different from the way he was during the days or the other evenings. I don't know quite what would have happened if I had gone through with it, but I know it would have been different from any other affair I had.

"Ken," I said. "You must stop. Please, you must. I don't know what to do. Please, stop."

And he did, saying, "Oh, God, I love you. I would never make you unhappy—you know that."

"Let's just lie here quietly. I cannot have an affair with you, not under these circumstances."

So we lay there quietly, his arm around me. There was some street light coming in through the window, so it was not totally dark. We were holding hands, talking now and then, when I thought I saw a shadow moving.

Ken was almost asleep. I sat up and watched a man come in through the door. I couldn't believe it. I watched as the man walked a few steps toward us. He stood at the foot of the beds.

I said, "What do you want?"

The man put his head down, as though he was suffering extreme embarrassment.

"I am so sorry," he said. "Please forgive me. I am O'Sullivan. I have been hired by Mrs. Tynan to follow you and have been following you since Madrid, and this was the first time I could get what she needed for the divorce case."

"Well," I said, "you have what you came for. Now you may leave."

"Yes," he said. "I'm sorry."

And he left.

Ken had, of course, awakened fully by the time the man was at the foot of the beds. He had sat up, but he said nothing.

As soon as the man closed the door, I got up and locked it—something I should have thought of long before.

"Ken," I said, "I'm very sorry. I know that this isn't your fault, but I will never be able to see you again until your wife calls off her dogs and I'm sure you can understand that."

"Of course. Where are you going?"

"I'm going to Oona."

"Well, let me make the arrangements."

We quickly dressed, packed, and went down to the lobby, and he arranged to leave. He didn't say very much. He knew there was nothing to say. I didn't want him to feel that he had done something terrible to me—because he had. I always lived under the threat of Bill taking the children away. And what happened in that hotel—despite the fact that we were in separate beds, and I was wearing my nightgown—for that to have gotten out would have been scandalous.

We went to the airport together.

"I know you'll go straight back to Matthau," he said. "But don't forget he's married, too."

"Ken, let's never ever talk about this again. Please. I have great feeling for you. I have love for you in my heart—I always have and I always will. But we will always have separate lives. One has an instinct about these things. For us to be together, we would really have to turn the world upside down. You'd have to turn your whole life's work around and I'd have to turn me around. Let's leave each other smiling. I haven't told you, but I've had an awfully good time. The only thing that really spoiled it was O'Sullivan."

When I arrived in New York, I couldn't believe what I saw. Walter was standing there, although I hadn't told anyone exactly when I was arriving. I was so happy to see him I couldn't contain myself. I jumped all over him.

We both laughed, and he whispered, "I love you. I love you with all of me."

I finally said, "Maybe I'm not terrific at marriage. Certainly those two marriages to Bill say that to me. Maybe this is what I'm good at. I am not sure that I should ever get married again."

"Well, I am. I want to marry you."

That did make me very happy. I didn't care if he married me or not—I just wanted him to *want* me to marry him. It makes me think of what F. Scott Fitzgerald wrote about there being only two basic stories, "Cinderella" and "Jack the Giant Killer," because one showed the charm of women and the other showed the courage of men. All the examples of my life show that the great stories are just the opposite—they demonstrate the charm of men and the courage of women. Specifically, it applies to almost any love affair I know about when the woman decides to want more than the affair she is having. That's when the trouble starts—when someone wants more than the other is giving or wants to give or can give.

One of the big secrets of love is to act as if you're getting everything, as if there's nothing more that you could possibly want.

In January of 1959, Walter went to Mexico to get his divorce, which is what people did in those days, and he came back the same night because he had made a date to take Aram to a basketball game or something like that.

In the meanwhile, Aram had called and asked, "May I bring Pop up? He just wants to come by and say hello to you." I hoped there wouldn't be a collision, but naturally they all came up in the same little elevator. And I could hear Walter saying in the hall, "Gee, I didn't know you were so short, Bill. You're really short. You know you're short? I didn't know you were short." And I thought, Oh, my God.

I had to go to the theater—*The Cold Wind and the Warm* was still running—and Bill said, "Let me drop you off."

"Oh, no, Bill, it's all right."

"Oh, come on. Don't be like that. Let me drive you down to the theater. I'll get a taxi and we'll go."

I said okay, and as soon as we got inside he turned to me and said, "It's Matthau, right?"

"What do you mean?" I said.

"A married man," he said accusingly. "You're going with a married man."

"No," I said. "He's not married."

"You know, you're a congenital liar. I've always told you that."

"He's definitely not married," I said, and we both began screaming at each other.

"You're such a fucking liar," he screamed. "I can't believe you're still lying to me. The worst thing I can do is take the children away."

"Do it," I said. "Do it."

"You're sleeping with a married man."

"No I'm not."

I'm not quite sure why I didn't just tell him that Walter had gotten his divorce that morning. Maybe it was because I was still afraid of him. It was the same old fear I always had. It didn't go away just because I was living another life.

Walter and I had had our marriage license for a little while, and then, on the morning of August 21, 1959, we woke up and decided to get married that day. So I quickly dressed.

"Oh, I must have a new dress," I said. "You know—something borrowed, something blue, something something, something new." I told Walter I would meet him at my apartment in about an hour and that he should find some people to be witnesses for us. We were both terribly excited.

I went to Jax on West Fifty-seventh Street, one of my favorite clothing stores, and my friend Corby, who ran the store, found me the perfect dress: white on white on the palest beige, a beautiful silk dress, which I wore with a gardenia at my waist. I ran home and Walter was on the telephone trying to get some people together, so I jumped into the bath and got all dressed up for the wedding, although Walter still had not heard whether or not we had enough witnesses.

Walter was just coming out of the shower as the telephone rang and I picked it up. It was Ken Tynan.

"Saroyan, I've been calling you for days. I have come here just to see you to tell you that my divorce is arranged for and that we will be free to marry very soon. I must see you immediately, right now if possible."

Walter had pulled the receiver slightly away from my ear so that he could listen, thinking it was one of the people we had asked to be witnesses.

"Oh, Ken," I managed. "How nice of you to call. I haven't been here. I didn't know you called."

"Never mind that. What about this afternoon?"

"Oh, no, Ken. I can't make it this afternoon. Walter Matthau and I are getting married."

There was a dead silence and then suddenly he screamed *"Congratulations!"* and hung up on me.

Walter was very quiet for a while, and when he did speak, he said, "I didn't know how far Ken Tynan and you had gone."

"You know exactly how far. I haven't seen him for nearly a year."

The last time was when he had insisted that he see me about a matter of great urgency. It would not take more than ten minutes, he had said, but he had to see me. I met him at Romeo Salta's for lunch, and he began a barrage of accusations and told me we were now in the jet age—in danger of nuclear destruction—and one had to live to the fullest. And all of a sudden, there was a loud ring coming from my purse. It was my alarm clock.

"What is that?" Ken said.

"Ken, you said ten minutes, and that is all the time I have. I want you to know that I am deeply involved with Walter and we intend to get married."

Ken said the most unbelievable thing of all.

"He's a married man."

"And so are you. And I'm in love with him and I will always love you, too, as you know, but it is Walter whom I love the most and want to make a life with."

To which he said, "I'm glad you always lied. Honesty does not become you."

Walter and I got married at City Hall. He insisted we go by subway. I said, "Walter, I don't want to go to my wedding by subway." He was testing me, for subways. At City Hall, I tried to lie about my age, but I have never told a more pathetic lie, because I lied about a year and a half. You don't lie like that. I should have lied five years and been done with it. I was like that man who kept saying "one percent" in his sleep—married to an old friend of mine, who married him for money, security, and lack of complexity. Money comes and goes. "Security" should be struck from the dictionary. Lack of complexity—"a good simple man"—doesn't exist. Everyone on earth is a pretzel inside, no matter what seems to be on the outside.

. . .

About a year or two after Walter and I were married, we went to
the theater one night, and during intermission Walter went to the
loo and I stood in the lobby not really looking around, but looking
at the floor (a habit of mine) and daydreaming.

I saw all these feet.

I then became aware that one pair of feet had not moved in
a while. It was one pair of big feet in front of my feet. I slowly
looked up and up and up and there was Ken. And losing all poise,
I gasped.

He laughed, and kissed me on the cheek. I kissed him and
regretted my lack of aplomb.

I was to see him again, a few times. He also telephoned now and
then.

But one day his beautiful daughter, Tracy, telephoned to tell me
that she was saying good-bye to me for her father—he could not
speak. He was dying of emphysema.

I couldn't get over the fact that he would even be thinking of
me at such a time.

I think he died a day or two later.

Tracy telephoned and said, "Carol, if it isn't too difficult for
you, would you come to the funeral? I know what it would mean
to my father."

Walter went with me.

I remember Ken often these days. I remember how he always
said he would die young. I remember that, although he had a
brilliant mind filled with all the knowledge one could have, he was
first and foremost a romantic person.

Most of all, I love the fact that he was a passionate man about
life and living and knowing things and changing. I will always love
that about him. I find it is a very rare quality. Passion has been out
of fashion for so long.

Rings on My Fingers

I have had many, many wedding rings. Bill gave me two beautiful wedding rings for our marriages. The first was a beautiful gold and diamond ring with "I love you" written on the inside in Armenian. The second one had the biggest diamonds I'd ever seen on a wedding ring. I think he thought that's what I would really like and he was right—for that marriage.

I wondered what Walter would give me. I knew he had no money. He and a friend bought a ring in the five-and-ten. It cost thirty-seven cents. I don't know what it was made of. When he put it on my finger at the ceremony at City Hall, I thought I would die—of greenness. My fingers turned green, and soon my arm turned green. I think it was made from what nails are made of.

It was the ugliest ring ever to be seen. I had to tell Walter how beautiful it was so he wouldn't go to pieces.

He mumbled something about "someday. . . ."

Walter later gave me a white-gold wedding ring with a chip of a diamond in the middle. It wasn't beautiful, but compared to what I had it was the wedding ring of an empress.

A few years later, I told Walter I'd lost the ring. We were in Israel at the time, and the jeweler in the hotel had shown me an Eastern wedding ring that had five different stones in five different rings, all connected. Walter bought it for me, and I put the ring with the diamond chip away. To this day, Walter doesn't know I still have it. I would never throw it away.

About four years later, I got a new wedding ring—gold with diamonds in it. I saw it at Tiffany's and thought, That's the one for me.

"Walter," I said. "I think we should renew our vows and get new rings just to remind us how new our marriage should always stay."

He said it was all right with him.

After that, I saw a very pretty diamond ring and I thought it would be lovely to have that since quite a few years had passed since the last wedding ring.

I suggested it to Walter and he said, "I think it's a good idea. But let me have it engraved before I give it to you."

He did, and it said, "To a great American."

. . . .

Marrying a Prince
. . . .

Although Walter had gambled ever since I met him, he did not gamble for the first six years of our marriage. That was because he was in such terrible debt from the gambling he had done before we were married that the bookies wouldn't take his bets. He owed a few hundred thousand dollars—far more than we ever thought we'd have. It was hard for Walter to stop.

One day, I got a call from a girlfriend who had seen us in a restaurant the night before.

"My God, Carol," she said, "I've never seen two people so in love." Actually, we were having dinner during the run of *Will Success Spoil Rock Hunter?* and he had the earplugs in, listening to a game. I knew he had a big bet on it, so I was watching his face closely, knowing everything he had was at stake. Then he won, and I was so glad, and he was so happy he gave me a kiss.

But even without the gambling, our marriage was filled with pressures of almost every kind: Walter's ex-wife, my insane ex-husband, Walter's two children (they lived with their mother), my two children (they lived with us). We each brought our old furniture with us.

The hardest thing in the world is to make a whole new life, and no one really wants to help. People want you to stay the same, to stay the way you've always been—the way they are used to you. But there was one sustaining factor, and it was the depth of love to which we were not only committed but were helpless in the face of. I learned so much from watching Walter—his innate decency, and above all, his attractive mind, and even above that, his smile. Our life together, even with all the problems, was the most beautiful part of my life. We seemed to live in an angel glow. The very few things we had looked beautiful. We looked beautiful. We felt beautiful—voluptuous, sensual. Being with Walter was perfect. All the uglies took care of themselves. We lived only for each other, and there truly were angels on our pillow—dreams of gold. The dreams of gold were the *now*. When he smiled, life was at its fullest.

When I have troubles and can't sleep, I send my foot across the bed to Walter's—which is warm and alive—and the trouble dims as little by little I have moved into his arms. After awhile he asks me if I can spell a word that he has thought of—and I begin to think about it. That is the wonder of Walter.

Nothing has ever equaled it for me. Nothing ever will. Despite everything, life gradually seemed to come together, woven by the silken threads of our love.

When we were first married and quite penniless but really, really happy, there didn't seem to be any work for quite a long time. We lived on borrowed money from a usurer, a gambler. We knew it would take years to pay him back at 14½ percent interest.

We moved into an apartment on West End Avenue. I had only gone to the West Side before on my way to Europe. I think Walter was testing me.

I made the apartment look terrific, even though it was made out of spit. We had an insane painter supplied by the building who said he could not do anything the way I wanted to do it. He loved gold walls.

"Look at me," and as he tapped his forehead he said, "I have a steel plate."

He scared me. I was hoping he would die—so I could repaint. After a few months he went to live in another country.

We lived in the apartment for almost ten years and I was so happy there that I rarely left. The same elevator man was there every day for all the years we lived there and he would always say, "What floor, miss?" when he saw me.

It was a very big apartment, which was good for us because we did have privacy. And, boy, did we have privacy. Privacy with Walter is indescribably rich in laughter, sensitivity, brilliance, and games. We both loved games.

I was very disappointed in some of my friends' reactions to our getting married. Gloria said I wouldn't have gotten married if she hadn't gone away that weekend. Gloria wasn't pleased, because she was aware of all the responsibilities I had—that is, in having to support my children—and she worried about that, particularly after she learned Walter was a gambler. But she was glad I was happy. Oona knew a lot about Walter from the letters we exchanged and was very happy for me. My mother was in Europe and was pleased I was married. Daddy was at the wedding. He adored Walter. He always told me there was something Lincolnesque about him. One of the best friends that I had and the one Walter liked the most was delighted. Lillian Ross, one of the best journalists in the world, came with us when we got married at City Hall. She and Walter were crazy about each other.

As for Walter's ex-wife, she called me up after the wedding and sounded very friendly. "I just don't believe that you married Walter," she said. "You had all those rich, famous beaus. How could you marry him?"

I was stunned—even though she knew how much he owed the bookies and how much she was going to get for always—when she said that. "Oh, well," I said. "For security." I'd told him to give her everything he had. "I'd rather be married to a poor man than a guilty man," I said. But it didn't work that way. Walter was poor and guilty.

Truman would yell at me when Walter's back was turned. He carried on terribly. "You know I like Walter—it's nothing to do with that," he said. "But you're not in a position to marry for love. People don't do this anymore. People marry for money, not love."

"But Truman—"

"Never mind 'But Truman.' The love you can get on your own time. What am I going to do?"

"You don't have to do anything, Truman."

"Look at all the problems."

"Yes, but they're working out slowly. You don't really think I would let a few problems throw me. Once you have learned how to walk you never forget it. I walked away from the problems, not Walter."

"Sweet baby, Walter is the problem."

"Why are you nagging me with the truth?"

"Honey, I wanted you to have everything—you don't have anything. Here you are on West End Avenue, ready to die. I can't help remembering you in that Park Avenue apartment."

"I'm alive. I'm completely alive for the very first time in my life."

He got so angry. "Oh, you should have married a rich, rich man. Then you could sleep with Walter all the time on the side."

"I would never do that. I have a very weak stomach. I could never go to bed with anyone I didn't care about."

"You're just as innocent as you were when I first saw you."

"You think it's okay for women to cheat?"

"Otherwise, they're cheating themselves."

Truman was a very serious man, serious about what people were really like and what life really did to them. In my case, as a close friend, he was anxious for me to achieve some security. "There's no such thing," I said. "The word should be taken out of the dictionary." The only security you can have in this life is love. As old as I am, I still believe that.

I tried to explain. "The air is sweeter with Walter. The color of light makes me beautiful. And this is one time when I would say with absolute sureness, 'Yes, he loves me. He loves me with all his heart and soul.' I believe it. I trust it. Truman, do you know what kind of happiness I feel? I felt as you felt when you wrote, 'As for me, I could leave the world with today in my eyes.' "

When I said that to Truman, he stopped and stood like stone and stared at me until I saw his tears. He did a total about-face. "Oh, honey, if that's the way you feel, you did do the right thing.

Honey, I had no idea. People don't love anymore. I'm so happy for you. I had no idea."

Walter and I seemed always to just manage. He couldn't get a job. But it was wonderful, being able to stay in bed with him. After a while, though, Walter did begin to get work, and then became more and more successful, and we had a floor beneath us.

· ·

Once There Was a Russian

· ·

When Walter and I had been married for a very little while, he was offered the lead in *Once There Was a Russian* by Samuel Spewack, who was also going to direct it. (Bella and Samuel Spewack had written quite a few Broadway hits.) Walter was to play Rasputin. After a few days, he came home and said that one of the parts had not been cast yet.

"They need a young girl. It's not a big part, but it might be fun. We'd have fun together. I'd love you to take the part."

I did. I was one of two concubines. The other was Julie Newmar, one of those very tall blonde girls with overworked mammary glands. She had the bigger part. She actually had the bigger everything.

She was very strange. I tried to talk to her a few times. When she opened her purse, and I don't know exactly what was in it, the stench was something unholy.

I jumped up from the shock of it.

"What is that?" I managed to utter.

"That's my lunch," she said. She pulled out a piece of wax paper that had not entirely covered a piece of cheese and proceeded to eat it.

As far as I was concerned, the whole theater should have been torn down immediately. The food was that old. And she had other foods as well in her purse, all mixed up with her makeup.

I suggested that she shouldn't eat it.

"That looks rotten," I said.

"Oh, no. You know nothing about food. This is what makes it wonderful."

I couldn't believe it.

Though my part was a small one, I was onstage a great deal of the time. It was a lot like being a model. I couldn't quite get along with Julie, but we talked now and then because we had to sit side by side on stage.

The play was quite terrible and she was terrible in it, but she was smart enough to know that. She didn't have a part to be good in.

Walter hated acting with her because she couldn't act and hated her because she thought she could. They had terrible fights. I had never before seen Walter fight with a fellow actor.

I didn't really think the play was actually going to open in New York. It wasn't just that it was badly received; people truly despised it.

Walter was magnificent in it, and I think that's the only reason there was an audience every night of the tour. It was the first time I had ever seen Rasputin played in a sexy way, and there was something quite wonderful about it.

Yet the fights between Walter and Julie grew more intense. Walter threw a chair or two, yelling, "What are you doing? Is that what you call acting?" Walter and Sam fought because Walter thought he wouldn't direct her properly. It was all the most terrible possible atmosphere in which to make a play happen.

I think it had about twenty-six young male producers. Or so it seemed. It was definitely more producers than I had ever seen before. They were all dressed for the part of producer—they were smoking pipes and growing beards and trying to look deep.

By opening night the chaos had reached its zenith. Walter's satin pants were torn badly. He went to the wardrobe mistress. "I know how busy you are," he said. "I'm so sorry to bother you, but would you mind very much sewing these pants so I can make my entrance on stage tonight?"

"Matthau," she said in a Germanic accent, "there's no time. Look what has to be finished before the curtain can go up. God willing, we should be a hit, then I can sew your pants."

Walter went back to his dressing room and I found him there

sewing his own pants. I don't know how he did it, but somehow or other he sewed those pants in such a way that there was no way they would ever be torn again.

"My God, what happened? Why didn't you call me?" I said.

"Well, you know. I thought this would be faster, and also I knew that they had to be sewn up like a goddamn coffin."

Opening night nerves ran rampant. It wasn't just a matter of being terrified. It was a matter of hoping that no one would shoot you while you were on stage.

When the curtain went up, the applause for Walter was fantastic. They also applauded Julie Newmar, although not as enthusiastically. (My entrance went unnoticed, but my second entrance didn't—I came out in a nun's habit.)

Before my scene was over, Julie got jumpy and threw her large hooped skirt over my head, as though it was an accident. Half-dead and not daring to breathe, I somehow found my way out of her skirt. As the first act continued, I began to pack up my makeup and personal things because I was convinced there was no way that this play wouldn't close during intermission. I had heard that there was a play once that did, so it was in the realm of possibility. In my mind, a certainty. No one laughed. People walked out. Hatred came in waves from the audience, rendering the actors useless.

But for some reason or other, the curtain went up on the second act, much to the horror of the people that were in it. I was especially horrified, knowing that most of the things I had to say were in that awful, awful second act. But everyone brazened it out, and finally, finally, finally, the final curtain went down.

What was left of the stricken audience slowly disappeared into the night.

As we went to our dressing rooms, we all passed a sign that had been put up. It read: "This play has closed this evening."

There was a great sigh of relief. One didn't know quite what to do about the party afterward.

Some press and photographers got themselves into Walter's dressing room, having been brought in by Julie Newmar. She obviously thought that everything had panned out. She had seen the sign, but she didn't think it concerned her. She knew she had a fantastic figure and thought that things would work out for her in some way or another. That's what she was like—a one-man show.

Walter's mother was in the dressing room with Walter as the photographers and interviewers arrived with Julie Newmar. At which point, Walter went totally mad and threatened all of their lives and told them they had two seconds to get out.

"Oh, Walter," Julie said in a coaxing voice.

"I've never hit a woman. I never want to hit a woman. I am going to kill you if you don't get out of here."

She ran. She ran faster than I've ever seen anyone run. She ran like a huge gazelle.

"Walter," his mother said, "how can you be that way? They're nice people. They're just doing their job. Why don't you let them in and talk to them?"

That was about as benign a sentence as I had ever heard her speak. At the time, I thought she said it because she loved seeing Walter be as miserable as she always was. By now, of course, I know it.

The lesson of the play was that there comes a time in one's career to pick and choose carefully. A job wasn't just a job, as it always is at the beginning of an actor's career, when his first responsibility is to work. Walter would now have to begin picking much more carefully.

The reviews were in tune with the evening. Walter just could not look at them. When you make your living as an actor, being in such a flop isn't funny.

Dick Avedon, probably the best man who ever lived, called the next day. I'd known Dick since I'd come back to New York.

"The best thing is that it's over," he said. "Let's get some fun out of it. Let's go to the theater and put your costumes on and let me take some pictures of you and Walter."

This was an incredible offer, particularly under the circumstances.

"Get your costumes on," he said again, "because one day you'll look at these pictures and you'll have a great laugh."

"Listen, Walter," I said, "people would do ten flop plays for an Avedon photograph."

But Walter felt so exhausted by the whole experience that he thanked Dick but said he just couldn't do it.

"I'll never look at the pictures, I know it—even though they're yours. I think I just want to forget the whole thing."

But as time passed, we all laughed at the awfulness, the meaninglessness, the stupidness of it. I have never been in a play again. Not specifically because of what a flop that one was, but because our life needed me more and more all the time. There was not a minute of a day or night that wasn't absorbed by being close to Walter, who was about to become one of the biggest actors ever on Broadway. He always was the best.

. . . .

Pregnant in Paris

. . . .

Right about this time, Walter did a movie for very little money, but to this day I think it is the best movie he's ever been in. It was *Lonely Are the Brave*, written by Dalton Trumbo and starring Kirk Douglas as the last of the cowboys, a true free soul, and Walter as the modern-day sheriff who for some minor reason has to bring him in. Kirk Douglas was marvelous in it, and Walter, chewing gum and trying his best to let the cowboy get away while still having to do his job, was superb. Gena Rowlands was also in it, and there was a quick shot at the very end of a man driving a truck in the rain who turned out to be Carroll O'Connor.

Lonely Are the Brave was not a box-office success, and I think the problem was the way it was presented. It should have opened on its own in a small art theater. Instead, it opened on a double bill in all of the Loew's theaters on the same day and was never given proper attention. I've always thought it should be rereleased.

It is interesting to note that in what has now been a long career in movies, that picture and that performance are still Walter's best of all. It is really about something—about dreams, independence, responsibility. Today, very few movies are about anything other than approximating last year's most successful money-maker, and that's where it all goes bad for the actors, the directors, the writers, the producers, even the studios.

But what ended Walter's dry spell wasn't this magnificent movie but a play called *A Shot in the Dark,* in which Walter gave an outrageous tour-de-force performance (even though he appeared only in the second act) as Julie Harris's husband.

Harry Kurnitz's play was a comedy about a French family, but on opening night there was not a single laugh in the first act. I'm not sure why, but the audience seemed unsure of what to do and needed to be told whether to laugh or to cry. And when they saw Julie Harris on the stage, the signal to laugh still was not there. Although they may have loved her, felt for her, known she is an amazing actress, the audience was not sure whether it was okay to laugh when they saw her. And remember, this was the opening night and they had not read any reviews yet.

But when the second-act curtain went up, Walter appeared in full comic stride and gave what amounted to a truly remarkable, elegant performance suggestive of Charles de Gaulle with a touch of Ralph Richardson and a little mincing walk taken from his mother thrown in. Naturally, the audience went wild with laughter. The real trick was to repeat this performance for an audience convulsed with laughter, and that is what Walter did so well on the following nights. Although he was not in the third act, it was his presence in the second that made it go. And go it did.

Walter was nominated for a Tony Award. I wrote a wonderful speech for him, thanking his beautiful, young, rich wife. Walter did win and made that speech so successfully that it was picked up by a lot of winners that night, including Margaret Leighton, who said, "I feel just as Walter feels, and I want to thank my beautiful, young, rich wife."

During Walter's speech I got so excited that I got pregnant. And of course, once he won the Tony, jobs were being offered regularly. Later that year, we left the children with a housekeeper and went to Paris for Walter to appear in the film *Charade,* which was written by Peter Stone and directed by Stanley Donen and starred

Cary Grant and Audrey Hepburn. There were a lot of other very good actors in it; it was a very good script; it was freezing in Paris and I was very pregnant.

The first people we saw socially were Mary and Peter Stone.

The next day was Walter's first day of shooting. At the end of the day, Peter came over to us and motioned for me to come close.

"You know," he whispered, "I have had to have dinner with Cary Grant every night since I've been here, and he is a very nice man, but I don't think I can do it one more night because it isn't very interesting anymore. And I'd love to show you guys a little bit of Paris. I know a great restaurant we could go to. I think I'm going to tell him that my lawyer just arrived and that I can't go to dinner with him. But have your driver take you to Chez Louis, where I will have made a reservation for the four of us."

We said, "Great."

We got into the car and went to Chez Louis. Very soon afterward, Peter and Mary showed up and sat across from us. I was sitting facing most of the restaurant, which included the front door. After we'd talked for a while, Peter said, "God, wouldn't it be awful if Cary came here for dinner tonight? I'd have to kill myself."

It was only seconds afterward that I looked up to see Cary Grant arriving with another man.

"Don't look," I said to Peter, "but your worst nightmare, the thing you are most afraid of tonight, has just happened."

"C'mon, Carol. You're crazy. C'mon, that would be a million-to-one chance. Chez Louis is not the most famous of restaurants, and I don't even know if he knows of it."

"I do know he knows this restaurant. I'm looking at him this very minute."

"Carol, you are driving me insane."

"Don't go insane. Just make up something to say, because he's on his way to this table to be polite and greet Walter and me. He doesn't know that the two backs he's looking at are yours and Mary's."

I think Mary slipped under the table at this point, but Peter couldn't.

Cary came to the table.

We all—especially Peter—gave him a very, very warm response, and we all said almost in unison something along the lines of "Please do join us."

Peter piped out something about just finding out his lawyer's plane was late. Cary had the manners to ignore that, and Peter had the manners not to pursue it.

Cary excused himself, said he was dining with a friend, and would see us all tomorrow.

Peter was still a wreck an hour later. To tell you the truth, I think that to this day Peter is a wreck whenever he remembers it. I think he has great style. How many people do you know who would lie to Cary Grant and stand him up for dinner? I tried to convince Peter of this at the time.

"You don't understand, Carol," he said. "I have to do a movie with him. It's important that we stay friends."

"You don't understand, Peter. Cary Grant doesn't care whether you have dinner with him or not. It would never occur to him that someone wouldn't want to."

These days, whenever I run into Peter (which is not often enough), I say, "Peter, I will never feel that Walter has made it until you stand him up for dinner."

Cary Grant did not waste any money. Walter and I started our stay in Paris at the Hotel Raphael (I think, one of the most expensive of all the hotels at the time). We stayed there until Cary Grant moved out. When we asked him why he was moving out, he said it was much too expensive. We had noticed that they had added some $100 telephone calls to the States to our bill, but I would go to the cashier and point to the charges and he would say, *"Je regrette, je regrette,"* and it would always be straightened out. Still, if Cary Grant had the guts to move to a lesser place, we ought to move to a still lesser place, which we did, and which was divine. It was the San Regis on the Rue Jean Goujon, where I had stayed many times before. It had all the romantic things one hopes to find in Paris—lace curtains, blue velvet covering the lace at night, a tiny balcony, a huge brass bed with Irish linen sheets covering the down and the feathers and the softness of lavender-scented sheets.

We were very happy at the San Regis until it seemed as though I was going into labor. I was at the end of the seventh month. I went to a doctor, an idiot who said that I was indeed in labor, and that I should go to the hospital immediately or I might even die.

As he was speaking, my labor pains were disappearing. So I thanked him very much, and as I left he said, "You are taking your life in your own hands."

And I said to him the only sentence I knew in French. *"Admirez la beauté de ses tapisseries."*

He looked at me sadly and I never saw him again.

I realized what had happened. I had been in false labor—which was to come and go throughout the remainder of my pregnancy. And while it wasn't ideal, at the same time it didn't mean that I had to go to a hospital.

I did have to stay in bed a lot, and my friends came to see me. When Truman, who had a house in Verbier, Switzerland, first came, I fixed the covers of the bed over and over again so he wouldn't quite see how huge my stomach had gotten.

Truman stepped in and said, "Oh, my baby is having a baby. I cannot for the life of me understand it, but then again, of course, you know I do. You two love each other so much that of course you should have a baby. You really are brave after the difficult time you've had with Saroyan. Now darling, I've come to be with you to stay with you and baby-sit you while Walter is working."

The days Truman came, we would sit and talk and gossip and have a very good time. When I felt well enough, we would go for a walk to a restaurant. Actually, it was a lot of fun.

Charlie and Oona were also living in Switzerland, in Vevey, which was very close. Once Charlie had called Truman and said, "I've just finished my autobiography. Come and have lunch with us tomorrow, and then, if you will, I'd love you to take the book with you and tell me everything you feel and think. It would be a great help."

Now this was a very difficult thing for Truman to do, because he was in the middle of writing something himself and he never stopped for anyone when he was writing. He just couldn't. But he loved Oona, so he felt he had to do this.

"I started to read," he told me, "and it broke my heart. I wanted Chaplin to have a great autobiography. Instead, he was writing about the people he'd met, and they're all lesser people, none of them could take a reader's interest the way he could. It was the book of a poor little English boy who will never be part of the royal family.

"So I went to work on it. In pencil. And I took it down to him. We started to talk about it and Charlie threw me out. 'Get the fuck out of here,' he said. 'I wanted you to read it. I wanted you to enjoy it. I don't need your opinion.' " And he never spoke to Truman again.

Oona and Truman, however, remained great friends, and one day they both visited me and we all had lunch at a restaurant they knew but I had never been to. Later on we went to a special showing at Balenciaga, who still existed in those days, and we saw some of the most beautiful clothes ever made. Oona ordered some dresses, and Truman said to me, "Honey, I'll buy you whatever dress you want."

"Oh, darling, no. Of course not. I can't wear anything now anyway."

"No, for later," he insisted. I wouldn't hear of it, but I gave him a big kiss for having thought of it and we continued giggling and having a good time.

Then Truman suggested we go to some place that he had mentioned before and have some tea.

Oona looked at her watch.

"Oh, dear, I really must get back to the hotel. I told Charlie I would be home by now."

"For God's sakes," Truman said, "you're home every day all the time. Carol will never be pregnant in Paris again, and all three of us have never been here at the same time before. I'm sure Charlie will understand."

She seemed a bit intimidated, almost as though she was about to come with us, but I could see she was nervous about it.

"Truman," I said, "darling, don't you know that that's what every woman really wants—a man who wants her to be with him and is jealous if she's not."

He simply looked at me. Oona looked so relieved.

"That's true, Truman," she said. "That's part of being in love. I think I'd better go back to the hotel."

And she did.

"Is it really that way?" Truman asked quietly.

"Yes, it is. I don't think Walter would like to come back after work and not find me waiting for him. He would think that very strange. The only reason I can be here now is because Walter is going to be working for another two hours. But you see, Charlie is sitting in the hotel waiting for Oona, and he is jealous of everyone who sees her when he isn't with her."

"Yes, I guess that's true. You girls are really terrific females, but it would be fun to have you both to myself for just a day sometime."

I told him what a sweet thought that was, but to be happy for us that someone loved us. I told him how wonderful it was to finally be with the one who was going to love you all your life. Of course, one can never be sure, but it felt that way. He agreed—but Truman seemed sad a few of those afternoons.

I finally had rather severe labor pains one night, but in the morning when I woke up, they were gone, absolutely gone. The picture was very nearly finished shooting, yet I knew it was time for me to leave.

"I think if I get on a plane today," I said to Walter, "I could make it home. Otherwise, what will happen is the baby will be born here. We really don't have the money to stay here once the picture is over. I think I better take my chances today. I hate to—without you—but—I don't know." I went.

I got on the plane. As it took off, I could still see Walter standing there in the cold and I thought, how can I stand a single day without him? I knew I was doing the right thing, but every minute without him seemed like forever.

As the plane went way up into the air, my pains came back, as they would in any rotten novel or bad movie. I couldn't believe it. These pains were the worst I ever had, and they really frightened me. I did not take my coat off. I did not undo my seat belt. I didn't go to the loo. I didn't eat anything. I sat straight in my seat and was terrified to move at all for all those hours until we began to land in New York.

As we descended, someone tapped me on the shoulder. I turned around to see a truly dreadful-looking man.

"You see," he said. "You're fine. You had nothing to worry about. I'm a doctor and I have been right behind you throughout the entire trip."

I undid my seat belt, stood halfway up in my seat and called him a barrage of names that I don't think he will ever forget.

"Don't you ever call yourself a doctor again," I finally said. "You do not have a single human quality. You knew I was pregnant. You knew I was frightened. You knew I couldn't even take my coat off or eat anything or read anything or go to the loo, and you remained silent, knowing I was in total terror of having the baby on this airplane. Whereas if you had only announced yourself, I would not have been quite as afraid. On second thought, taking a good look at you, I would have been more afraid."

The man looked at me in amazement, and that was that.

But the passengers around us gave me winks and smiles and one person make an "okay" sign with his thumb. I fully expected them to burst into song, perhaps "The Marseilles," as I disembarked.

I had already filled out my customs form. I declared only one thing: "one baby."

I had Charlie exactly one week later. Walter came home the day after. A feeling of such happiness came over me when I saw Charlie for the first time. We had expected a girl and were going to call her Amy Rose, but if it was a boy we were going to call him Charles, after my father and Charles de Gaulle and Charlie Chaplin. When I opened my eyes, the doctor was holding him up and saying, "You've had Charlie and he's wonderful," and he put him all naked against me with a sheet over us.

We fell asleep.

When I woke up again, a nurse was holding Charlie, and Walter was there, holding what seemed to be a huge suitcase filled with perfumes and a simply beautiful Pierre Cardin coat that he knew I had been admiring. The room was filled with flowers and love. It was the happiest moment of my life.

Dinner with the Guinnesses

Truman shared his house in Verbier with Jack Dunphy. Jack was the gift of Truman's life. And Truman knew it. They had been living together for many years.

Jack is tall and thin but well built. He's Catholic and he drinks a little, but not excessively. He's extremely intelligent, extremely private, yet, a simple man. There is no truly simple man, we know that, but he gives off that quality. He's written plays and poetry, but people who meet him at dinner don't know they're sitting next to a major talent who's produced very little. And he is the only person who really knew Truman.

One day when Truman was visiting me in Paris, I could see that something was terribly wrong, something that had nothing to do with my having a baby or anything like that. Truman sat down to pour the tea I had arranged for, and as he did I could see from the corners of his mouth and somewhere near his ears that there was a lot of tension.

"Truman," I said. "Tell me what's wrong. Tell me right away. I can't stand it."

He then went into a barrage of cursing Jack Dunphy. "That fucking goddamn Jack. Do you know what he did to me? You're not even going to believe it. It was so terrible that I'm still not able to get over it."

"My God, tell me what happened."

"I simply am in a rage. I'll try to tell it to you as calmly as I can, but I'm in an absolute rage."

"Truman, what happened?"

"You know what Jack's like."

"Yes, he's like an angel."

"No way. No way. He's not an angel. He's the worst, the meanest person we know."

"No, that's not possible. You always exaggerate about Jack."

"No? You don't think so? Now you just listen to this. You know how nice Gloria and Loel Guinness have been to me all these years? I know a lot of people's gossip is that he was a Nazi during the war—but that's ridiculous. They're two of the richest people in the world, and they've invited me to the most fabulous occasions I have ever been to. I've been their houseguest, and so has Jack, in all parts of the world. And they do entertain royalty and everyone else royally.

"I've taken them out to dinner a few times, but nothing to speak of, really. One simply cannot compete with that kind of money. But in my own way I have entertained them as well as I could and I have enjoyed doing it. But now they had made a special trip to Verbier just to see me and that asshole Jack. And that's quite a mean little trip—private plane or no private plane.

"In any case, I decided I would go all out. They were going to stay for the night. I had the most beautiful linens on their bed, the best soaps, the best towels, and the house was ravishing, filled with flowers that I did myself, knowing Jack would not help me."

"Truman, he always helps you. You know that."

"Never mind. He had no interest in helping me. Of course, I did all the cooking."

I must say that Truman was a superb cook.

"I planned their meals to perfection," he continued. "I had everything organized so that there would be no difficulty and of course, last night, as I brought the hors d'oeuvres in and we were talking, I could see that Gloria was really charmed by the whole thing. Truly she was."

"Well, then," I said, "everything was fine."

"It was until the middle of the most perfect dinner with the greatest wine. The conversation was going so well and their enchantment with us was so obvious, when suddenly Jack turned to Loel and said, 'What are you doing here, you big fat Nazi?' He said it loud and clear and it was unmistakable. There was nothing I could say. The only polite thing I could have done was to shoot myself. So I did nothing. Gloria tried to smooth it over, but of course, there was no way and I think she felt awful. They left immediately.

"Honey, you never saw anything like the first-rate tantrum I threw. I told that motherfucker off like he never heard. And of course, not much good came of that. He just looked at me as though I were crazy. And so I just said, 'You make my life miserable. I hate what you did. How could you have done that? You know how much they mean to me.' He said, 'I'm afraid I do.' I said, 'Then why would you do it? The war is over and has been for years and no one really knows that that's true. How could you do that?' And that son of a bitch said, 'It was easy.' Now how would you like that to happen to you?"

"I might not like it. But I would get down on my hands and knees with gratitude to a man who had the courage and dignity and decency to do what Jack did."

"Oh, you're never going to give up. You're sitting there with another baby in your belly and you think—"

"I'm going to tell you what I think. I think that Jack is probably the only person you know who is worth knowing. Of course, I love what he did, just as in your heart you did and you know you did and that's why you love him so much."

He chewed on that for a while and said, "Of course, you're right. But it doesn't mean anything to be right."

"Oh, yes, it does. It isn't even a question of being right. It's a question of being human. And you know that Jack was telling him the truth and that no one tells anyone that rich the truth. Jack was brave beyond brave. No one has to tell you that. You know that."

"It's stupid to do that. It's too late. You can't say it. What good does it do anyone to say it at dinner?"

"It did good. I'm sure it did something wonderful for Jack, and before you know it, it will have done something wonderful for you. Jack is a poet and Loel Guinness is a man who has been reputed to be a Nazi for a long time, although somehow it always has remained unsaid. You have got to love Jack more than you ever have for this."

Truman was very quiet for a while. He then said, "Carol, that is why I love Jack and you know it. But Jesus Christ, the times that he picks drive me crazy."

"I know," I said. "Anyway, you do appreciate him. I know you do."

"Yes, I do. And I know all about the Guinnesses and what they are and were and will be in any given situation. You know that."

"Of course I know that," I said.

Truman never mentioned it again. They loved each other to the end. While there were a few sleazy, vagrant interruptions due to Truman's bigger-than-life-sized fascinations with the ordinary, they nevertheless had a deep and true love for each other.

. . . .

A Lily and a Rose

. . . .

Billy Rose was rich and famous. He won a shorthand contest when he was a very young boy. He snowballed that into a capital-gains deal beyond any other. He married famous women, including Fanny Brice and Eleanor Holm. He was a producer of spectacular Broadway shows and owned the Diamond Horseshoe, a nightclub that had the tallest girls in the world dancing in it. He was very friendly with Bernard Baruch, an important financier at that time, an advisor to presidents. Billy started as his secretary. He got great tips from Baruch on the stock market and became one of the richest men around.

Billy owned an island near New York, and whenever I called him he would say, "Now, when are you and Walter coming to spend a weekend with me on my island?"

"Billy, we must plan it. I'll find out our schedule from Walter and we'll call you. You're very sweet to ask us."

I said this knowing we would never go because I'd heard from two people who I absolutely love, Al and Dolly Hirschfeld, what a weekend at Billy Rose's island meant. (Al, of course, is probably the most civilized person I've ever met in my life, and Dolly has never changed. She always has and always will look like the angel on top of the Christmas tree.) I got off the phone and immediately called Al.

"I think Billy really wants us to come for one of his weekends. Wouldn't you go just one more time so we could go when you go?"

"Carol, you know I would do anything in the world for you except that. I will never do that again as long as I live."

"What exactly happened that put you off going so much?"

"Nothing big. It's just that he has so much money—that bone-marrow kind of money—that the minute he doesn't want to watch the television anymore, he simply turns it off and doesn't ask you whether you might like to continue watching it yourself. He's rude in a money way, and once you are there you are imprisoned with him until the boat comes back three days later. He is not great company. He expects you to be the experts, to amuse him, to shine and scintillate for him. He wants you to follow him around all day, no matter where he goes. And he actually spends most of the day checking up on his stocks and bonds and making notes about them. But because he's so rich, you can't just go and do anything you want, such as sit down and watch television. If you happen to take a book out of his bookcase, you more often than not find that there isn't even a book there. It's a facade of books. In a way, it's hilarious. Maybe you ought to go once, but remember, you'll have to march."

"I'm not going."

Still, I called Billy now and then when friends had ideas that needed money to put them into motion. He always listened. That could be one of the reasons he became so rich.

I admired Billy. He had one of the most beautiful houses in New York, furnished with priceless antiques in his decorator's impeccable taste. However, he had to show up somewhere in the house, and it turned out to be in the powder room, which was done with a wraparound mural above the chair molding to the ceiling. It was the most exquisite copy of Fragonard. The ladies were like rose-buds, with beautiful bosoms and the sweetest lace and satin clothing ever painted. But the faces were the faces of Walter Winchell,

Leonard Lyons, Fanny Brice, Fred Allen, Milton Berle, and the like. I thought it was terrific to do his own thing in the middle of the environment he aspired to.

One of the things I telephoned him about was a play by Lillian Hellman called *My Mother, My Father, and Me*. Walter was in it, as were Ruth Gordon and several other very good actors. Lillian had, I think, adapted it from something else—whatever the case, it was not an original Lillian Hellman play. When it opened in Boston in 1963, it seemed to be in big trouble. Lillian had Mike Nichols come up and give her some advice, which he did. And she fired Gower Champion as director and replaced him with Arthur Penn. That alone was a sign of confusion, since I would not really think of them as comparable or interchangeable. And so they were killing the play in Boston. Lillian was bringing in new pages, and the cast was rehearsing until all hours of the night. Everyone was in a state of total exhaustion. Walter was so tired. He'd come back to the hotel after leaving the theater at three in the morning and have the phone off to everyone and tell the switchboard he would not take any phone calls until 11:30 in the morning. A little while after 9:00, the telephone began to ring and ring. I got to it as quickly as I could.

"I am so sorry," the switchboard operator said, "but Miss Hellman is on the telephone and says it is extremely urgent that she speak to Mr. Matthau."

"Just a minute," I said. There was nothing I could do under these circumstances except wake Walter up, and so I did.

He put the phone to his ear.

"Uh-huh. . . . No. . . . Uh-uh. . . . No, no, no. . . . Just forget about it, Lillian. . . . Forget it. . . . No way. . . . Bye, Lillian."

He hung up the phone.

"What?" I said. "What is it? What's the matter?"

"The matter is that Lillian is in Filene's Basement and has found you the perfect mink coat and wants me to come down and get it for you. She then said she could put the money out if I was too sleepy and I could pay her later, and I said no again."

I couldn't help thinking how adorable she was. I also thought it was sort of interesting because in those days, I was wearing a fur coat from Maximilian that Walter gave me after Charlie was born.

How could she have found me a fur coat on sale from Filene's Basement that was superior?

The next day, I saw Lillian at rehearsal. We were sitting in the audience watching the director make vast changes in her play. She wore a curious expression, which I assumed was due to her vanishing text.

"Carol," she whispered.

"What?"

"Is Walter always that cranky in the morning?"

"Well, Lillian, if you ask him for a fur coat in the morning, he's cranky."

She laughed.

"I'd take you over to see it but it's gone. I knew it would be gone."

The director continued to make changes.

"Want to walk back to the hotel?" she asked.

I usually did walk back with her in the late afternoons. I found her fascinating, funny, and very brave. It's true that she looked a little bit like a short George Washington, but she had the most beautiful clothes you could ever imagine. She adored beautiful things, and her Vassar-graduate and man's-woman kind of personality, topped with her brilliant lies, made her very sexy.

Always when we reached the lobby of the Ritz, there were never less than three of the handsomest men in the world there who had been waiting for Lillian to arrive. They always stood up and were truly happy to see her and she them. And they all had a lot to say to one another. One of the men I remember was Robert Lowell, and somehow, they were all something like that in looks or manner—tall, dressed as very rich men dressed—simply, with great tweed jackets, and so handsome if you loved WASP looks, which Lillian did. So many of her beaus had that look. Lillian could drink them all under the table without ever getting drunk.

She'd ask me to join them in her suite. I would excuse myself and tell her I would be back after I changed for dinner. When I got back, the atmosphere would be filled with laughter, fun, intelligence, and trust. It was Lillian's atmosphere. She had a gift for that. Those various men were there every single late afternoon of the run in Boston. There was no question that they were very much taken by her. As was I. As was Walter. There was no one else quite that interesting. She simply understood, in an objective way, the politics and the style of the times she was living through.

The play flopped terribly in New York, and she was beside herself. She blamed the wardrobe mistress, the carpenters, the ticket takers—absolutely everyone but the playwright, the director, and the actors. She might have blamed Ruth Gordon just a little bit because there was quite a jealousy between them, despite their recognition of each other's talents.

The producer, Kermit Bloomgarden, wanted to close the play immediately for lack of ticket sales. Lillian got a very bright idea, or rather, she thought she did. She telephoned me.

"Carol, Walter told me that you know Billy Rose. Now, I know that if someone subsidizes the play for a few weeks it will catch on and run. It's a new kind of play that they are not used to seeing, and it needs just those few weeks of subsidy and I think it will be a hit. What I would like is for you to call your dear friend 'ugh' Billy Rose and tell him that I telephoned and present him with the following offer: If he keeps the play running for three weeks, which won't cost much because everyone is waiving their salaries, I will give him half my rights to the property in perpetuity and a third of all my future works."

I was filled with apprehension. I was afraid to call Billy and I was afraid to fail Lillian. I could feel my heart beating. I could hear it. Front, back, front, back. It almost hit me in the back each time. I said something to Lillian to give the impression that I received many phone calls like this. Unfortunately, I think she heard my heart pounding.

"Carol, he will never be offered a deal like this again, so you can be very strong when you make this offer."

"Of course, darling," I said fliply, as I did not like being so transparent.

"I'm at home. I'll be waiting by the telephone. Call me as soon as you talk to him."

I got off the phone, paused for a moment to think *Oh my God!* What is Billy going to say? Then I called him. He answered his private phone, which was next to his ticker. He sat there more than anywhere else in the house.

"How are you doing, kid? Have you picked a weekend yet to come to my island?"

I made up some excuse about Walter and a television show in California.

"Fine. When he comes back, we'll do something."

"Billy, I have another one of my business deals for you." (I had presented him with two others that two out-of-work actors had given me.)

"Okay, kid. Shoot."

And I told him exactly what Lillian had told me to say, because I had written it down word for word as she said it. I finished and he was quiet for a minute.

"I need a little time, kid. I'll get back to you in twenty minutes. I need to think about it. Just give me twenty minutes."

"That would be wonderful, Billy."

I hung up and immediately called Lillian.

"Stop dying," I said. "We'll be called back with an answer in twenty minutes."

"Hmmm. I know that son of a bitch, and I somehow think he's gonna screw us in some way or another."

"Not really. Because if he was going to screw you, he would say yes immediately and then plan how to screw you. Otherwise, he'd say no."

"No, no, no. That's too simple for him. Remember how he got where he is and how much he likes the feeling of power."

"Lillian, I better hang up."

I did, and after exactly twenty minutes, Billy telephoned.

"Carol, I have a message for you to give to Lillian Hellman, and I would like you to give it exactly as I say it."

"Of course." I reached for the pen and paper.

"Tell Miss Hellman that this is a deal that I wish I could have offered Goebbels."

Silence.

"That's it?" I said. "That's the whole thing? Can't you add a little nicety, a 'thank-you' perhaps?"

"I hate Lillian Hellman."

Apparently there'd been some clash between the two of them some years before that Lillian hadn't bothered to mention when she'd asked me to call. To this day, I don't know what it was about.

"I'm sorry that you feel that way, Billy."

I called Lillian and told her exactly what he'd said.

"This is the deal he wanted for Goebbels."

She did not take it well and proceeded not to take it well for about half an hour.

"Well, darling," she finally said. "Thank you anyway. Let's have dinner tomorrow night and think of someone else."

I'm doomed, I thought. I'm going to have to spend the rest of my life asking rich men for money.

Lillian and I remained friends, and toward the end of her life she would come out to visit Los Angeles and we would go shopping every day. She couldn't see very well, and she could barely walk, but every day she would say, "Let's go shopping." She was insane in a store; she wanted everything. If she was too weak to speak, she would just point. And I think she should have had it all. Because she worked hard all her life, she wrote every day, she was completely independent, never asking for anything from anyone. She had very good taste and loved to live well.

I thought Lillian was a marvelous woman—tough-minded, brilliant, and a good writer. I remember one day saying to her, "Your love affair with Dashiell Hammett sounds so wonderful, Lillian. It must have been terrific."

"Well," she said, "there were a lot of problems. It was terrific in some ways, I suppose."

"Oh, but it was so romantic."

She looked me straight in the eye.

"It did sound romantic, didn't it? That's the fun of being a writer. That's what writing is for."

Frame-up

Sidney Lumet wanted to marry Gloria and he went after her like no one ever courted a woman. (Sidney doesn't marry girls; he marries ideas. His first was the young star of the young medium of TV. Rita Gam. Second was Gloria Vanderbilt of the great American Vanderbilt family. After Gloria there was Gail Jones, the daughter of Lena Horne. The next was the perfect WASP: Heidi Gimbel.) An up-and-coming film director, he turned his big guns on Gloria and said, "I love you, I love you, I love you." But all the men she married did that, I must say. They really wanted to marry her.

And Gloria is almost a perfect female in the sense that she will take on every political belief, every single feeling of the man she is with. It really happens inside her. She becomes a part of him. When she married Sidney Lumet, she had to make herself a lot smaller in every way.

And all of the money Sidney had really seemed to go for her laundry bill. This was a girl who was not only very rich at that moment but who spent it all. So then she had to go to work and when she did, she made twice as much as she had inherited. And spent it, too. All of it. To this day she works harder than anyone I've ever known, and successfully. She designs clothes, perfumes, jeans, and sheets. She makes money and she spends every penny. She's fantastic that way.

When Walter and I married, she did not approve. For a wedding present, she gave me a compact. For face powder. She felt I had the responsibility of marrying someone rich, just as Truman said, for the sake of my children. "No," I said. "I don't want to die for the sake of my children. That's a death to me." I might have died on the spot for them if they were threatened, but to just die for nothing was ridiculous. I didn't fight with her, but I didn't want to see her, because I wasn't going to spit on this great life I was having with Walter. I couldn't do that.

Time went by, and Sidney called. "She wants me out of here," he said. "I'm so unhappy." He was crying. I thought, Oh, my God, because when Gloria leaves a man, she doesn't just leave him. She leaves him for dead. He was going through hell, I just could hear the pain in his voice, and I felt simply terrible.

"Sidney," I said, "move out of the apartment. That will help you a great deal. There's something about a pedestrian act, just that little difference of getting from door A to door B, that's a relief. Once it's over, it's over. Just move now."

"I can't," he said. "I've been looking everywhere for an apartment, and I can't find one. I don't know what to do." He was really in a hysterical state.

"Sidney, look. Walter and I are going to Greece for a film. We'll be gone for three months. I'm mailing you the keys. I'm putting them in the mail tonight. Take the apartment. In three months, things change."

"You would do that for me?"

"Of course." Actually, I would do it for anybody in that kind of pain. Except Hitler.

I pasted the keys on a card and mailed them to him with a note. "Darling Sidney, please use the apartment. It is yours. Nothing will make me happier than knowing that you were beginning to get better."

We came home in three months and I asked our housekeeper if Mr. Lumet had been there. She said no. I couldn't understand why, so I called his office.

"Oh, honey, baby, sweetie, how are you?"

"Fine, Sidney, but you didn't need the apartment? Is everything all right now?"

"You know, it was the goddamndest thing. I found an apartment the next day and I moved right into it, but you'll never know how much this meant to me. I'm looking at the keys and your note right now."

"I'm glad, Sidney. And you sound so happy."

"Oh, yes, I'm happy. I've met a new girl. I'm in love." It was Gail Jones.

The keys didn't come back. I called him again in just less than a month. "Oh, I'm such a pain in the neck," I said, "but I don't want to bother getting new keys or changing the lock."

"Oh, sweetie, baby, honey, I'm looking at them. I'm looking at them right this minute."

The keys never, never came.

Sidney and Gail invited me to their wedding, but I didn't go. When Gloria found out that I hadn't gone, she wrote me a letter that was so naked in its love that I was stunned by it. My God, I thought, I'm a fool, just a fool. *Who* would ever love me like this? She can do anything she wants, I will never fight with her again.

I called her right up. "Oh, darling," she said. "Come right over. I've gotten married to Wyatt Cooper, a writer and a wonderful man who was a friend of my mother's."

"I never meant to make you unhappy," I said when I saw her.

"Oh, I know. And I never meant to make you unhappy. Of course, I was so surprised at first. But knowing how you are when you think someone is in any kind of pain, I could understand it."

"What? Understand what?"

"When I found your keys, and the note you had written."

"Really? When did you find it?"

"I come into town twice a week, and there are two drawers in the apartment I always use; one is my nightgown drawer and the other one is my lingerie drawer. The keys and note were in my nightgown drawer, which I was absolutely going to use, and they were on top. I looked at it, and of course what he was saying to me was, 'This is your best friend and she prefers me and she hates you.' "

That's why the keys never came back.

Ken Tynan said a very funny thing about Sidney. We'd go to big cocktail parties, and they were always there, Sidney wheeling Gloria around, and Ken would say that it reminded him of a little tugboat getting the *Queen Elizabeth* out of the harbor.

Wyatt Cooper was the great love of Gloria's life. They lived together and they thought together. Theirs was a most romantic love affair. What he said and wrote about Gloria was poetry. He made all the demands of her that are made in real marriages. She still mourns him and will—always.

Tom Buckley (a very dear friend of mine) once described an idyllic afternoon in Southampton. He saw Gloria and Wyatt walking on a lawn that went all the way down to the Long Island Sound. There were pink and white flowers lining the path. He said he couldn't help watching them. She was so beautiful in a lacy white dress and carrying a parasol, and Wyatt was in a white suit. They were holding hands—the look of it was dreamlike and magical. When they reached the water, they stood there talking together and laughing lightly. Tom said it was like looking at a fairy tale and he would never forget that moment, seeing love so alive, so young, and so rare. The memory of it has become a part of his life.

Gloria and Wyatt had two brilliant, brilliant boys, and he was a great father. He died unexpectedly, and I went to be with her after it happened. After school, those boys would come home and do their homework in the living room while Gloria sat there doing needlepoint or something. They'd be playing music and talking, doing their homework; it was lovely to see Gloria with them.

"The only one who ever really left you anything," I said, "was Wyatt."

The Odd Couple

One Sunday afternoon in 1964, after Walter's great success in *A Shot in the Dark* and *Charade*, Candy and Hal March invited us to their house in Westchester for dinner. Hal had a TV show that was very successful and Candy looked like a piece of candy. It turned out to be a very big party and a very big and very beautiful house. Candy was most gracious, and at some point, Walter and Neil Simon were introduced and struck up a conversation.

"I've just written a play for you," Neil very shyly said.

Walter liked the way he said that.

"I would love to see it," he said.

He read *The Odd Couple* the next day. He fell in love with it. He called Neil Simon to tell him how wonderful he thought the play was and that he would love to do it as soon as it was ready.

"It is ready," Neil said.

When the deal was made a few days later, Walter said he would not be in the play unless he was allowed to invest ten thousand dollars in it. This turned out to be a difficulty.

"Walter," Neil said, "this play is completely taken."

"Well, then I am not going to be in it. Not unless I can put my ten thousand in."

"All right, Walter, take a piece of mine."

Walter had never invested in any play before, nor had he ever wanted to. But he knew that this play was probably the best bet he would ever make, and indeed it was. It paid off over and over and over again.

Mike Nichols was set as director. Art Carney was playing the other leading part.

Walter asked Neil if he could play Art Carney's part.

"It would be more of a challenge to me," he said. "Or perhaps we can each play a different part each night."

Neil was aghast.

"No way, Walter. Don't ever have that thought again. I wrote this play for you and I wrote this part for you and that's that."

The rehearsal began. All the people involved knew that they were part of a great, big, fat hit. Which is rather amazing when you think that usually—no matter how good a play is, one is never sure of its effect on that big dark chasm that is the public.

It went on the road with problems in the second and third acts. Neil wrote and rewrote and rewrote. Walter kept learning new lines after each performance, night after night. Then, at the request of Mike Nichols and Neil Simon, he would go over them with Art Carney, cueing him late into the night.

I felt that a very strange thing seemed to be happening with this play. I felt that both Mike and Neil thought that Art Carney was the true artist of the pair, certainly a more delicate matter than

Walter. He was the one who on opening night was going to send the play directly to heaven. Not Walter, whom they respected as an actor, but not necessarily as an artist. They felt that he was far more in their range of understanding than someone like Art Carney. They handled Art in such a soft way that when trouble spots were hit in rehearsal, they yelled at Walter, which made things rather difficult for him.

I saw the play every night in every city. I sat next to Neil. I had only met him at the party in Westchester and seen him in the theater and knew nothing about him. But I made little notes as the play was being performed, and at intermission, and finally at curtain time, I would talk to Neil about my reactions.

"You see, Neil, this is the history of a marriage," I would begin, and continue for some time. (I didn't know that no one says anything like that to Neil Simon. He is not interested in hearing anyone's opinion at those moments—particularly those of an actor's wife. But I only knew that years later, because he is a gentleman. And I love him.)

On the day of opening night in New York, there was a morning rehearsal. Then everyone was sent home to rest up for the evening performance. I kept everything silent at home. I so hoped that Walter would get even the smallest nap, that his brain would stop working for at least one hour.

Every once in a while, I peeked into the bedroom and to my horror, I saw him sitting up in bed fully dressed. He had showered and shaved and was ready for the theater. And now was frantically writing in his script, line by line, page by page.

"Walter, what are you doing? It's too late for all that. You have done more work than is even possible. How can you do any more?"

"Please shut up," he said. "I have to do this."

"Do what?"

"If Carney forgets his lines here, I can do this. If he forgets it here, I can do that. You see, if I write it, then I can see it. And if it happens tonight and I have seen it written, I will remember what my alternatives are because I don't know if he's going to blow it."

He continued scribbling until he'd gone through the entire script. It's interesting about Walter. So many people think he

phones in his performances. He never once went to sleep during
all those weeks—even months—without a tape recorder playing
the play. I don't know of anyone who works that hard and yet
seems never to work at all. He insists on maintaining his relaxed
manner when he is working, in order to make the rest of the
players feel more comfortable. That, too, is acting. It is not Walter.
Walter is not a relaxed man.

When he kissed me good-bye to go to the theater, he said,
"Don't worry, darling. This will be a very big hit no matter what.
And you can get a lot of maids in the morning."

He left. I went to get dressed. It may have been the only night
in the world that I didn't care what I looked like, even though I
had a brand new dress to wear. It was the first dress I had bought
since we were married in 1959. I swear it's true. It was now 1965.
My dress was so beautiful I was afraid to move.

What a hell it is for actors, I thought. No matter how good they
are, no matter how brilliant they are, in a sense they are really like
chorus girls. Each performance they play they will never see again.
Opening nights usually aren't Walter's best performances. Yet,
he'll be on that stage playing those cards and chips out to that big
black nothingness—the audience. It is his riskiest gambling.

When I arrived at the theater, the house was almost completely
full. It was probably the most celebrity-filled first-night audience
I have ever seen. I sat behind Jean and Walter Kerr. Walter was the
New York Times theater critic—the most important critic in America.

The curtain rose and the play began. To be honest, I watched
Walter Kerr more than I did Walter Matthau. Kerr is a man who
knows how to laugh. It was a pleasure to hear him. I felt he adored
Walter and that his wife did, too. Within a very few minutes, I
knew we were home free.

Sitting there, watching the culmination of so many years of
Walter's life and really only a small piece of my own, I thought to
myself, it's incredible that this has happened.

Walter had been in hits before. He had been nominated for two
Tony Awards and won one. But the magnitude of this was something else.

Walter is a giant on the stage. He just is. There is no explanation for it. Also, within a very few seconds of seeing him, the audience falls in love. And all else pales.

On this night, it was all heightened.

Now, placated by the fantastic laughter of the audience, the laughter of Walter Kerr, and Walter's acting, I sat back and watched Walter's total triumph. Toward the end of the first act, Carney started saying lines from the third act, and Walter had to reverse and crisscross and do a pirouette and a double flip-flop over his left shoulder. And when Carney forgot one of the last lines in the act, Walter walked with his back to the audience to the rear of the stage, and Carney's eyes followed him. Walter held his hands behind his back (so they were visible to the audience) and he began to mumble this and that and the other thing. And then, to the back of the stage, he said Carney's line loud and clear. He turned back to Carney and the audience and said his own line: "You see how crazy you're driving me?"

And that was the curtain. And it was safe.

The rest of the play was more and more an actor's dream. The standing ovations were for Walter, who insisted on including Art until Art wouldn't come out anymore. I don't know how many ovations there were.

When we left the theater, we took a taxi ride to *The New York Times* and waited in front of the building for the newspaper. And then we read the review, which was a rave beyond rave, and the review of Walter's performance was as good as an actor had ever received. Walter was at that moment as happy as I have ever known him to be. He was like a little boy being given the pot of gold. I think that when you have worked that hard and when every detail has meant that much to you, you need to feel knighted. He did, and I loved seeing him so happy.

Then we went to the party. It was Walter's party. Mike said so, Neil said so. They all did. They, who had all worked so hard, were very generous. They saluted Walter.

How sad that that triumph was Walter's last appearance on Broadway. But because of it, everything began to happen at once. Those great big movie money offers came in, the telephone never stopped ringing, the front door never ceased to open up with more flowers and telegrams and vitally important business letters. And then came that very special telephone call from Billy Wilder.

Walter had the deepest respect and affection for him. Billy Wilder had tried his best, ten years before, to make Walter a star in the movies by putting him in his film version of *The Seven Year Itch*. "If Walter Matthau goes on the stock exchange, buy it," he was reported to have said.

Now Billy said hello to Walter and offered him a part in his next movie, *The Fortune Cookie*.

"How much do you want?" Billy evidently said next.

Walter looked at me modestly. I put up five fingers, each representing a hundred thousand dollars. At which point, Walter's look turned to utter disgust.

He left it up to Billy. Also, he had never accepted a job without a finished script and never would—unless it was for Billy Wilder.

The answer was yes and the deal was made and we were off to the races.

But as I sit here and remember this, I cannot help but realize that the very thing that catapulted a fine actor into an enormous success and unheard-of money has ended up imprisoning him today.

Walter is a powerful dramatic actor—and a part that would force him to drop a few veils and exploit that quality has not come his way. Walter's very guarded—anyone who tells jokes all the time is. That's a very useful defense for someone who's really scared out of his wits. I want Walter to play everyman. I want him to drop a few veils.

Walter's Mother

Before I met Rose, Walter's mother, he described her as the most fascinating person, a true combination of Gertrude Stein, Stalin, and Marilyn Monroe. The closest to the truth was Stalin.

Walter and his older brother, Henry, had dinner with Rose every Friday night, and she would stand them up against the wall and throw poison darts at them all night. The first time Walter wanted me to meet her, he said, "Have dinner with me tonight at my mother's."

"I'd love to, but I can't."

He asked several more times, but after a few months, he said, "You really have to come with me. She doesn't have much time."

"My God, what's the matter?"

"She could die."

"Is she sick?"

"No," he answered. "But she could die."

I thought to myself, we all could and will. But this was different. It seemed a very real fear on Walter's part. His whole personality was, in some ways, foretold by his mother. He feared her. He loved her. He wanted her love more than anything. That was never to be. Because she was a woman who, as Maureen Stapleton put it, "invented the Depression." There was simply no way to please her. Her anger raged on until the day she died. Some of it was left on her face as a corpse, despite that insane smiling makeup job they do in funeral parlors.

Of course, Walter is extremely grateful to Rose because she has been the inspiration for some of his most brilliant performances.

He played her meanness in *The Sunshine Boys* and he used her walk for *A Shot in the Dark*.

"Speak English and walk fancy," Harold Clurman had directed him. So Walter used the walk of his mother when she was in a great hurry to tinkle.

And Walter uses her in many other ways—her depression, her sadness, and her disappointment are always in the air.

She had a peculiar trust in me. Every once in a while, during the deepest part of winter, she would go to Florida. Walter, of course, gave her all kinds of money for these trips, but I know, being the total money psychotic that she was, she walked there. She would give me all of her bankbooks to hold in the safe-deposit box that I didn't really have but told her I did. And would tell me never to show them to a living soul and to just take care of them for her.

Every time she came home from Florida, I returned the bankbooks in what I thought was a beautiful new pocketbook. I knew it would keep her very busy trying to figure how to take the pocketbook back to the store and get cash for it. There really was no way to do that because I usually charged them. So I would buy the pocketbook back from her. That transaction always pleased her.

She often told me, "You're a good girl. You're a nice girl. You're sweet." But after Charlie was born, she would say, "Why did you have to have a baby? All the money that baby will cost— why did you have to have it?"

"Rose, we wanted a baby together. That's why."

"That's a reason?" But of course, as time went on, she, like absolutely everyone else, fell in love with Charlie, our son, and Charlie adored her.

I took Rose to the opening of *A Shot in the Dark,* and she talked during the play, of course, mostly wanting to know Walter's exact salary. Knowing how she was about money, I always made it twice what it was. She had no real interest in his performance. During intermission, I introduced her to a few Rockefellers, a few Vanderbilts, and anyone whose name she knew—all the famous first-nighters who were there, and they all were very happy to meet Walter's mother. They paid her enormous compliments about having produced such a talented son. She used her high voice and was very sweet, but as each one walked away she asked how much money they had.

Rose used to tell Walter stories about the time she heard Chaliapin (a great basso) sing in the old country. And Walter was always dazzled when she told it because she was remembering something that had been a great and happy event for her. He would continue to question her about him to keep the memory of that happiness going. She so rarely was happy.

"What do you remember about Chaliapin?" Walter would always ask her.

"He was very tall."

"How tall was he, Mama?"

"Oh, seven or eight feet."

I know that Rose had to be impressed by Walter's talent, but somehow she could not say it to him. She couldn't go all-out happy. It just wasn't her style.

She made me laugh years later when she was recovering from an operation at a very posh place in Long Island. I think Walter visited her at least ten times a day. And always brought little gifts, big gifts, smiles, friends, funny stories, affection, and anything he could think of that might help to make her life a little softer. One day, he said, "You know, Mom, I really am a very big movie star, and you know when you get to be this big a movie star, you don't pay for anything."

As he said that, a slight smile seemed to come to her lips. He went on to say, "You know, William Morris gives me this limousine to use and I can have free tickets, the best seats to all the plays, films, operas, concerts. And it's ridiculous for you not to take advantage of some of this. You've met a lot of nice ladies here that you seem to like."

"They can all drop dead," she muttered.

Walter plowed through. "Mom, some of these ladies have been very nice to you, and you really like them. Wouldn't it be nice to take a few of them out once in a while to an opera or the ballet or a concert? You'd be picked up by a limousine and then taken to a wonderful restaurant and then go to whatever you'd decided you'd all like to see. It would be a change for everyone, and it's free. It's totally free. It does not cost one cent. It does not cost one-half a cent."

"Well," she said. "Wally, I don't know. Maybe I'll think about it. I'll think it over and let you know." Pause. "Who would be paying for this?"

"The William Morris office."

"You mean, you're really such a big star that the William Morris office will pay for all this?"

"You got it. That's it. That's exactly what it is."

Of course, that's exactly what it wasn't, but Walter arranged everything with the William Morris office, knowing that once his mother told the other ladies, they would love it so much she'd have to accept this offer. And they did. And she did.

After a few months they were going out twice a week. She saw plays, ballets, concerts, operas, circuses—any entertainment event that the ladies found in the newspapers. The limo drivers were complaining because no one tipped them. Walter made more arrangements.

The bills came in. The more she spent, the happier Walter was. And one day, after about five months, she telephoned Walter. (I always listened in.)

"Wally, I'm sick of the opera and the plays and the concerts and the ballet. I'm sick of going to all these great things. Wally, I don't want any more of these nice events." She took a thoughtful pause. "So Wally, do me a favor."

"Yes, Mom."

"Ask the William Morris office to send me the money."

Another Visit to the Pharmacist

I was not completely untouched by the sixties, I must admit.

Someone told me about amyl nitrate, something wonderful to take as the moment of truth was about to hit during sex. Of course, I had to know what that was and how to get it. It turned out that every drugstore had it and you did not need a prescription for it.

So the next time I was near my New York drugstore on Madison Avenue, the very one I had gone to for years, I went and saw my old friend the pharmacist, who once sold me all those boxes of Kotex. He was very glad to see me, and I bought a few things and then, very casually, I said, "Oh, do you have any amyl nitrate?"

"My God," he said, "do you know that everybody has been asking me for that? I really don't understand why. I actually only have one box left. Something must be going on with amyl nitrate."

"You bet there is," I said with a gleam in my eye.

He was used to me by this time.

"What's going on? What is it this time? Why does everyone want it? I have only this one box left, and a lot of customers who really need to have it. It's very important for them."

"What customers have to have it?"

"You know, the ones who have had heart attacks."

"Oh," I said, but I still wasn't sure what he meant.

"What do you want it for?"

"Well, I heard that when you are having sex and are about to live the golden moment, that if you crack it open at the time, that golden moment lasts and lasts and lasts and is bigger and stronger than ever, and that's why everyone wants it. They want big golden moments."

"Is that what it is?"

"That's what it is."

"Well, okay. I will give you my last box. I'll order some more on Monday, if it means so much to you."

"It does. It means everything to me. What could mean more?"

"Well, the next time you come around, be sure to stop in and tell me how it is."

"Oh, sure. I will. If it's that great, I think everyone should know about it."

He looked at me oddly for a moment.

"You know," he finally said, "I didn't know you were so sexy."

I gave him a long hard look. I was in a rage.

"Why didn't you?" I said.

So a week went by and I found myself walking by the drugstore and decided I needed a few things. I went in and asked for this and that.

"Well?" the pharmacist said.

I looked at him blankly.

"How about it? What happened?"

"When?"

He was exasperated.

"You know," he said, "you told me about it last week. All that baloney about the golden moment and all that stuff. Did something happen?"

"Oh," I said. "Oh, my God, you see, what happened is I put the little box in the drawer of my night table and then just before I get into bed, I take one out and then as I'm getting into bed, I put it under the pillow. But what happens is terrible. I get so excited and I go so crazy, I forget all about it. Even though I swear each time to try and make myself remember, I just don't remember."

"My God, you don't remember. Well, will you be around town for another week or so?"

"Yes."

"When you come around again, let me know how it went."

"Oh," I said excitedly, "I will."

And of course the following week, the very same thing happened. I just kept forgetting about it. I couldn't help it. I guess I was overly excitable or something. I didn't quite know how to do it. What was I going to do? Was I going to say, "Walter, wait a minute," while I scrambled over to the other side of the bed and grabbed it from under the pillow?

A month went by and now I was truly determined, but then something awful happened. It seems that one morning Walter was feeling sexy and came over to my side of the bed to make love. I wasn't in the bed, but very sleepily, he was trying to find me. And that's when his hand felt this little glass thing under my pillow.

He looked at it.

"What the hell is this?" he said when I came back into the bedroom with the breakfast tray.

And then I told him all about it. He listened without saying a word.

"Where are the rest of them?" he finally said when I was done. "You must have more than one."

So I opened the top drawer. He saw the little box and took it.

He then took them all out of the box, threw the box away and took tons of Kleenex and smashed them up and flushed them down the loo.

"Walter," I said. "How could you do that? They're getting scarce."

"Carol, that sort of thing is for the Nixons. We don't need that. Okay?"

"Okay."

When I went to the drugstore the next time (not wanting him to know what Walter had done), I said to the pharmacist, "Same old story. I just forgot."

"Wow!" he said. "You must have some terrific marriage."

I do.

H Wood, U.S.A.

In Walter's contract for *The Odd Couple,* there was a clause that allowed him to take time off to do a picture and then return to the play. At the end of 1965, Walter had been in the play of *The Odd Couple* for almost a year (including the pre-Broadway tour). Also, the play was a very strong hit and could continue its run, especially on the assumption that Walter would be back after a short period of time. So we flew to California—Charlie, Ray (who had come back to me to take care of Charlie), Walter, and I. Aram and Lucy were in college at the time. We moved into a rented house on Alpine Drive in Beverly Hills, and Walter began work on *The Fortune Cookie.* He played a crooked, fast-talking lawyer who forced his cousin, played by Jack Lemmon, into suing for an injury he didn't really have.

We got to know the Wilders and the Lemmons and spent most of our time with them. Billy Wilder is one of the most attractive men I've ever met and certainly one of the most intelligent. He knows about the best of everything. To go shopping with him, which I did once in San Francisco, is a rare treat because of his interest in anything that is beautiful or well done. His appreciation of life is very special. The Lemmons became family to us. When we finally settled in California, Jack's decency and Felicia's laughter always made us feel all was well with the world.

There were big social demands on Walter, who was not used to accepting any while he was working, but somehow, along with the high spirits of his success and working for Billy Wilder, he seemed to have a great deal of energy and did far more than usual.

I spent most of my time cleaning the rented house. I think I was cleaning it until the day we left.

One Sunday night, we had dinner at Mike Nichols's rented house. He was about to shoot *The Graduate* and was not married at the time. Lillian Hellman was his houseguest then. They were very, very close. Walter seemed to be having lots of fun, and it's always fun to be with Mike Nichols and utterly fascinating to be with Lillian Hellman. Elizabeth Taylor and Richard Burton came by after dinner, at the height of their famous couplism.

Richard was very interested in having a conversation with Lillian. It seemed he loved to talk about writing and was something of a writer himself. Of course, Lillian liked to talk about politics and sex. Soon, I heard Elizabeth Taylor say, "C'mon, buster, let's go."

After they left, Lillian wanted me to go upstairs with her, and I noticed as she climbed the stairs that her breathing was very heavy.

"Lillian, your breathing sounds terrible. What is it?"

"Emphysema or some dumb thing like that."

"My God," I said.

We went to her room because she wanted to show me her new wigs. She'd bought a lot of them. Naturally, I tried them all on. I told her, "All those wigs—you ought to marry a president." I had been told all presidents' wives wore wigs so their hair would never look messy.

And then Walter yelled from downstairs that it was time to go home. We left.

Although Walter had not mentioned that he had lost a lot of money on a game that afternoon, I knew he had. He had started gambling again after the opening night of *The Odd Couple,* and it had accelerated. I think he had lost so much in the last six months that he himself was in a state of shock.

We got into the car, and as we drove home Walter's quiet signaled something rather strange to me. It was almost as though it was my fault that he had lost so much money.

But this was not Bill Saroyan, I thought to myself. Walter is far too intelligent to accuse me, as Bill had, but at the same time, I knew that emotionally he had to blame it on something or some-one other than himself. I was worried that I was that someone.

He may not have been thinking that at all, but it was my interpretation of the very silent ride home. So unlike Walter.

An hour later, Walter was in the middle of a heart attack. We were both extremely ignorant. We had read about things like that happening to other people, but never imagined it would happen to us; we had no idea what was going on. We telephoned a doctor we knew slightly, and he said he would come over. When he arrived, he told us he was not sure what was wrong, but he gave Walter a shot of morphine, which made him throw up. He said it could be a heart attack and that he would be back very early in the morning and left.

As this was going on, I looked at Walter, who was in terrible, terrible pain until the morphine took hold, and it seemed as though a dark gray curtain had descended over our lives. Yet, while I knew instinctively that it had been a severe heart attack, I also knew no one else should know it.

I telephoned Billy Wilder. I knew they were about three-quarters of the way through the picture and that there were some scenes that didn't require Walter that still needed to be shot.

"Billy, there's nothing to be upset about," I assured him, "but Walter won't be able to come to work tomorrow."

Billy was gracious, as always.

"Tell him to do whatever the doctor says," Billy said. "And I'm sure he'll be fine in a few days. Maybe he just needs a little rest."

Despite the grayness, I tried to make a joke or two with Billy so things would seem normal, although I knew deep down that we were drowning in nothingness. Even so, just in case, I wanted Walter to be able to finish the picture.

I then telephoned Jack Lemmon, as I was to do every night for the rest of Walter's illness. Jack is one of those people with that rarest of all things, an evolved heart. He listened quietly as I told him the story. He asked what he could do to help.

"Walter asked if you would please come by on your way to work in the morning," I said, "and collect the money to give to the bookies."

Walter had asked me to ask this. He felt that was a matter of honor.

Jack showed up at the front door at 4:30 in the morning, freezing, to collect the money. He took a look at Walter.

"Good God," he said.

"It'll be all right, Jack, you'll see. You know how Walter is. Every once in a while, he's like a hypochondriac."

Jack laughed and then looked at me very seriously.

"Carol, I want to tell you something now, and you must never forget it. You can lie to me anytime you see fit and I will accept your lies."

He obviously knew how sick Walter was, but he also knew how much we wanted them to wait for Walter and give him a chance to finish the picture.

The ambulance came. I paid them to turn the siren off. Walter was sleeping.

They did give Walter a chance to finish the picture. And they did something else. Because this had happened on location, they continued paying his per diem, which was no small matter and which I'm not sure they had to do. They also continued giving me the services of a car and driver whenever I needed them. The Mirisch Company, Billy Wilder, and Jack Lemmon were first-rate in their behavior during the entire illness, which lasted from January to June.

After only a few days of Walter's not appearing on the set, the press started asking questions and were told that Walter had hepatitis. At which point, according to Elizabeth Taylor, everybody went to get shots. But this was the best way of handling it, because people at that time knew so little about heart attacks that had I told the truth, the industry would have considered him a dead man. And the truth of the matter was that he wasn't doing very well at all.

I have been looking out of windows all my life. I think a lot of people like to look out the window. I do. I love train windows. I love to ride in the darkness of a train all night and see that occasional glowy light from a little house here and there on the landscape. My favorite view is inside other people's windows. I could tell you the whole story of a life by just going from window to window.

Looking out of a hospital window is different from looking out any other. Somehow you do not see outside. That which is inside devours you; your emotions—fear and love and questions of life and death—fill the room. Outside that hospital window is nothingness, because everything that you love or care about and desire and need and had and have and cannot live without is in the room.

It frightened me that I didn't know anything about heart attacks. Is Walter dying, I thought? He can't die. He mustn't die. I won't be able to stand the pain.

My next thought was that I would have to suffer. I would kill myself right away. And then I remembered our baby, Charlie, just three years old.

My God, I thought, I could never leave Charlie. That trap, that trap. The trap of love. The forced numbness, so that all those things that have to be done constantly to keep the one you love alive are done. You have to be the most watchful, you must learn everything, see everything, know everything you can, and that must all happen in a very short period of time.

I had to move fast. I fired nine doctors. I fired all the nurses. I changed hospitals. All seemingly risky things to do, but the risk was greater if I didn't. One of the doctors that I had fired had said to Walter, "Let's try to wiggle our toes, shall we?" and I quickly ushered the doctor out of the room and told him never to come back.

"What is the matter with you? Why not?"

"Because," I said, "Walter is a sick man. But he is still a man. You must talk to him as you would a man." And that was that.

I had never seen Walter afraid before. From things I know now, I feel that there's often a kind of nervous breakdown that follows an event such as this, which forces one to face one's mortality and vulnerability. It reminds one so emphatically of all that one is not and can never be.

I saw tears in Walter's eyes as I watched him trying to sleep. I thought, how terrible to cut him down just as he was coming up over the mountain. Walter had had the first huge success of his life. It had been a long time coming, and I sometimes think that Walter never really expected to succeed in his profession on that level. He knew that he was good and would always be able to work as an actor, but "star," "movie star"—these were not things he thought about. Or, for that matter, really cared about.

I think most people, certainly actors, worry the big worry: Will I ever work again? Will I ever be able to? I think that Walter was thinking more about that all the time.

I kept close to the doctor. I kept saying, "I'm a gambler's wife. Give me the odds," and "Tell me exactly what is happening physically. I will look up the words, but I want to understand what the possibilities are—the good ones, the bad ones, the alternatives. I cannot sit here and contemplate life and death. Will he live or will he die is like dying. It's too big for me. I want to think about a valve or a clot or something that could go here and do that or do this and go there. Anything but life and death."

We were in the hospital for a very long time. Walter was quiet and weak and after a while, I realized that the graph had begun to go the other way and that it was possible—in fact, I was sure—he was going to live. A strange thing happened to me. I had always loathed any reference to anything that had to do with nature's musts—and there are two words I never use that have to do with going to the loo in a big way. To me, it was the ugliest thing in the world—the words, the thing itself, everything about it. But one afternoon, after being in the hospital for two months, I used the loo in Walter's room and there was a little something left over from the nurse emptying Walter's bedpan. It did not disgust me. It meant that he was alive, really and truly alive, that his body was functioning once more. And I was grateful.

One night, about a week before he was allowed to leave the hospital, Walter watched an old television show that he'd done quite a few years before. It was one of the "Profiles in Courage" series and he played President Andrew Johnson, who had had the Articles of Impeachment voted against him but was never thrown out of office. Walter played him brilliantly at a high velocity. As he watched himself, tears were streaming down his face.

"Darling," I said, "why are you crying?"

I died a little each time I saw Walter cry, but I knew how necessary it was. I had been warned by the doctors of the dangers of not expressing rage, disappointment, anger, and all one's other wounded feelings. (It is interesting that many women don't express these emotions for fear of showing a lack of grace, and men are brought up with the idea that they must maintain control. These responses actually change the body chemistry and can place one in a very dangerous position. Manners, which in some ways make life easier, can also make you sick.) Still, I could not help being saddened by Walter's tears as I knew this man who had never cried and who looked at life in such an amiable way would never be able to do so again.

"I will never again have that kind of energy," he said, mesmerized by the television screen. "It cannot exist for me again."

"That's all right, Mr. Matthau," said a nurse who was in the room at the time. "You can play Abraham Lincoln. He was a nice, quiet man."

Although at any other time Walter and I would have laughed, the tears were still coming and I was trying to kiss them away.

"Don't give it a thought," I whispered. "You're going to be a big, big movie star. You won't need that kind of energy."

"You definitely are crazy," he said. "I think that's why I love you."

Two months after the heart attack, everything that had happened began to settle in my thoughts like a kaleidoscope of uncertainty. Part of my life had truly come to an end. Being young was over. Having fights with Walter was over. That would be a true loss, because we had great fights and we had great fun having them. I was suddenly taking care of everything, riddled with responsibility. I didn't have the strength I needed. My youth had ended. It would all be different for me forever.

"Walter will forget this, as he must," the doctor told me, "but you never will."

And I never have. Although that was in 1966, the fear never leaves me. And that is the true insidiousness of a heart attack—it can come out of the sky and turn all of your life into strangeness and force upon you a whole relearning of who and how to be.

After Walter was well enough to come home, I had to be aware of how he was feeling and I had to see that his diet was correct—it had to be salt-free at that time. I saw that he took very small walks daily and that he rested most of the day. I screened as many telephone calls as I could, as they took a lot of his energy. I saw that he did not get worn out by having too many visitors, although energetic visitors in particular seemed to tire him and make him feel weak again. But I adjusted to all of these things, and he was getting better and stronger all the time.

I had one problem, which was becoming more and more serious. It stopped me from sleeping, until finally I wasn't getting any sleep at all and I was afraid to fall asleep. It was a dream.

The dream always started in our bed, in our room. At that time, I always slept on the side of the bed near the telephone so that I could answer it. It was usually turned off at night anyway, but as I dreamed about it, it rang very loudly and steadily.

"Hello?" I would say.

No one answered. I had the receiver to my ear, but it was still ringing. It scared me.

"Hello? Hello?" I kept saying.

And the telephone would ring at the exact same pace.

I was terrified.

"Hello? Hello?" I would start screaming. "Stop ringing! I'm answering!"

It kept ringing. I don't know why it was so frightening, but it was, beyond words.

Dreams accentuate feelings. If you are terrified, you are more terrified than in waking life. If you are happy, you are happier in a dream. And this—to have a telephone keep ringing after you answer it—was the unknown.

The unspeakable terror as I would scream into the ringing telephone "Hello? Hello?" would finally wake me and of course, I would realize it was the dream and the phone hadn't been ringing at all.

My heart would be pounding. I would be in a state of terrible anxiety for a long time afterward, but then, after a while, I would calm down and go back to sleep.

Almost every night, the ringing would start at least once.

Sometimes the dream came twice during the night.

And sometimes I would have the dream as many as four times.

As it would happen, I would say, "I won't have this terror. I'm having the dream," and yet, even as I said it to myself, I would feel the terror. It didn't matter whether I was aware that it was a dream or not, it just upset me terribly.

I couldn't make up for the sleep during the day because there was too much that had to be done that only I could do. After about eight or nine months, I was so exhausted I don't think I really could have gone to sleep if I had the chance. But I knew that somehow I had to because I was feeling weaker and weaker and I could not allow myself to become too run down to take care of Walter. Because he had really started a good, strong recovery, and that was the whole point of taking care of him.

When I was in bed beside Walter, I would say to myself, "I'm sure the dream has got to end sometime. I've got to sleep sometime." The exhaustion put me in a sort of halfway world, a semi-sleep. I would begin to sleep, but because of the dream I would try and keep a part of myself awake, and once actually did.

And one night while I was beside Walter, trying to sleep but only managing a light slumber, I heard the ring of the telephone.

"Oh, no, oh, God, no," I said to myself when I heard that ring. And in this exhausted, sleepless-but-sleeping state, I listened hard as the telephone rang. And what I heard was strange—it was not the telephone at all.

The ring of the telephone was the beat of Walter's heart.

I had the dream because my head was close to his chest and because I had gotten so used to listening hard to his breathing to see if there was any change.

It was all quite simple. Walter's heart was beating quite strong and very steadily.

Once I understood it, I never had the dream again.

And then I was able to sleep. But I did not sleep without listening for Walter's heartbeat, which wasn't an ideal way to sleep.

So, for the first time in our marriage, I began to sleep in a room by myself.

It was something of a help, because once I fell asleep, I could stay asleep for much longer than I had before.

On the other hand, I was nervous about not being there to hear his heartbeat going strong and steady. I got up many times and went in and listened.

After a while, I slept.

To this day, when I am in Walter's bed, I cannot really sleep. After all these years, it's still a window I cannot see out of.

The Academy Awards Wow!

One Sunday in 1967, Walter had an accident on his bicycle while riding down the Pacific Coast Highway. He fell off in traffic and someone brought him home. I called the doctor who had treated Walter for his heart attack.

"Okay, you're fine," said the doctor after checking Walter's heart, and he left.

After an hour or so, Walter had a terrible pain in his arm, and there were little pieces of gravel and maybe even some glass in his face that looked dangerous to me. I thought he might get an infection. I called the doctor back.

"Why don't you go to the emergency room at UCLA and have them look at it," he suggested. He was a cardiologist, and once he had checked Walter's heart out and it was okay, he didn't care if every bone in his body was broken.

I thanked him profusely for his generosity and hung up on him. We went to the emergency room, and it was very crowded, but some young intern recognized Walter.

"My God," he said, "look at you. And you're up for an Academy Award tomorrow night."

"I fell off my bicycle," Walter said, and told him the story.

The doctor immediately X-rayed his arm and put it in a cast. He showed Walter the X rays of the broken bones and then asked for another doctor, who came in and very deftly took the pieces of gravel and glass out of Walter's face. There was some blood, but they cleaned it all up and told him not to sleep on his face.

"Maybe you can get away with it in front of the camera," the second doctor said. Walter hadn't even been thinking about this. They also gave him some painkillers in case the arm should bother him during the night. That was the extent of it.

Walter went home, got into bed, and went to sleep. The next morning there was to be a rehearsal, but Walter did not go to it. There was, after all, only a chance that he would win as the Best Supporting Actor for *The Fortune Cookie,* which he'd finished once he'd recovered from his heart attack. (It wasn't quite fair that he'd been nominated for a supporting role, as his part was really equal to Jack's. When Walter had read the script in New York, he called Jack and said, "How can you let me do this part? It's much the better part. All you do is sit in a wheelchair and feed me the lines." Jack, with his incredible generosity, had said, "Isn't it about time?")

In the middle of the afternoon, Walter said he thought he could make it, whereupon I immediately began to get our clothes ready. My dress, which I had spent a month looking for, was the most beautiful and the most expensive dress I have ever had, which somehow seemed to fall into the spirit of the whole thing. I couldn't wait to get there, to say nothing of the relief I felt that Walter was well enough to go.

I was thrilled at the thought of actually being at the Academy Awards. I had watched it for as many years as I could remember with my pals in the East—all of us piling into one big bed and laughing and making fun of the speeches and the sentimentality. And then there was that occasional real cheer. The best fun of all was the clothes.

It was always a great evening because the vulgarity was truly beautiful. Years later, a director who was producing the Academy Awards was determined to get rid of the vulgarity—without which there would simply be no Academy Awards.

Walter was placing bets with his bookie, trying to find out the odds in Las Vegas on his winning or losing. He looked especially handsome because in my mind's eye he was holding an Oscar, even though one of his arms was in a sling. I thought there was something very unusual about showing up like that.

We were laughing and playing word games on our way there, and then we arrived. As we stepped out of the car, we both saw for the first time the rafters—like people straight out of the French Revolution, a mob that could, in a second, go in any direction. They were rooted to nothing but the stalls they were sitting on. They were dying of the cold and the length of time they were sitting there and were screaming cheers of love and occasional obscenities. It was a whole huge, thunderous, roaring, incredible sound—the closest sound to an earthquake that I have ever heard.

Walter knew immediately what to do. He waved and greeted them and was just about the best movie star you ever saw.

Then we were in the auditorium and I realized that this was not what I had been laughing at on the bed at home years ago. There is a big difference between watching on that bed and actually taking part in it. It is not funny. It doesn't smile. It is lethal. It is the death of one person and the birth of another—oblivion for the loser and renewal for the winner.

The room had more cameras than people. The cameras looked at the people and were unable to hide how much the people wanted the award. They really wanted it. It meant money and success. It meant everything they ever wanted. Everyone was there to win.

When we were in our seats, I leaned over to Walter and said, "Of course, if you don't win, I never want to see you again."

Walter laughed because he does not think that way, and being as self-absorbed as he is, he was probably simply thinking about himself or a bet he had going. (I was surprised he had come without his earplugs.)

In a blurred way, I saw a lot of faces I knew, but I didn't talk to anyone. I could not manage any fake charm at this moment because I knew that if Walter didn't win, it would be a big loss.

Just before the big moment came, I whispered to Walter, "Don't forget to kiss me."

The moment came. I remember the kiss, a rush of lights and applause, with Walter moving gracefully toward the stage. Walter managed to stay Walter—an incredible feat. I had rewritten the speech I had written for him for the Tony Awards naming his beautiful young and rich wife as the person he most wished to thank. Walter was very happy. He announced to the press that he was going to raise his salary immediately. And he did.

I had forgotten about the pleasure of seeing a man who had worked that hard for that many years finally get something—or what is considered something—back. We did the whole thing; we went to the Governor's Ball, which is known to be the Newark, New Jersey, of balls, and then later quietly went to see the man who was most responsible for what had happened, Billy Wilder.

Billy had tried years before to get Walter in this position, and to Billy it was as though his belief in Walter had now been acknowledged by everybody—his baby won the race. We sat with Audrey and Billy among all their beautiful paintings. They were incredibly happy and sweet. We all were. It was fun.

Of course, for many months to come I did not remind Walter that it was *not* the Nobel Prize. I love the idea that it is possible for some people to enjoy their success and their money and have fun and leave their neuroses and bad luck behind. So many are unable to get the most out of the good things. They bring all that baggage from the very beginning with them right up through all that is fresh and new and different and can change life for the better. You can close a book—or walk away or fly around the world—because you can't get rid of the old baggage. I think one of the arts of living is letting go so that all the roses can bloom.

Walter has been nominated for an Oscar again, but since *The Fortune Cookie,* always in the category of leading man, for *Kotch,* and *The Sunshine Boys*. He hasn't won again—yet.

I was particularly unhappy the night Walter did not win for *Kotch,* because that was the year Charlie Chaplin came to America and accepted an honorary award from the Academy with Oona at his side.

Oona's sweetness was so incredible. We got so dressed up and then as we sat down in our seats, Oona squeezed my hand and said, "Can you believe it? We're at the Academy Awards together." And so we were.

I wanted Walter to win, to show off for Charlie. I told all this to Charlie later.

"Oh, little Carol," he said, "don't you know that I know how this is done, that I know the chicanery, the greediness, the insanity? Name it, I know it. You can't go against all the odds. Don't you know that I know what a wonderful actor Walter is? That's my business. So don't worry. I know you're married to a great actor."

Walter was sitting beside me and had listened, of course, to all that Charlie said. I saw on his face the most winning look I had ever seen before or again. To have been complimented by the great man himself was so significant to Walter. No statue was needed to refresh his memory.

He will never forget that moment.

. . . .

The Movies

. . . .

The success syndrome had taken a real hold on us. I say "us" because indeed that *is* what happens in a marriage, whether with success or failure. Now added to *The Odd Couple* success was the Oscar. We went back to our New York apartment, but our life there became totally different from what it had been before.

Walter began accepting parts again, but only in the movies. He liked California, and as he became strong again his career zoomed ahead. We could never have imagined the kind of attention that success brought. It's quite amazing in its coarseness—in the way that it is the end of your privacy—except for the money. The money has true refinement. And it gave me a chance to hear my favorite sentence in the English language over and over again: "You rang, madame?"

And the person that such success happens to is caught unaware and does not know what expression to wear. The usual expressions don't seem to fit at all. One can no longer eat quietly in a restaurant—or eat at all for that matter—as one is now bound to maintaining a certain weight. One must be wonderful to all the people previously ignored. One must be a hail fellow well met with a sense of camaraderie to all the janitors one sees as one is leaving the set at the end of the day. One's temper must be saved for one's wife. One no longer really needs that wife, as the women are plentiful (and not really to get something definite from one, but just to have been near one of the greats).

Walter was totally unready for it, having been knocked around by his mother, told off daily by his ex-wife, and never really treated like a prince until he met me (and that, I think, is why he was so taken by me). But since everyone was now doing what previously only I had done, I, too, needed a new face. So I bought a lot of new clothes.

We went back and forth for a while. Walter would work in California and then, between assignments, we would go back to New York. We did this until it was time for Charlie to go to school, at which point we bought a little house in Pacific Palisades.

I tried to hang on to our apartment because it was one of those big, marvelous older New York apartments, but it was impossible; people knew when we weren't using it and asked to borrow it and there were finally people we didn't know in it (friends of friends), and it cost us the same to keep it going when we were away as it did when we were living there. The grocery, the housekeeper, the laundry, the cleaner, the drugstore—all the bills seemed to keep coming until I arrived and threw everybody out and finally decided to get rid of the apartment.

On our very last day in our apartment, the elevator man who had said "What floor, miss?" for ten years shook hands with me and said, "Good-bye, miss. It has been a pleasure knowing you."

"Same here," I said.

Lying and Lying in Bed

Walter and I were lying. And then lying in the dark. We would talk about how lucky we were to have each other. How inconceivable life would be without the other. Once or twice before, Walter had fallen asleep without saying these things so I had hit him over the head with a frying pan. Ever since then, he has said them every night.

"You're wonderful. You're perfect. You're all I will ever want. I love you, I love you, I love you."

"Thank you, Walter."

"Can we go to sleep now?"

And I'd laugh and then we'd curl up and go to sleep. Or we'd talk about the different people we'd seen at parties. New York's most beautiful model was at one party—she was the girl of the moment. And I said to Walter, "Isn't she beautiful? She's considered the most beautiful model in the world. What do you think?"

"Hmmmm." Walter took a long, considerate look. "She looks like a hungry chicken hawk on a frosty morning." It wasn't the worst description, because although she was beautiful, she was model-type beautiful.

We spoke of marriages, and when you speak of other people's marriages, you are, of course, saying something about your own. A delicate sparring begins. Once I saw an actor at a party sitting with his arm around a very naked starlet who was about seventeen. His wife was at the other end of the room talking to friends of hers. They caught each other's eyes, and he threw her three kisses and continued pinching the girl. The wife was a very sensitive and intelligent person who knew exactly what was going on and I think spent most of her marriage deciding whether or not to leave it.

Fidelity is a constant issue wherever there are men and women. I think the terrible thing about it is that most women are so afraid of life, of being Out There, that what marriage becomes is a sort of suit of armor with which to face the world. And I do mean a suit.

Walter and I went on to speak of some beautiful women we have known who marry and then, when their husbands want a divorce, have a big stick-up and get themselves involved with alimony, insurance, and everything in perpetuity. They become "alimony queens." When they are asked out by a man, they have to think, "Does he have as much money as I'm getting, because I wouldn't give up everything for anybody."

"Why should I share my diamonds with him?" asked one woman.

These women don't simply stay bitter. They get more bitter all the time. And lonelier. There is an entire world of bitter women. They are not good company. They talk about their loneliness so bravely that you immediately realize you have to focus everything you say so it ends up something like: "What a miracle of a human being you are. I've never met anyone with such sensitivity and courage." Then, after a suitable period of time, you gently hint that you will be leaving the country almost immediately for a very long time, but you will try to keep in touch.

When Walter and I are in bed, we look out toward the ocean and see the dark silhouettes of trees against the dark gray and pink sky. That is the color of that coastal sky in the Pacific Palisades where we live. We make shapes out of the trees.

"Look at that part of the tree. Does that not look like Olivier as he looked when he played Richard the—bad one, whatever the number is," I say.

Walter knows the number. Then he says, "It is so beautiful to just be in bed and to look out at the whole world, the rim of the Pacific Ocean."

"Yes, take a good look, because it might be in Arizona tomorrow."

He laughs, as we all do when we talk about earthquakes. That night he said, "That was a beautiful dress you wore tonight. How much did it cost?"

"That? Oh . . . my mother gave it to me a long time ago and I just had it altered."

"I love you because I love your sweet lies."

"I love you because you know I'm lying and you let it go." I hate this business of nailing each other every time you hear a lie, particularly because you know the truth is a bore.

"How much did the dress cost?"

"Walter, you know how I feel about things. I told you that quote I read in *The New York Times* years ago."

"What quote?"

"We are not here to see through one another. We are here to see one another through."

"Carol, how much did the dress cost?"

"It really is a very old dress. I just changed it around a little bit."

"Carol, I want to know how much the dress cost and when you bought it."

When I told him, he quickly went all the way to the other side of the bed and stayed there the rest of the night. I knew that even though he was sleeping he was seething with rage, so I went to my sitting room and telephoned friends who were in other parts of the world, telling them that this diseased gambler that I was married to and whose gambling I never spoke about was mad because he thought my dress was so expensive. I actually didn't think it was so bad. There were women at that party who had dresses with unheard-of prices. Mine was three thousand dollars.

Even I knew how rotten I was, I told them, winning all of my friends' sympathy. That was a lot of money for one dress, and it was really a dress that only other women would like.

I remembered that I used to dress to please a man; I couldn't care less about other women. Why was I doing this?

So after getting off the phone with my friends that night, I ended up rereading *Lucy Gayheart* by Willa Cather who, along with Jane Austen, is one of my favorite authors. And suddenly, I ran back to

Walter's bed and kissed him and kissed him and told him how much I loved him and that I wasn't going shopping anymore, nor was I going to do any more rotten things. And he was perfect and I was awful. And that is the way we always made up.

. . . .

The Gardeners

. . . .

Dear Oona,

Just so you will know: Walter is a very selfish man who happened to get the greatest housekeeper of all time because I was the very best, until a few years ago when I got sick, and now I am only slightly less than my best. I'm having gardener trouble. Walter doesn't want to know, he doesn't want to hear, he does not have time to deal with it in any way because he and his bookie are tremendously busy most of the day and night. And I get fucking mad.

We have a dead tree in our garden and we have spent thousands and thousands of dollars trying to keep it alive. I think it's a worthwhile thing to do. It's just that I'd like a little encouragement from him.

"Aren't you perfect? You are keeping a dead tree alive."

Something like that would do, but simply isn't forthcoming. I attend to all business and house problems. That in itself is unusual, particularly for a spendthrift. Oona, I definitely think Walter is a little crazy. I have about twenty-five gardeners working for me. I have less than an acre of land and most of it is house. I simply cannot explain it. I cannot fire anybody. I just keep adding people. And someone has to help me with this. I've asked Walter.

"Have I complained?" he says. "Do you know what another husband would do if his wife had twenty-five gardeners?"

"Walter, I just need you to help me. We have to be like a unit in front of these gardeners. Even though we disagree about everything, in front of the gardeners we have to agree on everything.

They have to know that this marriage is solid as a rock forever and everything has been agreed upon. Unless they see that, I have a terrible time, like when that awful man wanted to put the weeping willow at the bottom of the hill so all we could see was the top. I told him the whole point is to see it weep. And he said, 'I don't agree with you.' I said, 'You don't have to agree with me. I pay you. And the garden is going to be my way and if it's distasteful to you, then leave. In fact, you're distasteful to me. Please leave right this minute.' And he did. And Walter, I know exactly what you wanted to say to him the next day. You wanted to pull him off to the side and say, 'You don't need to be upset. You know my wife is very, very sweet. She's just a little crazy and you have to realize she's crazy.' And so I had to sit on your shoulders the entire day, from the minute we got up to the time we went to bed, so you couldn't say that."

Walter is a man who has three houses that are all perfectly run and very beautiful and always ready for him. What I am saying is that he has my guts, my heart, my soul. He's taken all of me and hasn't the slightest notion of what is involved here. He doesn't want to hear about the houses, he doesn't want to know about them, he never says that anything is nice, and always says when something is wrong. Which to me is the absolute reverse of how one should live. I know that by letting someone know when it is right, they will learn faster and better what to do to make things better and better all the time. There's a hideous name for it and it's positive reinforcement, and you know, Oona, that's like saying penis instead of prick. I can't stand those terms.

Anyway, I'm mad as hell. The gardeners have driven me nuts. Walter is ignoring the situation and pretending that I am in a very good mood. How he manages to do this I do not know. That may be the result of the fucking positive reinforcement he's not doing.

None of this would matter at all except by 9:00 at night, I'm feeling dreamy and I'm in my bath and planning to surprise Walter with a beautiful new nightie and the surprise part is that I will leave the price tag on it, whiting out one zero. And of course, I can't wait.

But when that part of the evening is over, my mind instantly attacks the gardeners again and I go into another room and write lists of grievances. I have about a thousand crank letters that I have written to Walter over the years. It somehow gets me sleepy after about a hundred pages and I finally fall asleep. The next day, it doesn't seem to be all that terrible. They are the meanest letters I've ever read in my life. I must tear them up before I die so that he never sees them.

The Flop

It had the sound of morning California success—Spanish gardeners, lawn mowers, the pool man, the laundress bringing in her own family's laundry, the governess bringing the car out of the garage while the little boy waited, dressed in the school uniform (a uniform more suited to Eton or midwinter Groton, but insane in the blazing, glaring sun of the desert that is Hollywood, U.S.A.).

We were asleep in what the real estate people probably referred to in ads as a "to die" master suite. I left the soundproof paradise and walked into the upstairs living room, opened the windows to make sure that the rich, money-filled sounds belonged to big fat us. They did that morning.

I bathed and put on a new no-makeup look and made Walter's breakfast. For the "plus" for his tray (a custom from the first day of our marriage to keep away the bleakness of being poor, the pain of needing a job, and all those anxiety-ridden, mean things running riot in the emptiness), I picked a deep red garnet rose, to which I added a little English ivy. I added one other thing. It may be the sleaziest act of my life. God, I hope so. But California flowers have no scent. It's as if there's only a stem, a graceful buildup to nothing. I couldn't stand it, so I put a few drops of Rocha Rose in the water. Now, his tray was perfect.

Making the breakfast was a big thing. It was as though we were still "real people." I always told Walter that there just weren't any real people anywhere. There were poor people, people to help, people to hate, but I had never seen a real person in my entire life. There had been one—Mozart. Actually, two—Thomas Jefferson. We parted oceans on that. He knew there were. I knew there weren't. He said his whole acting career had been based on playing what he regarded as "real people." I told him his career was based on playing brilliantly because he knew that no one was real and no one else knew anyone who was real, so how could they criticize him? We disagreed on everything, but we didn't talk much, so it worked out.

As I brought the tray in, I saw instantly that our drop-dead master suite was exactly that. There were newspapers and magazines all over the bed—some crumpled and some opened again, black ink underlinings on some—and Walter was covering his head under the pillow making muffled sounds.

"I can't stand it. It's so terrible. I can't tell you," he said as he read the reviews of his latest film, *The Secret Life of an American Wife*, his first since he repeated his Broadway success in *The Odd Couple*.

"They hate me," he said. "They all hate me. They hate the picture and they hate me. I'm finished. All our fun is over. We're going to have to go back to playing Scrabble every night. Let's buy the best Scrabble set they have right now before we don't have a penny left."

"Don't be ridiculous. Any actor of your stature doesn't sink with one flop," I said. "Actually, you could survive a few flops."

"Oh, boy, are you wrong. This is it. Do you know what this means?"

"Well, there are a lot of things we can do. We can sell the Rolls Royce and the beach house. We really don't need that many people working for us. There are many ways we can still live very nicely without spending all that money."

"You really don't get it. It's much worse," he said. "I'll have to be nice to everyone again."

Civil Lies—Civilized

I really feel one must lie big and one must lie a lot. I do not know if a single person on this planet could get through twenty-four hours without some semblance of a lie. Life simply calls for it. Some lives scream for it. Lies are part of being civilized. Not lying is aggressive and cruel. I think lies and dreams and fantasies and aspirations are the best of each of us. I certainly would not want anyone to stick to the text when they think about me. I would hope that some of those sweet, cute little lies that I told had taken hold.

If I had any tendency to tell the truth, I would have had nothing but unending troubles. But since I don't and never will, I'm having a wonderful time.

As I've mentioned, when Walter and I were in City Hall filling out the forms for our marriage ceremony, I took a year and a half off my age. After I did that, I felt awful. Not because it was a lie, but because it was so small a lie. I remembered a friend of mine who had married a man for his money, a man who talked in his sleep and always said the same thing: "One percent."

"You can't stay married to a man who dreams about one percent," I told her. "When you dream it can be anything. Eight hundred percent or eight thousand. That's the whole point of dreaming. He can get one percent when he's awake."

So during the ceremony I kept thinking, One and a half years. That is the stupidest thing I ever did in my life. And predictably, the next day my sister managed to say something or other to Walter that gave me away.

Wars are started by the truth. Peace is proclaimed with lies.

Certainly anyone who has lived past World War II knows that. Only liars are good politicians and good leaders. Only liars can get it off the ground. But I am talking about a certain kind of lying. The lie is not always said outright, but it is always in the air.

I have always loved *Alice Adams,* both the novel by Booth Tarkington and the movie with Katharine Hepburn. Alice was not born into money, but she took on so many sweetly transparent little affectations of grace and breeding in order to give herself the air of someone who was. And then she fell in love and rather floridly invited her beau for dinner. Even though it was the very hottest night of the summer, Alice had made her mother and family so nervous about the dinner that they made a tremendous Thanksgiving meal. They all sweltered in that tiny little dining room so near to the kitchen where the oven had been on all day. Alice was, of course, mortified, destroyed, and did not know how to use her charms to cool off the room.

But I loved Alice Adams. I loved how she braved it out and I loved it that she wanted everything to be better than it was, especially herself.

That is one kind of lying. There are other kinds, of course. There are the routine lies.

"How are you?"

"Fine. How are you?"

"Fine."

That exchange is, of course, a total lie. I understand that a lie can occur with someone about to go to the electric chair. But really, what else could one say?

"I'm terrible. They're going to kill me."

One can't say that. Not only because there's not enough time to say it, but because in the face of real tragedy, there simply are no words.

Brave men lie, beautiful women lie. Bores tell the truth. They simply don't have the imagination to do otherwise. But one can tell wonderful lies about bores, so they do have some use. When men and women are having affairs, what woman could possibly say "I didn't come"? It is exactly like saying "You gave a rotten party." I cannot imagine anyone saying that. It is totally demoralizing for the man and it is coarse and common of the woman. But a sweet little lie in its stead would at least make it *civil lies—civilized*—possible for it to one day happen. It's just a matter of breathing slightly differently and saying "Oh, darling," and then "oh, oh, oh, *oh!*" It doesn't kill anyone to tell that sweet little lie.

One night, I was at a big New York party with Sydney Chaplin, Charlie's oldest son. We were both starving and made our way to the buffet table. We filled our faces until we were sick. Then Sydney said, "Did you have enough to eat?"

My mouth was so full that I had to nod yes.

"Me, too. How do we get out of here?"

"Oh, no, Sydney."

"C'mon, we've got to get out of here. It's a terrible party. If we don't do it now, we won't do it. We'll be here forever. Is there anyone in this room that you want to talk to?"

"No."

"Good. I just thought of something to say."

"Okay."

So we quietly got our coats and were now close to the door when our hostess, who had spent the whole evening telling everyone what a great lay she was, said, "You can't possibly be leaving. My God, you just can't."

"I'm so sorry," Sydney said. "But we must go right away."

"Has something happened?"

"No, but I've got to go home to feed the octopus."

Her mouth was open. She didn't understand what he had said or why he had said it. No matter—it worked.

I am just touching on small little lies. I know there are big lies to be told and I know I've told some of them. I'm really not saying these things about lying for liars, I'm saying them for those wonderful puritans, those strong and fine people who refuse to soften even a small moment in anybody's life with a tiny little white lie, an adorable, perfect little lie. A sweet lie. A good lie. A lie that is actually part of the deeper truth.

A Party for Oona and Charlie

The major social move we made after coming out here to the West Coast to live was to give a party for Charlie Chaplin and Oona. It was 1972 and Charlie was coming back to the United States to be honored, first in New York and then by the Motion Picture Academy with a special Oscar. Gloria was going to give them a party in New York, and we were giving them a party here. Charlie was no longer in the very best of health, so Oona suggested that I make it a luncheon. I asked her for a guest list, so with the exception of a few really close friends of ours, the selection was theirs.

When the invitations went out, absolutely everyone I'd ever heard of began to telephone us about the party and how they had to come because they were very dear friends of the Chaplins. A lot of this was nonsense because I knew all their friends. Still, I would relay the messages to Oona, and she would very rarely say "yes" to anyone who wasn't already on the list.

I found myself in a hysterical state, being totally unable to call people up and tell them they couldn't come to the party. Finally, I explained the situation to Walter and said that he had to help me. Walter did it so charmingly, so sweetly, that I think most of those people had more fun during that conversation with Walter than they could have had at the party.

So now the list was locked, and we had ninety-three people for lunch on the Sunday before the Academy Awards. We very rarely gave parties and when we did they were very small, because for some reason that I'll never understand, entertaining has always made me nervous. Even if someone planned a year in advance to come for a peanut butter sandwich, I would get completely hysterical with anxiety.

Now I had all of the Hollywood Charlie knew coming and all of the window dressing (new Hollywood) that Oona and the children wanted to see and just two or three of our friends. Naturally, I didn't do a seating plan for that many people, but I did arrange for Charlie's table because there were certain people he wanted to sit with.

And the party had to be collapsible. By that I mean that Charlie's moods were always changing, and every once in a while he'd remember how terrible Hollywood had been to him and he'd threaten not to come to California at all.

I didn't really feel sure he was coming until he boarded the plane (and even then, not absolutely sure). In the meantime, Porthault tablecloths, Baccarat crystal, the best possible wines, and the most beautiful flowers were arriving endlessly. Finally, the party began. Charlie kissed and hugged everybody, though actually he remembered no one except the one person he wanted to see more than anybody else. And that happened to be Martha Raye.

She arrived in a Rolls Royce with a chauffeur liveried in the same colors as the Rolls. As she came through the door, she immediately spotted Charlie, ran toward him, and jumped into his lap, where she stayed until she left the party. He was genuinely happy to be with someone he recognized and particularly Martha, whom he had adored since she'd played the woman he'd tried repeatedly to kill in *Monsieur Verdoux*.

The party went very well, with people who had not seen one another for such a long time getting together again. Charlie and Walter were walking around the garden, and Charlie looked out to a brilliantly bright blue sea with what seemed to be thousands of tiny sailboats floating gracefully.

Charlie gazed out at the sea for a long time and then said to Walter, "Now that really must have cost you a fortune."

Charlie was that way. He saw life in terms of movie sets or scenes or ideas for movies. He loved seeing Lewis Milestone and Groucho Marx and Danny Kaye and Oscar Levant and Frances Goldwyn. Charlie was very anxious to have the Goldwyns there, but he was disappointed that Sam was too ill to come, because when Charlie's troubles had happened, Sam had been the only one to speak up for him.

It was the last time Charlie was to be in California. A few days before the party, I had had lunch with Oona and Charlie at the Beverly Hills Hotel. Charlie had asked what I thought of his being here.

"I think they are too late with too little. And California is filled with crazies, so one has to be careful." But I added that I was thrilled that he was here, and so was everyone I knew.

He talked brilliantly and coherently at lunch. It was not the way he acted in front of a lot of people. "It's marvelous to be old," he said. "You can get by with so much. When I had dinner with the queen, I was seated next to Princess Margaret Rose, and she kept saying things like, 'When you did this it was so wonderful,' and 'What did you mean exactly when you did that?' Then she'd wait for a while and ask another question like 'What did you have in one film that was just like what you had in another film?' I simply became exhausted trying to answer her so I finally said, 'Dear Princess Margaret, you must forgive me, but you see, I have had a whole series of little strokes and I can't remember a single thing.' So you see, you can simply get out of everything if you're old enough."

After the Academy Awards, I saw him do almost exactly that. We went to the Governor's Ball together, and many, many people came to the table to greet him. Oona would more or less give him the name of the person or remind him of something about the person so Charlie would have something to say.

However, when one man came over to greet him, I saw Charlie's face sour. He refused to even look at the man, who kept trying to put his face in front of Charlie's. And Oona was trying to keep her head between them while she whispered to Charlie, "It's Jackie Coogan." She said it about three times, whereupon Charlie turned his back to both of them. Oona sort of smiled and said, "I'm so sorry," and the man went away.

Then Charlie turned back to Oona and said, "Will you stop

that?" She said she just wanted him to know it was Jackie Coogan, who'd costarred with Charlie in *The Tramp* fifty years before.

"I know it was Jackie Coogan. I knew it the minute I saw him," Charlie responded. "He wants residuals. And there you are making that big fuss."

. . . .

Among the Porcupines
. . . .

Once while at dinner at Barbara and Marvin Davis's house, I sat next to Merv Griffin. Not being seated at the same table with Walter, I was smoking. Walter hates for me to smoke. I had my own lighter, but as I took it out, Merv quickly said, "No, no, no. Let me light this for you." And he lit my cigarette with the most beautiful gold lighter I had ever seen. I don't know what made it so beautiful—it may have been the color of the gold, it may have been the shape of it, it may have been that it was so obviously tactile. It was a very perfect-looking object.

"Oh, how beautiful," I said. "That's the most beautiful lighter I have ever seen in my life."

"That's exactly what I said an hour ago to Frank," Merv said, referring to Sinatra, "when he lit my cigarette with it as I was fumbling for my own lighter. 'It's yours,' Frank said to me, and I said, 'I couldn't possibly take it, and he said, 'It's yours, kid. And that's that.' So I didn't know what to say. I told him I loved it and thanked him profusely and meant every word of it. And here it is."

"How wonderful," I said. "I think that was adorable of him. He must really like you a lot."

"Well, we've been friends for a long time, but this lighter is really something else again."

"I think it was a lovely thing to do. Especially because I love having my cigarette lit with it."

He smiled like someone who had eaten the whole box of candy. As the dinner wore on, he lit my cigarettes many times, and the lighter seemed more and more beautiful to me each time. It became like a magic object. I couldn't take my eyes off it. It was plain and perfect.

Toward the end of the dinner, I took a cigarette and waited for Merv to use the magic object. There was a pause as Merv began to look for it. He went through his pockets. He turned them inside out.

"My God, what's happened?" I asked. I got down and looked underneath the table to see if it had fallen, and so did he. And he suddenly looked at me.

"Don't look for it anymore," he said quietly.

"Why not? We have to find it."

"I know where it is."

"Where?"

"We can't talk about it now," he whispered. "I'll tell you later."

"I can't stand it. I have to know."

"Barbara has it in her purse," he whispered even more quietly, referring to Sinatra's wife, who was seated on his other side.

"Don't be silly. Why would she ever do a thing like that? For what reason?"

"I can't get into it now, but it is in her purse."

"Why? Didn't she want you to have it?"

"No, she didn't. She didn't know Frank had given it to me until we were at the table, and she was incensed. I could feel it."

"She hasn't said anything."

"What's the matter with you? Of course she hasn't said anything."

"Doesn't she like you?"

"Oh, yes, she likes me."

"She doesn't like you if she took the lighter."

"You don't understand about things like that."

"Oh, yes I do. She stole your lighter."

"She doesn't see it that way."

"How else can she see it?"

"She thinks it's hers."

"It is hers, isn't it?"

"Now, you just watch this."

And he began to rummage around the table again as though

looking for the lighter, and he turned to Barbara and said, "Barbara, have you seen my lighter?"

"You mean the gold one that Frank gave you tonight?"

"Yes, that's the one."

"Yes, I've seen it. It's in my purse where I always keep it," she said sweetly.

"Oh, well, Frank gave it to me as a gift."

She was silent for a moment and then she smiled and said, "Frank isn't right about everything."

. . . .

Parties

. . . .

There's always tension about going to a party to have a good time. I know that the dying process begins the minute we are born, but it accelerates during dinner parties.

It's a silent, secret, slow-motion summertime all the time.

Of course, there are always pleasant dinner parties. Funny things happen at them, like they would happen anywhere. I remember one night being at Jennifer Jones's and Norton Simon's when they were still living at the beach. They had twelve people for dinner and everyone seemed to be chatting amicably. I was sitting next to Cary Grant. And he said to me, "Do you see him?"—pointing in an inconspicuous way at a person directly across from him at the round table. He was pointing to Warren Beatty.

"I used to be him," he said to me.

Needless to say, I spent the rest of the dinner telling him he was much, much too magnificent to have ever been Warren because that is what that statement called for and I do know how to play tennis. That was the ball he wanted to bounce back and I continued to do it throughout dinner. (But Warren is a man of many aspirations, and I cannot help admiring him and his work.)

At another dinner party, I sat next to Gregory Peck. He told me that "as you get older you must make a concerted effort to expand your life. To do more, to go more, to have more, to want more, be more, see more, everything more. As a rule," he explained, "it all starts with the children moving away and you think you need a smaller house. That is a big mistake. The minute they leave, get a bigger house." And so on.

I thought he was right. The next day I began a shopping spree of more and more and more, and I think I've spent some of my happiest days just taking his advice.

Jack Lemmon will not sit next to me at dinner because I always eat up his entire dinner when he isn't looking or when someone is talking to him. He can't believe that I am still doing this. Even now, if he comes to a dinner party and finds my place card next to his, he immediately rearranges it.

The greatest effort is given to place cards. Place cards are the most difficult things to do. It's like writing biographies. And it's really a waste of time because most people walk around changing them anyway. Of course Walter, who doesn't understand the concept of seating man-woman-man-woman, says the best thing about these seating arrangements: "Are we eating or fucking?"

. . . .

Thirty Pounds

. . . .

On one of our trips to New York, Gloria and I had lunch, and she made a big fuss about how wonderful I looked because I had lost thirty pounds. I had lost it on purpose because I had been too fat, and now I was too thin. (You do know when people say "chic," they mean thin.)

Thinness is one of those things women think is wonderful but men don't. They like the girl they love to be juicy like a Renoir. They don't like to see or feel bones. The ideal is to be like a perfect piece of fruit that is about to burst. And then burst.

"You look so perfect," Gloria said. "You must not lose one more pound, because this is your perfect weight, and you know

when I paint you, I use circles. So you must not lose your round-
ness. This is just perfect. What does Walter say about the weight?
Isn't he ecstatic?"

"I haven't told him yet."

. . . .

Gossip

. . . .

Maureen telephoned one night, saying, "Any gossip?"

"You know, Maureen," I said, "I really do have some gossip
tonight."

"What? What have you got?"

I told her what someone had just told me. In fact, Milton Berle
told it to me himself.

"Maureen, do you know that Pola Negri left Milton Berle for
Hitler?"

There was a long silence. And then, in a completely changed
voice, she said, "I am never going to have another drink as long
as I live."

. . . .

Mikey and Nicky

. . . .

Elaine May and her husband, Dr. David Rubenfine, first came to
California in 1969 to visit Walter for a weekend. None of us had
ever met, but Elaine had an idea for a movie she wanted to do with
Walter. They had some telephone conversations about it and it was
decided that they would come and spend some time with Walter
and see if they could get a producer and work something out.
Everyone knew that Walter was very bankable and that Elaine was
brilliant so it wouldn't be too difficult to do.

I answered the door and looked at Elaine, and before I could look at David, she said, "My God, I have a part in a script that I'm working on that you would be perfect for."

It was the best hello I ever had.

"Come right in," I said.

Walter came rushing down the stairs, and we all began to talk, so it wasn't until four or five in the morning that we finally took their suitcases into the guest house.

David had an incredible mind and Elaine appreciated it. And he was so in love with her that it was really something to see.

The weekend was spent putting together *A New Leaf*. Walter was to play a very rich man who is losing all his money and has to think about marrying a very rich but clumsy girl. Elaine was to play the girl and direct from her own script. Paramount was called, all the necessary arrangements made, and by Monday afternoon the deal was on.

Elaine and David were leaving late that afternoon to go back to New York and they did one of the best things I ever saw. About a half hour before the car was scheduled to pick them up and take them to the airport, they telephoned their mothers, who lived in Los Angeles.

"Mom," they each said. "We're here, but just for an hour. Actually a half hour. But if you can make it quickly, could you meet us just so we can kiss and say hello?"

Both mothers said they would come as quickly as possible. Elaine and David were standing in front of the house, having their bags put in the car as the mothers arrived in separate taxis at the same time (all of which had been brilliantly figured out by David). Whereupon, Elaine and David both screamed with pleasure and love and happiness and hugs and kisses and "I love you's."

"Isn't this terrible?" Elaine kept repeating. "This is so frustrating. You'll never know how awful this is for us to have been here for only an hour and a half on business. Oh, you look so beautiful. You can't imagine what it's like to see you. We love you. We just love you so much. Oh, God, we miss you. Oh, God."

"I don't know how to say this," David interrupted, "but we've got to get in the car, Elaine. We're late. This could cost us a lot of money on the deal."

The mothers, upon hearing about the possible loss of money, shoved them both into the car and slammed the door.

The mothers turned to each other and exchanged one or two cool hello-hellos.

Then Walter realized that their taxis were not there anymore so he came out and introduced himself and drove them each home.

I thought I had never seen anything done in greater style. Elaine and David were superb. They called us from New York, and before they could say anything, I said, "You are the two most brilliant people I have ever met in my life. And you left your mothers happy, which is the incredible thing."

The next time I saw Elaine, she gave me the same greeting as the first time.

"You are going to be so wonderful in this part I have for you. I can't believe it."

Elaine and Walter had a lot of fun and a lot of fights and made *A New Leaf.* Quite a few years went by. Then, one day in 1975, after all those years, Elaine telephoned from Philadelphia.

"I want you to be here by Monday to start shooting," she said. "We're in the middle of the picture."

"What are you talking about?"

"You know, *Mikey and Nicky,* the picture I've been telling you about. I sent you a script, didn't I?"

She had left a script at the house which was actually quite wonderful in a way. It was a family story about two gangsters who are old friends but have to kill each other. It was written in such a lean way, and the part for me, as Nell, a gangster's moll, was very good. But I said, "Wait a minute, Elaine. I didn't even know you'd started this and—"

"You knew you were going to do the part."

"Yes, but I really didn't talk it over with Walter."

"Fuck Walter. I want you to do the part. If Walter wants to do a part in it, he can. But I'm having another script sent to you immediately. Put Walter on."

Walter took the telephone and proceeded to say "yes" to everything Elaine was saying and then hung up. He looked at me.

"If you go do this part, that's it for us."

"How can you possibly say that? Then why did you keep telling her 'yes'?"

"I don't want to get involved with this. You've got to call her yourself and tell her you can't do the part. That's not for me to do."

I called her back.

"Elaine, Walter doesn't want me to come to Philadelphia to do the part. Please try to get somebody else."

"I can't get anybody else. Nobody can do the part the way you can. You are the only person who is right for it. You know exactly what to do. Nobody else will."

"Elaine, try to get somebody else, because he says no and you know I don't like to upset him."

"Put him on again."

And he got on. And said "yes" over and over again. "She can do whatever she wants," he said.

"Put her on," Elaine said. I took the telephone from Walter. "You just heard him yourself. You can do anything you want."

"Yes, I heard him, but there's an old saying in Armenian, 'When I say "la," you know I mean "lalablue." ' "

"Carol, stop being so crazy. You've gone insane. Just get to Philadelphia and come on and do the part right away."

"Please try to get somebody else right away. Please."

"Walter will be fine. You'll be here doing the part."

"Elaine, you don't want to break up my marriage."

"Are you going to tell me that this would break up your marriage? That's insane."

"Well, Walter is insane. He's standing right here and he's ready to kill me."

"Carol, I—"

"Okay, okay. I'll be there on Monday." I hung up the phone and turned to Walter. "Why are you doing this? Why didn't you say the same thing to Elaine that you said to me so she didn't think I was lying?"

"This life isn't enough for you? You want to be an actress, too?"

"No, but she has this idea in her head about me doing this part. It's just one of those things."

"Let me see that script."

He read it.

"It's a very good script," he said, "but why does she see you as a gun moll? What makes her think you're so right for that?"

"It isn't at all a gun moll. It's a wonderful part, and Elaine explained that since I'm the opposite of a gun moll, it will make the part special."

"She thinks you're a gun moll. So if you want to ruin your life and go to Philadelphia to be a gun moll, then I don't know what to say about that."

"It is so stupid for you to say that. I'm not going to be a gun moll, I'm going to do a part."

"But you are not an actress."

"How do *you* know?" In fact, Walter thinks I'm the best actress he's ever seen. But he will say anything, depending on the circumstances.

I decided to take the part, but I was very surprised when I got to Philadelphia and saw how things were going. Elaine had been doing a sequence in a graveyard with the two leads, John Cassavetes and Peter Falk. And they didn't seem to be able to get out of the graveyard.

Meanwhile, Walter was going mad.

"Well, are you finished? You've only got a small part. How long is it going to take you?"

"They haven't gotten to me yet."

"What the hell are you doing there?"

"You heard her. She told me to be here."

"Yeah, but did you hear me? I told you not to go."

Then, finally, after two weeks, Elaine was ready to do the scenes I was in.

John Cassavetes was very driven and very talented, but he always wanted to improvise and use his own words rather than the writer's. With Elaine, even though she was the writer, he was very free to do that. Peter Falk and he wanted to make the script their own, as they had done in most of the other pictures they made together. On the other hand, the author does stand for something. In my opinion—everything. But they reverted back to their "Hey you, cat man" stuff which was obviously not an improvement over the perfect script Elaine had written for them to work with—a script in which each line advanced a point that had to be made or fleshed out a character. All in a style that was as good as Hemingway's.

In any case, when they asked me if I knew my lines and I said of course, I immediately fell into disfavor with both of them. "That's terrible," they said.

"No," I said. "It's not. You still think only Ethel Merman knows her lines." I tried to explain that I had not been in the movies and was very rarely an actress and knowing the lines was at least some base from which I could try to get a performance.

"No, that is not the base," John said. "You are the base."

"Well, whether you are right or wrong, I still know the lines."

After a while, he didn't seem to care because knowing my lines was not doing me any good. You see, he made up all his lines, so when I had to respond to him, I couldn't use the lines Elaine had written. I had to respond to what he had said. It was hell.

In one scene, John had to slap me in the face in a way that would look as though he had done it very hard. Well, it not only looked as if he was doing it hard, he actually did it so hard that I instantly burst into tears from shock and hurt and confusion. I couldn't continue the scene. Elaine continued to shoot.

"Cut. Do it again," Elaine said.

I admire Elaine May's acting and writing talent, but I'm not sure that she has the temperament to direct. She goes into a nightmare when she directs. She has the intelligence, but something emotional happens and she leaves the real world. She can't say, "That's it. We're finished." She thinks something extraordinary will happen if you wait long enough. I understand that feeling. A lot of people write that way. And she's so happy when she directs that she doesn't care about time. She has directed some things, like *A New Leaf* and *The Heartbreak Kid,* brilliantly. And there is not a better movie writer. I wonder why she can't find peace in being the best actress and the best writer.

Both John and Peter were in great awe of her. I've always felt that actors who are in awe of their directors or writers give performances that are somewhat less than they could be. I have spotted awe in a number of supposedly very good performances.

Understanding the part is always necessary. Awe is never necessary.

I think acting should be illuminating and I think it should have a sense of beauty. I'll see anything of Tennessee Williams's because even in his worst plays there's that aspiration toward beauty. One might say that Lee J. Cobb was too big—physically—to have played in *Death of a Salesman,* but his performance on stage was riveting and one that could reach into your whole inner life. I think if it had been played by the little man it had been written about, it would not have been that memorable first *Death of a Salesman* that we saw. To play the person you are is the most difficult of all; to illuminate the person you are playing is more possible.

So there I was in front of the camera, simply sitting down helplessly, wretchedly, desolately, not knowing what had happened or why it had happened. I had to say to myself, "Well, I'm not going to say anything. This is probably a mistake. He would not do it again. He has the most beautiful wife and she loves him. I'm not going to say anything. I'm sure it was an accident."

The cameras began to roll. They had put a lot of makeup on one side of my face to cover the bright red from the slap, and it looked fine, I guess. So as the scene started, I tried to summon up all the energy I had had before, which was almost, but not quite, possible.

He then slapped me again.

I again burst into tears, and Elaine again kept rolling. I again sat down in shock. John stood there laughing as he watched me, because he thought that's exactly what his character would have done. (Of course, he laughed that way in a lot of his movies. I guess he thought it was more sinister, and it was—at least, it was the first time he did it.)

"Cut," Elaine finally called.

As I walked back to my dressing room, John was behind me on his way to his. I turned around very quickly and was directly in front of him.

"John, don't hit me that hard ever again. Do you understand? Don't do that. Ever."

"Do what?"

"Don't slap my face like that again. Do you understand?"

"Yeah, yeah, yeah. I understand."

About five minutes later, we were back doing the scene again. And of course, he slapped my face like that again. But this time I did not fall to the ground. I grabbed his arms.

"John, I'm through being a nice guy. If you ever do anything even remotely like that again, I'm going to twirl you around in the air and throw you out the window. And you better trust that I can do that, because between my adrenaline and martial-arts training, I could kill you. And I'm old enough not to care."

He didn't ever do anything like that again. In fact, I felt we became friends. I don't want to say he was a bully, but I think when he realized he was trifling with the troops, he decided to stop. I once asked him about it.

"Well, a lot of actresses I've worked with seem to want that. It makes it easier for them to do the rest of their scene."

"Maybe that's true, but it's not true for me and it will never be true for me. It paralyzes any possible performance I might have."

"I understand. I'm really sorry. I didn't mean to upset you. You know that. The problems I'm having are with Elaine."

"Then keep them with her, because I admire you and I want to continue to admire you."

Part of John's problem was that he always wanted to know about the scenes that followed the scenes he was in. He had to have some idea about what happened afterward, because everything was connected for him. And he didn't like to wait for Elaine to give him that time to sit and talk it through. But he never took it out on me after that, and that change made acting with him quite an experience.

For instance, during a scene when we would go under the coffee table and supposedly have an affair, John always had a new poem to recite. He recited Yeats, Shelley, and Keats. And would always ask me when we broke whether I had ever heard them before. He knew a lot about a lot of things. It made me very sad when he died, because he loved his wife, he loved his life, and he loved what he was doing. I respected him. He did not have millions of dollars and he used his own money to try to do something. Success or failure is beside the point. It is the aspiration that counts, and his glistened like no other.

When my part in the film was done, I was leaving Philadelphia, and I went to say good-bye to John.

"You are such a wonderful actress," he said. "I hope we get a chance to act together again someday."

"John, you have just seen my entire career."

Whereupon he got mad as hell.

"If you were my wife, I would punch you right in the nose. Do you know how awful it is when you have a talent like that to say a thing like that? I could punch you—"

"Thank you," I said quickly, cutting him off and running away. I was flattered, of course, but terrified of what might come from him next.

It took a very long time to edit *Mikey and Nicky* because there were all sorts of complications. Because of all the improvising, it was very difficult to cut together, and the studio people were tearing their hair out. And when it was ready to be released in 1976, they gave it very short shrift—it may as well have opened in one drive-in in Iowa. Actually, it did play for one afternoon in Westwood, Los Angeles.

But there were showings for critics, and I got the most remarkable reviews I've ever read, starting with Vincent Canby's in *The New York Times,* to Judith Crist's in the *Saturday Review,* to Sheila Benson's in *The Village Voice,* right up to Charles Champlin's in the *Los Angeles Times,* which said that if the picture hadn't been such a bust, I surely would have been up for an Academy Award nomination.

So it was an ideal situation. No one saw the picture and I sent everyone I knew my magnificent reviews. "Jesus Christ," said Peter Falk, who'd been a friend since we took acting classes together with Sandy Meisner in New York, "you stole the whole fucking picture." It was absurd.

Every once in a while, there was talk of its going to Cannes and I'd cringe a little bit, but by now I think the movie is quietly dead.

I got some offers to do other pictures, but I knew better than to take any. Walter and I saw the picture together. He said I was brilliant in it. He knew I'd die if he said anything else.

"Elaine really does know what she's doing," he said.

I was so afraid to go and do *Mikey and Nicky* because Walter so disapproved, and yet when it was all over and he saw it, he seemed to be closer to me than ever. So I guess what counts is not what you do, but how you do it. He seemed proud of me, so it was okay. Of course, that is what's known as living dangerously, because I could just as easily have been awful in it. And then what?

Dachau Is Across the Street

When Walter and I went to Munich in 1979 for the filming of *Hopscotch,* Oona joined us. Walter was shooting most of the time, so Oona and I made big plans to do nothing and a few other plans. We decided to go to Dachau, which was close by, because (as Oona said) what else can you do, except just try to pay your respects in some way. We both agreed that it was a good idea to go without Walter because it would surely have a terrible effect on him.

Just as we were leaving, Walter came in and said he was through for the day. He asked us where we were going.

"Oh, well," I said, "we've hired a car to pick us up and take us to Dachau. I know that isn't really something you could stand doing."

"No," he said, "I want to go with you. I think I should go with you."

We both assured him he certainly didn't have to think about it.

"Darling," I said, "please don't go. It will depress you so terribly. And you are working so hard. Maybe you should just rest. We'll be back fairly soon."

He then started to have a terrible fight with me, saying that I just didn't want him to go with us, which of course was ridiculous.

"Don't be stupid," I said. "I always love to be with you. I just thought I was saving you from something."

"Don't save me so much. I know where I want to go, and it's Dachau."

So the three of us went.

The driver said he had no idea where it was we wanted to go. He said most of this in such a thick German accent that we realized we were with the one person who had probably spent many a happy hour there. He was grumbling while we left Munich when suddenly I saw the smokestacks. I pointed them out to him.

"See smokestacks?"

"Ya, ya, ya."

It was a short ride with a little house here and a little village there. It was gingerbready and cute as hell.

I pointed out to the driver many signs that showed the way to Dachau. After all, the German government had made a quasimuseum out of it—one had to pay to get into it, so it does seem you paid for Dachau, no matter what you went for.

We arrived, whereupon a guard with a gun in his boot screamed out to Walter, "Pay money" and the amount of money which Walter had already paid. Walter told him he had already paid. Walter wanted to kill him, and there's no question he could have—easily.

We then went through the organized tour until we broke away from it to continue by ourselves. I suddenly realized we were walking on top of unmarked graves. They had laid the pathways so peculiarly that it was almost hard not to. It was a very German configuration.

We went through the barracks, we went through it all. It was fiendishly clean. It made me think a lot about clean. What is clean? The floors, the walls, the loos at Dachau were scrubbed and polished. The loos were in the center of the dormitories, which were the beginning of something less than civilized, the beginning of constant humiliation.

We then got to the crematorium. That is where the ghost remains. It is in the form of a stench that is death itself. In fact, in order to see the crematorium, we had to keep perfumed handkerchiefs over our noses. All the scouring and scrubbing and cleaning has not removed that lethal, unbearable stench. The crematorium has in it two places to hang people, conveniently located near the ovens where the bodies were thrown. Also, there is a small wall built for people to stand against so as to be executed and then thrown into the ovens.

While we were in this actually very small room, a small, dark, hunchbacked man, looking something like a Jules Streicher version of a Jew, approached Walter.

"May I have your autograph?" he asked politely.

It was shocking.

Walter shook his head.

As we came out of the crematorium, I saw that the only way out of Dachau was through the ovens we had just seen. That was the only way anyone could have escaped.

It was the flattest piece of land I have ever seen. There was not one tree. It was so flat that there was no way anyone could take a single step without being seen.

The crematorium is the last building you walk through, and as we walked away, the drizzle of the day, the tourists, the unmarked graves, the flatness persisting—all served to make one feel how barbaric this century had been. This century that had accelerated technology to a point almost beyond reason, and yet all its science and all its knowledge did not stop this country from being the most barbaric and backward country I know of. To make it even more diabolical, it was so breathtakingly well-organized.

We walked out the gates. I became aware for the second time of the most important thing about Dachau that there is to know. It is that, quite simply, Dachau is across the street. A regular street with stores and apartments above them that had obviously been there for decades, before Dachau was constructed. And there were souvenirs to be bought. And all those people who lived across the street—who "didn't know anything"—surely saw almost everything through a chain-link fence that covered all four sides of Dachau. That was the shocker. One always imagined it to have been somewhere up in the mountains or in the woods or at least out of the city. I had imagined that they had taken existing railroad tracks and added new ones and put this cauldron of hell in the most hidden place.

The Nazis may not have regarded this as necessary, since they never regarded Dachau as a death camp, although there were few that survived it. There was a hangman's noose, maybe two or three. There was a place to execute people, and it was in constant use. Why was Dachau not regarded as a death camp? Is death numbers? Didn't enough die to qualify? Is that what it is? I don't understand that kind of thinking. People were imprisoned and were starved there and killed there, but the book of records does not consider it a death camp. Auschwitz is considered a death camp because thousands of people a day were killed there.

Death. It's all death in Germany, rich Germany.

Frederick Vreeland, a career diplomat who is a very dear friend of mine, was stationed in Bonn for a while. I once asked him what that was like. And he thought about it carefully before answering.

"This is what it was like," he said. "One day I had to entertain a very high-born Prussian lady. I can't remember whether she was a countess or not. In any case, the ambassador could not keep his appointment with her so I was asked to keep it. We exchanged the niceties. I, of course, told her what a beautiful country it was.

" 'Yes, Mr. Vreeland,' she said, 'this was once the most beautiful country in the world. But it can never be that again because of what happened.'

"She went on to say, 'Don't you find it incredible when you hear so many people saying they didn't know, they simply didn't know. They had no idea. It was not possible to have any idea about it. They didn't know. And that goes on and on as the theme in Germany today. Mr. Vreeland, you look like an intelligent young man. Surely you cannot believe that all of these people did not know. I would like you to know that absolutely every single solitary person in Germany knew. Except for me.'

"And that," Frecky said to me, "is what it was like."

He, being a diplomat, had said the proper diplomatic thing to the woman at the time. I can't imagine what it was. Why do they attach their honor to that ignorance? It's a strange kind of thinking. Interestingly, the final crime is that my feelings toward them is as ugly as their thinking. It's hard to hate a person, but a whole people—it's an inhuman thought. And yet I am as guilty of that in relation to the Germans as they were in relation to the Jews, the Slavic peoples, the political dissenters, the aristocrats, the gypsies, the intellectuals, and I could go on and on.

I think there is a division between people who know something about the Holocaust and those who do not. The various school-books that I have read make far less of it than it was, and that is a terrible mistake. I think all the archives should be open, everyone should know the whole truth, because the ease with which it could happen again is the most frightening thing I know.

I'm not referring specifically to anti-Semitism. Anti-Semitism is, always has been, and I believe always will be a fact of life. It must be very hard for some people that such major influential figures in Western society as Jesus, Freud, Marx, and Einstein were Jews. It is so much easier for people to rally together in hatred than to rally together in love, understanding, and tolerance.

But I can't help imagining a lot about what new and great minds were killed in the Holocaust, about what we might know today had it never happened, and how far we might have come. The ultimate mind to me was Thomas Jefferson's, and in all the years since his time there hasn't been another like it. But how do we know there hasn't? We don't know. We don't even know the true numbers of the dead. We won't ever know that. It is almost impossible to believe that a people decided—and were allowed, even encouraged—to say who would live and who would die. That's where I feel my rage.

We sat silently in the car as we were driven back to the hotel in Munich. Then Walter and I continued the fight that had begun earlier that day.

"Please don't fight," Oona said. "Look what we saw this after-noon. How can you fight like that?"

"Exactly," Walter nodded excitedly. "On top of everything else, you spoiled my time at Dachau!"

Oona O'Neill

Oona O'Neill was born with a broken heart. But when she met Charlie Chaplin, her life really began. He was everything she never had and didn't dare hope for. He was charming, brilliant, loving, and funny, and sweet to be with. He was even fun to gossip with, for Charlie had what only whole men have—certain feminine qualities. He loved to decorate their houses; due to his painstaking care and interest, the one in Switzerland was a perfect replica of their Beverly Hills house. He loved women, but more than life he loved Oona. I can't think of any other man who married the girl of his dreams.

They had both known lovelessness—aloneness, deep despair, and desolation—in their youngest years. There is a bond between people who have known such fear and need in their earliest life. It is immediately recognizable in the other.

They both knew that they both knew.

Their jokes were about how rich they were and all they had, how they were in the company of kings and queens, and other fairy tales. Their main thrust in life was toward those fairy tales. They were never thought of as lies, they were aspirations and they made them come true by the force of their natures.

Charlie was in the midst of troubled times when he met Oona. A woman named Joan Barry had filed a very noisy paternity suit against him. But the way in which Oona and Charlie fell in love outweighed what was happening in his life. He fell in love in a way that he had never fallen in love before. I know that Oona did. Charlie was a man who had known many women, even loved some of them. Oona had never fallen in love before. She had had little-girl crushes as we all do when we're little girls, but that's it. All the love that she had been unable to give Eugene O'Neill—or anyone else for that matter—found a place to live and grow in Charlie.

Charlie's love was incredulous. He fell in love with Oona as a young boy would fall in love for the first time. That had never happened to him before.

They clung to each other through all that went against them in the outside world. It did not put a strain on their love because they had fallen so deeply in love they had already exiled themselves in an odd way.

She made him laugh and she moved him very deeply. She was the two girls that he always sought—the waif and the princess. And her light sweetness and bawdy sense of fun absolutely charmed Charlie to the moon.

Oona felt something she had always wanted to feel but had never felt before now—safe. Not only was he older and a great man, he protected her and she knew he would for the rest of their lives. She felt loved and cared for and pampered and nurtured and cherished. She grew in all the ways in which he made room for her to grow. She woke up every morning to spend the whole day and night with him. He did the same, with the exception of his work. He wanted to be with her all the time. She went to the set with him every day because he could not bear to be without her.

But that safety exacted a price. I guess we pay for every moment of happiness we ever have. Maybe the price for Oona was to allow parts of herself to go dormant. With her mind, she could have done anything, but part of her always had to be a little girl. Charlie's little girl. He always had to be The One. He had had that from the public for a long time, but then the public turned on him. He still had to get that, all of it, but from one person, Oona. He was not easy to live with; she didn't expect him to be.

Take clothes. Charlie wanted Oona to have the most beautiful clothes in the world. There was nothing she couldn't have. So when they were in Paris, she would go to Balenciaga and all the couturiers. Then would come the time for the fittings, which took place in Switzerland in a little town near Vevey. And Charlie would wait in the car for her while she had the fittings. And that would make Oona very nervous. She would say, "Oh, God, hurry!" And she wouldn't look at any other things, because he was waiting in the car.

They had many children, and Charlie was a stern Victorian parent, not unlike Elizabeth Barrett Browning's father. When they were little, he was the most loving parent in the world. He was full of kisses and hugs. He adored his children—until they began to have minds of their own. He would not take anything short of worship.

Oona's daughter Victoria, for instance, is one of the most romantic beings I have ever met. She actually is as romantic as she looks. When she was very young, I think fifteen or sixteen, she began to exchange letters with a man, Jean-Baptiste Thierrée. He was traveling with a circus he had created, Le Cirque Extraordinaire. I heard it was one of the more charming ideas in the world. Vicki was very taken by the whole idea of him. As they corresponded, they fell in love. And one day, he wrote her a letter to say his train would be stopping for ten minutes in Vevey and it would be so wonderful if they could meet, even if it was just for a minute or two. Vicki was dancing in the clouds and of course told no one. It was her secret, because she knew how much Charlie would disapprove of the correspondence and certainly of the meeting.

She put on her best dress and waited in the train station. He arrived and they met. I know they recognized each other instantly—I guess they might have seen each other's photographs in the newspapers. He spoke no English, but she did speak French. I don't know what was said, but she got on the train with him and left Vevey forever.

Oona felt destroyed. She truly didn't know what to do and didn't know what to tell Charlie. Charlie knew absolutely nothing about anything that had happened and thought that Vicki had run away for no reason.

After a while, they heard from Vicki and Jean-Baptiste, who told them of their love. Vicki told Oona and Charlie how much she loved them, and that perhaps the reason she was capable of being so deeply in love was because she had been surrounded all her life by their love. Charlie's rage mushroomed up like poison gas, and it took a long while for him to calm down. He vowed never to see his daughter again, but that changed as the years went on.

Oona once told me a story about being in London with Charlie. They were walking into the Savoy to meet their son Michael and his wife and their new baby. The wife was nursing the baby in the lobby and apparently Charlie had an absolute fit. "I cannot stand it, I cannot stand it," he kept repeating. "She puts me off my food." He carried on this way for hours. Of course, times had changed but Charlie couldn't accept it.

He had a strange relationship with his children. Oona was the buffer, because she understood them better. But she wasn't always successful. Even in that fairy-tale world, there was a shadow of a porcupine.

"I love my children," Charlie once said, "but I worship my wife." And so he did.

Oona always more or less expected that Charlie would die first, because of the enormous difference in age. In a funny way, that made their life together deeply romantic, because she knew he wouldn't always be there and she cherished every moment they had together. They adored each other's company. They didn't need anyone else.

Even after the children came, it was Charlie first for Oona, always. I think that her children, being adult now, can understand more about why they didn't have the priority and he did, which is something they may have resented when they were younger. I don't think Oona had any regrets. I hope not.

I think the notion that children are your life is the biggest myth in the world. They're not.

Love is your life.

I remember the Christmas Day that Charlie died. Oona always referred to his death as "the long good-bye." He had been sick for so very long. She would not leave him for more than a few minutes, and only then because it was necessary to arrange something for him. They had round-the-clock nurses, a house filled with people to care for Charlie, but she wouldn't let anyone else touch him. She was there. "He took care of me," she said to me, "and I am going to take care of him."

When Charlie died she went into deep mourning. I remembered the days when Oona and I read Willa Cather's *Lucy Gayheart* together. One Christmas she gave me every book Willa Cather had written—beautiful first editions. It was a remarkable present, and those books went everywhere I went. When I heard that Charlie was dead, I tore out that part in *Lucy Gayheart* we'd read together so many times and put it in an envelope and mailed it to her right away. It was about a young widow who came back to live in her hometown after her husband died. She had loved and mourned him deeply. After a lot of time had gone by, she began to take walks on Main Street in the afternoon. And soon after, she was buying and wearing pretty clothes on those walks. She soon began to wonder about her old hometown sweetheart. She'd spend a lot of time preening and dressing for the walk and fantasizing about running into him. The whole idea was very exciting, and one day she did run into him. And it was, as most of these meetings are in literature and life, sad. She found him so ordinary she didn't care what he might think of her.

That night, looking out the window in her room, she saw snow falling—white and lacy, with blue lights. Magical. She opened the window and watched it for a long time. Then she put one hand out, almost to her elbow, and then the other. And then she put her face out and let the snow fall on it, and it made her face feel wonderful. She looked up above the trees to the sky, which was filled with beautiful white snow, swirling, gently falling on leaves, trees, ground, rooftops. And she loved watching it. And suddenly she knew something. That old sweetheart is life itself.

But for Oona, life itself was Charlie.

After Charlie died and his coffin was stolen but returned when Oona refused to pay any ransom, I asked Oona to come and be with me at our beach house in Trancas. Trancas is north of Malibu and probably the most beautiful beach in these parts. I thought she really should get away from Vevey and that maybe such a complete change would help a little bit. She and Charlie had the greatest romance of all time, and they lived happily ever—but then he died. And then came after.

I arranged for us to be there alone so that she could be completely herself and not feel that she had to be any particular way. Few people knew how brilliant and how very funny Oona was.

When Walter and I went to the airport to pick her up, she could have been the very same girl I walked home from school with many years ago, with her raincoat and her long black hair. As we embraced, I think that I completed the sentence I was saying when I last said good-bye to her years before. It was always that way with us.

We went to the house. I had all her favorite things there, and we spent the days listening to music, reading, talking, not talking, laughing, cooking, walking on the beach, catching up on everyone we ever knew. Until one night when I said, "Oona, you haven't cried. We're alone here. You're free here. You don't have to be any special way here except how you feel."

"I know," she said. "You see, Charlie's brother died several years ago and Charlie and I visited his wife and we both adored her, but from the moment we arrived until two or three days later when we left, she never once stopped crying and carrying on beyond anything Charlie or I had ever seen. We both felt helpless. There are no words for that, and we understood it, because they were very, very close and happy together and had had a long and marvelous marriage. But as easy as it was to understand, it was hard to endure the way she ranted and raved on steadily. When we were finally on our way home, we decided that we would never ever again try to be of comfort to someone in that state, because you can't be. I made up my mind long ago that that would not be the form my grief would take if Charlie died before I did, which I always imagined he would."

"Shut up and cry," I said.

We both laughed, and I think she was relieved at last just to explain how she felt. Several days later I watched her from the big window as she walked toward the beach with her back to the house. And with the sun slanting in as it did and the glare of the water and the shadows, it looked almost as if she was only one-half a person, and that was the truth of it.

I told her my own problems. I told her that Walter said that I would never allow a single soul in the world to treat me the way Gloria does (he's crazy—she's adorable) and that I was still this little waif holding a tin cup and my eyes were rolling with pleasure at the thought of knowing Gloria Vanderbilt. Can you imagine him thinking a thing like that, after all the years—all the times Gloria and I had together, all our secrets and all our devotion—and no one is as devoted as she is. Can you imagine telling me that I was only interested in her because she's Gloria Vanderbilt?

Oona looked at me straight in the eye and said, "It's the only reason I'm interested in her." I fell off the chair.

She saw a few very old friends. And we began to have some people for dinner. Dinah Shore lives several houses away, and being neighborly, she invited us for dinner one night, with Walter. (After a certain amount of time, Walter began to visit the beach house because I told him that Oona was doing all right and that we both missed him, which we did.) Dinah has written a lot of cookbooks, as you may or may not know, and she makes sugary southern food and, like all cooks of great reputation, is a lousy cook. But we still thought it was sweet of her to bother with us.

So we went and realized she was not bothering with us at all. She had taken a shine to Walter and doted on all of Walter's inhaling and exhaling. With each word, she was trembling with reaction and smiling and beaming right into his face.

Finally, Oona and I went into a separate room.

"What are they doing in there?" I asked Oona. Walter and Dinah had gone into her very special and very dark television room to look at something, but more than we could hear the television, we could hear this riotous and hilarious laughter from Dinah at whatever Walter was mumbling.

So Oona and I crept to the doorway of the television room and watched as Dinah blew moonbeams of laughter into Walter's face. Walter was delighted to find that he was *that* interesting and *that* funny and had a somewhat perplexed but completely happy look on his face. Oona and I watched them, unobserved, for some time.

All we could hear was her laughter every four or five words of Walter's, and we finally got bored and went back into the living room and sat down and began to laugh.

"Why," Oona asked, "did you tell me all that junk?"

"What junk?"

"That junk about Dinah insisting that I come here for dinner because she so wanted to see me."

"That's the junk she told me."

Oona giggled. We began to snoop around the house and then went back and heard the same sounds coming from the television room.

Oona made an interesting observation.

"Do you realize that someone could come here and slit our throats from ear to ear and we could fall off the sofas, the blood would be everywhere, the killers would have left, and we would have bled to death, and as she came back into the living room, she would continue as she is this very minute? It would simply not matter to her."

"You're right," I said. "But you know they say that concentration is a wonderful thing."

Anyway, we found our way home along the beach, and Walter soon followed. He could not understand what we were talking about.

"I don't know why you two are acting this way. Lots of people like my jokes."

"What Dinah likes about you, Walter, is no joke," I said. And it wasn't.

So the days passed and I felt that Oona was all right, having a freer time, a better time. We had a lot of invitations, only a few of which Oona felt up to accepting.

Merle Oberon had invited us to have lunch at her beach house. She was a very narcissistic movie star who had married some very rich men (producer Alexander Korda, for one) and a few not so rich ones. And of course there was Bruno Puglia, who was the richest of all. She had made a few successful movies and was now longing for those golden times.

The lunch was stultifying and boring and sad. She had known Charlie and Oona and was doing "the right thing," but she had nothing to say to Oona, nor did Oona to her. All she could do was sit there and be Merle Oberon. She was married to a very young man who seemed to take care of her. He was quite charming in this way, which put him in a somewhat less embarrassing light. He seemed to really care about her, and *she* cared deeply about her.

As I looked at her, I tried to figure out what was under her skin. Silicone? What was it? She was very strange-looking. I could not connect this woman who looked somewhat mummified and pickled in brine with the beautiful, young, wild Cathy of *Wuthering Heights*. I realized that between her narcissism and Oona's shyness, unless I said something pretty soon, this luncheon was going to go to pot.

So I started to tap-dance the way I do in these situations, and Merle cheered up a bit and showed us some of her jewels. Pretty soon, we had stayed a polite-enough length of time to leave.

"You know," Oona said when we got home, "she was always a fucking bore."

"Well, when that kind of woman gets to that kind of age, there is a kind of tragedy that occurs. Everything they have is based on being young and beautiful and neither has great staying power. The loss of either is taken hard by these women who have nothing else."

"Charlie only liked her when she was married to very rich men," Oona reflected.

Of course, that was true. That was the wonder of Charlie. Although he became Charlie Chaplin, he never stopped being a poor little English boy. He was so much more interesting than all the people he ever met or wanted to meet, but I guess part of what was so moving about him was that he didn't know it.

Oona stayed for about a month. Before it was over, Jennifer Jones (Mrs. Norton Simon) telephoned and invited us to lunch. She is certainly one of the most beautiful women ever, and one of the best in every way. After making her invitation and settling the details, she said she wanted to speak to me privately before we came.

When I telephoned her, she asked what Oona would like. "What kind of day would she like? What is the best kind of thing we could have and do?"

And I truthfully told her that just being with her was what Oona would like, because Oona knew her from when she and Charlie had lived in Hollywood and had always loved her.

"How is she doing?"

"Fair."

"What do you think of this—I would like to describe the year I had after David died," she said, referring, of course, to her late husband, David O. Selznick. "It was the worst year of my life, and I almost didn't live through it."

"I think that would be great for Oona. She needs to talk to someone who knows what she is living through, especially you, Jennifer. And if you can bear to do it, if it isn't too painful for you, I think it would be wonderful for her."

Jennifer decided to play it by ear, and if it seemed right, that's what she would do.

We went a few days later to her beautiful house. It had some of the most incredible paintings I had ever seen, to say nothing of Jennifer herself, who looked radiant. We had a marvelous lunch and spoke of old times and clothes and girl things and gossiped in a giggly way. Then Jennifer said, "Let's go in the bedroom and take our shoes off and talk."

So we sprawled around the bedroom with our shoes off, and Jennifer told Oona about how it was with her when David died. It was a terrible story of loss and loneliness and abandonment and all the things that one fears it is. She told Oona that she did not think she could possibly live through it and did not know how she did. She then said she had gone to Dr. Milton Wexler for help and that his advice had indeed saved her life. She went on to say that, among other things, he had arranged for her to spend an evening with Norton Simon.

"Jennifer," he had said, "I would like you to speak to this man about our organization and the research we are doing on Huntington's disease. He is very rich and philanthropic and perhaps he will donate some funds. Please do this as a favor to me."

Jennifer had told him that she really didn't want to go, but had said yes only because Milton had been so wonderful to her. So she went and had dinner with Norton. At first, Jennifer had been very serious about discussing money for research, but somehow the evening had ended with Jennifer and Norton laughing and saying they were both a couple of hustlers.

They had had a great time together and went on to have a devoted marriage.

Oona was moved by the story, and after a while Norton came home and came into the bedroom and met Oona. He was most charming; no one who met them could fail to see the bond between the Simons.

As we left, I kissed Jennifer good-bye and whispered thank you in her ear. Oona invited her to visit in Switzerland sometime.

At the beach house that night, Oona said, "Jennifer really is darling and she is still beautiful and she's happy and there's something marvelous about him." She was silent for a moment. "But that first year she spent. I don't know how she got through it."

By that time, the greater part of Oona's first year was over.

It was time to take Oona back to the airport and say good-bye. When we went to the ladies' loo, I saw tears in her eyes and I told her how much I wished I knew a magic word or idea or something that could help. And yet there aren't any big ideas or big words to help someone in the face of such a loss. But there are a few little ones.

"Oona, you came here by yourself and you haven't traveled alone in all these years, so you really have begun now. I think it would help if you would develop some mobility. Just that very simple task of getting from Place A to Place B provides you with a greater sense of life than you can possibly know. When you arrange to rent a car or do this or that, you are doing a dumb, dreary chore. But it is these dumb, dreary chores that are part of life and that keep life close to you. Do these little things, because the big things are made up of these little things, and will come eventually. Little things get done, big things happen."

"I know, darling," she said. "I love you. I'll call you when I get home. And I love Walter. You have the last best man in the world."

We said our good-byes and I watched her get on the plane. She was still that half a person I watched from the window at the beach. I hoped so much that she would become whole.

Oona made a try at living after Charlie died, but it didn't work. She simply could not stand the pain of being alive without him. I went many times to be with her. It is unimaginable that either could live without the other. His death added to the tragic scent of genetics.

Oona O'Neill was born with a broken heart. Knowing that, it was wonderful to make her laugh. When she laughed, she sounded like a very soft little bell ringing. Then, too, there was that marvelous bawdy side of her, which was funny and always accurate. In all the years of knowing each other we never once had an argument. I used to wonder why. I know, now, why. She could understand eight sides of every situation. However, understanding is not a point of view. She knew what to let fall away and what to embrace.

Oona was brave. But she could not put an end to the deep mourning in which she lived until her death.

Oona, that beautiful bright red rose.

But the wind was blowing softly, taking petal by petal.

Oona Chaplin died of a broken heart.

. . . .

Avedon

. . . .

Avedon is restless. He probably has seen most of the world, but he feels as though he really hasn't seen anything. He wants to see something—wonderful—special—beautiful. I think he hopes he can help change the world and he knows it has to be changed. Despite all his success in his field, and everything he's done, he is still a young man finding his way. His friendship is one of the best parts of my life.

We met at a friend's one Christmas. We chatted a bit—enough for him to say, "I've heard that you are extraordinary, but I don't see it."

"I think you're right," I said. "I'm not. Because everybody is."

"Oh," he said. "Now I see it."

Little by little, I got to know Dick, his wife, Evie, and their son, Johnny. I was once in Paris with them when he was photographing the season's fashion collections. When it was over, Christian Dior (this was a few months before his death), said to Dick, "Please ask Madame Avedon to come to my salon and I will have a special showing. I want to give her a gift."

They had the showing and went to lunch. When they came back to the hotel, Evie said, "Nothing was quite right for me. It was all beautiful, but not quite right for me."

I was torn between being dazzled by her and wanting to kill her. It was then I noticed that her shoes were handmade, her blouse was silk—everything she wore was the simplest, the most beautiful. She looked just like a schoolgirl. She had her own style and it was impeccable.

She and Dick had a one-room apartment when they first married and he was just starting out. They had their big bed right in the middle of the room. They made no pretense. Dick was gregarious; he needed to be for his work. Evie, on the other hand, was extremely shy and only liked to be with people to whom she was really close. I think that got in the way a little bit.

I don't know any woman who doesn't want to be photographed by Dick. It has its own kind of status—due both to the beauty of his work and the fact that he would spend any of his precious time with you. His pictures are referred to as "Avedons." He told me how that started. It was on one of his earliest jobs (*Harper's Bazaar*). After the model had all the accessories on he looked carefully and made changes that completely changed the look. But he couldn't decide on the background. After much time had passed he decided on nothing. He used the plain white wall of the studio. It was a radical choice at that time. That was the first Avedon.

He acts not as the renowned artist he is, but as a boy who came in the back door. But if you know him, the first thing you know is that nothing is accidental.

Dick is obsessive. He knows exactly what he wants to do and how to do it. He sits right in the center of the world, although he is a true outsider. He could have been anything. He would have been as brilliant at anything else he decided to do as he is at photography.

Dick is astutely literate and seems to know almost everything everywhere. If there is a new kind of igloo being built at the South Pole, he knows exactly what it looks like and exactly how it should be made to look.

Dick is a loner, and his generosity is the deepest kind. He wants you to get what you want on your terms. If he gives advice, it is toward getting what you want as you dream it might happen. He understands dreaming when you're awake. He respects fantasy. He does not bury life in practicality.

He has been my friend for a long, long time, and we tell each other secrets. He is one of the very few people whose secrets I keep.

When I came to New York to be in the revival of Bill's *The Time of Your Life,* I needed some new photographs for outside the theater. I called Dick's office and spoke with his secretary.

"Does Dick have any time to take some pictures of me? I need them for the front of the theater."

"He would be delighted to do it."

She said she would call me back with an appointment, which she did. I wrote the appointment down, and then suddenly I asked, "Oh, what would this cost?"

"A private sitting costs five thousand dollars."

I wanted to kill myself at that very moment.

"You have to do me a very big favor," I said. "Cancel the appointment and don't even tell him I called. If you tell anybody about this, I will die. Don't mention it."

"I won't. But why are you canceling it?"

"I'm very poor. I don't have five thousand dollars."

"You know how he feels about you. You could work something out, I'm sure."

"Don't mention it. Swear you won't mention it."

"Okay, okay, okay."

I then began to think of some other way that I could get some photographs. But before I could think of anything, the telephone rang. It was Dick.

"Now be quiet," he said. "She had to tell me because she cannot make any appointments for me without telling me who they are with. I'm taking your picture. I don't want to hear another word about it."

"Dick, I cannot let you do that. It will make me miserable. You know that it will. I think it would be worth every penny, if not more. It's just that at this moment, I don't happen to have any money."

"Will you please be quiet about the money? I'm taking the pictures and that's that."

I carried on and carried on and said I couldn't let him do that.

"All right," he said finally. "I will make another price, you can pay it whenever you can and I never want to hear another word about this."

"Okay, but I'm paying and that's all there is to it."

"Fine. Just be there."

"You'll send me a bill?"

"Yes, I'll send you a bill."

He took the photographs and sent me a bill for two hundred dollars. The bill had a P.S.: "To be paid when your ship comes in."

Oh, Dick, I thought, what ship? What could you possibly be talking about? There's no ship for me out there. I know it. You might mean a little canoe lost in the middle of the Atlantic Ocean. How could you possibly have such faith in me?

In any case, time did go by. Quite a bit of time. One night Gloria gave a very big party, and suddenly on the television, which a few people were watching in the library, there was a news break saying that the *Andrea Doria* had sunk. Well, some of the people there knew some of the people on the ship. We all went into the library to listen to the rest of the reports.

People began to leave the party. I saw Dick going into the elevator. The door was just about to close.

"Dick," I called. "That was my ship."

I did try to pay him many years later and received a torn-up check in the mail.

. . .

In the summer of 1978, when Oona came to New York for the first time after Charlie's death, Dick had a tremendously successful show on at the Metropolitan Museum of Art—something that had never before been done for a photographer. Although he never confused photography with art, Dick has the eye of a painter. There were huge flags in front of the museum announcing Dick's show. He wanted to take us himself and did. Seeing it with him was wonderful—very special. Oona was thrilled. The show received a lot of attention. It showed thirty-five years of the full body of his fashion photography. The fashion world is his. He has used that as an opportunity to train young photographers who come to New York to learn. He trained them without receiving any money; he felt he was giving his time to a valuable cause. Many of these young men have become the most famous photographers of today. They might not be the first to tell you they were Dick's students, but they were.

The night of the show, Dick invited Oona and me to have dinner with him afterward at his studio, where we had the best meal we had ever had. It was caviar—the best caviar, all the caviar served as if it were mashed potatoes on mashed potatoes. And vodka. Afterward, we had brownies from Greenberg's, the best bakery in New York City, and then we fainted away.

Oona and I talked about it for days. Who else would think of a meal that way? It was simply perfect. So was the music. So was the conversation. Being with Dick is perfect. He never stopped telling me to write. We would be crossing Madison Avenue—against the light—and he would go on with why I had to write. Anyway, he's really a book, a very big book. I love him. I would really like to make this an interesting story by telling something rotten about him, but I can't.

I.P.L.

Irving Paul Lazar—I.P.L.—is an American phenomenon. All of his dreams have come true. He has insisted on it. He has the most beautiful wife and lives the life he imagined when he was a little boy. His house is exciting to be invited to. His guests cannot be guessed at. He knows people from all over the world. He mixes them all up. And he is a very special man of letters. He has kept writers up there and out in view long after their talents dulled—he felt that much loyalty. He understands the value of money and keeps understanding it as the world changes and its value changes. He is pristine in his tastes, an impeccable friend—he pushes you in the water when you least expect it and he stands there smiling, believing, thrilled that you made it to the top and out of the water.

He is swift. (Swifty.)

He is brilliant.

He represents the best writers in the world and understands the importance of their work for the future.

He is also funny and protective, and when you're with him you cannot imagine anything bad happening to you. His critical faculties are deep—and he tells you what he doesn't like in a short, fast, clear sentence that contains a clue as to how to fix it.

He lives an exciting life. He is an exciting man and it is exciting to be included in the life of this growing boy in his eighties.

He has reverence for the written word and being alive.

On the night of the Academy Awards, Mary and Irving Lazar give the best party of the year. For many years it was at the Bistro

Garden, but more recently it has been at Spago. Those people who are not up for Academy Awards or not presenting them all want to go, and all the winners and losers come to the party immediately afterward. It's always a huge success, and the best thing to do is to make sure you've set your video recorder to tape the awards before you leave the house, because there's no way to hear or see the show at the party. Everyone is talking with such excitement (mostly because they're at Mary and Irving's and not because of the show) and what with the screaming, booing, and clapping, there is total confusion as to who won what.

In 1984, Barbra Streisand was one of those who appeared on the show and came to Spago afterward. She had on an incredibly simple and beautiful dress. It was all white, and she has the most dewy and roselike skin you have ever seen—it matched the dress perfectly and she looked exquisite. She seemed very nervous for some reason and after a while, she came to sit next to me.

We'd first met when she and Walter fought terribly during the making of *Hello Dolly!* "You're just mad," she told him finally, "because the picture isn't called *Hello Walter!*" But we became friends after I publicly stuck it to Isaac Bashevis Singer for criticizing her four years of work on *Yentl*. I wrote a letter to *The New York Times* strongly defending her. I don't know if she was more amazed that I'd written it or that it was printed. But when it appeared she sent the most beautiful roses I've ever seen. Her then agent Sue Mengers, a darling girl who looks like a sinister marshmallow, had a few people over for dinner. Barbra asked if she could sit next to me. So we got to know each other, and when she sat by me at Spago I sensed her nervousness.

"Is something wrong?" I asked. I think my question came as a relief.

She told me that she was very upset because of the dress she did *not* wear to the awards.

"Why, Barbra? Why are you upset by that? No one could look more beautiful than you right now. And as far as I can tell, your dress is the only one here that no one can make fun of."

"Well," she said quietly, "this is an old dress that comes to my rescue every once in a while. It's a Dior."

"It's the best dress here. How can you be upset?"

"You see, the man who made the dress I was supposed to wear is very upset that I didn't wear it. And I like him very much and I didn't want to upset him, but I couldn't wear it. It didn't fit properly, it wasn't at all what I wanted it to be, and I think he knew this but wanted me to wear it anyway. I thought about doing it just to please him, then realized I couldn't. Whatever I wear, it must at least fit. I know the kinds of things people say about me—how terrible I am and how I take charge of everything, and it makes me feel awful that I made him feel awful."

I looked at her and saw how really upset she was about disappointing this man who made the dress she couldn't wear. I did know this about her: She sees every side of everything, a wonderful quality, really, but not one that makes one happy. "Barbra, you are at the very top of your life at this moment. You are the biggest star in the world. You live in the most incredible house of your own design. You are an artist in so many ways. And you are spending your perfect life worrying about this man who made your dress— the man you paid anyway. I love that about you, but at the same time I hate to see you spoil things for yourself and not get the full sensation of your success. You've worked all your life for this. You have to learn how to take some pleasure in it."

"I guess I do get pleasure from it. But it's natural for me to worry about every single thing."

"That's because you're a perfectionist. But being one can make you miserable. My money's on you anyway. I think you'll find a way to be as you are, and be happy as well."

Worrying about clothes, though, is easy to understand. When it comes to clothes, people are very competitive, especially if they're movie stars. I think every smart woman devises a look for herself. Margaret Sullivan had a look: romantic, young, pretty, smart. Katharine Hepburn made a look for herself as this wonderful old salty character. Marilyn Monroe had a look; it was like, "Fuck me with sadness." And Barbra is as much a phenomenon as Marilyn was. They both faced the worst obstacle courses in the world. They both had one thing going for them—talent. Everyone knows about Barbra except the Academy Awards.

Milos and Mozart

Walter and Milos Forman often said that they wanted to do a picture together. Walter loved Milos's work (especially *One Flew Over the Cuckoo's Nest* and *Loves of a Blonde*), and although he didn't know him very well, when he did see Milos he found him to be a pleasure. Milos has that marvelous vitality and kind of personality that seems to give reality a little kick up the stairs. He's very funny, yet filled with tragedy. And you see that all right away. He is generous socially, and when he and Walter met, they had a marvelous time right away. They had an automatic unspoken, untried, instinctive trust in each other's work. Or at least, I know that Walter did.

One day, Walter read in the newspaper that Milos was going to direct *Amadeus*. The real love of Walter's life is Mozart. He lives with Mozart all day and all night. He laughs with him, he cries with him. He knows every note and every nuance of every known piece that Mozart composed. It was the first thing I ever knew absolutely about Walter, and it is the only thing I know absolutely about Walter to this day.

"Walter," I said after seeing the play in New York, "Salieri is your part. Salieri will never be played until you play it. What a great part for an actor."

And it was. Love and hate side by side in one human being. The absolute passion for the beautiful music battling the rage that another had created it. All the feeling in the world went into that love—a love that went beyond life. The rage stood beside it with equal intensity and never moved. And in my mind there was only one actor who could embody this conflict.

"You cannot make a wrong move in that part. All you have to do to play that part is to show up." I went on and on in this vein for quite some time.

And he agreed. To play that part would have been something like a lifelong dream and ambition coming true. For Walter as an actor it would have been the pot of gold at the end of the rainbow.

I say this unashamedly because I have seen Walter on the stage, not just in funny movies, and because I know him so well. That part of him is the part of him I love most.

Now with this news about Milos, I suggested to Walter the following:

"Walter, telephone Milos Forman. Tell him that you want to play Salieri. That it is one of the dreams of your life, and that you will play it for nothing—that you are happy that you have made some of the worst pictures you have ever seen, because that has made you rich enough to do this for nothing. And he can take your minimum SAG salary and give it to any charity he wishes. Also that you know you have been slotted into doing mostly comedy and that's what the audience expects from you. Therefore, you realize this might be a problem for Milos and that is one of the reasons that you would like to test for the part."

"Milos is very intelligent," Walter said. "He knows that it is not possible to play comedy without the base of tragedy."

"For all his intelligence, he still has producers and money people to answer to. So be sure to say you wish to test for the role."

"Okay, okay."

Milos is one of our neighbors in Roxbury, Connecticut, where we go once every five years but are always planning to spend more time. Walter telephoned him there. I, of course, was listening in. I told Walter that I would get a big pad and pen and in case he forgot to say anything, I would put it in front of him with my notes as he was speaking.

Milos answered the telephone and a very friendly conversation began.

"What's the matter with you, Walter? Why don't you spend some time here? Your house is so beautiful. How can you stay away?"

Walter very quickly said, "I know, I know. I'm planning to come up there soon. How are things with you?"

And they exchanged notes and news about what each was doing. And then out of the friendly, laughing tones of the conversation, Walter rang out loud and clear with "Milos, I want to play Mozart."

There was a dead silence.

"Milos, can you hear me?"

"Yes, Walter," he said very quietly. "I hear you."

"Well?"

"Walter, Mozart was thirty-something years old when he died, and he was a tiny blond, blue-eyed, cherubic baby of a man. Now I know how talented you are—you could play anything, really. But I somehow don't know how I can give you the part of Mozart."

"Of course, of course," Walter said, and they continued to chat about other things and hung up rather quickly after that. So all the plans of testing and doing it for no money went into the air.

I, meanwhile, had been bringing in huge pieces of paper filled with scrawls of "no *no* no!" and "Don't say that" and "Salieri *Salieri* SALIERI" and "No more Mozart. He thinks you're crazy."

But when it was all over, I stood still for a few moments. I was feeling many things for Walter, for a man who would sabotage himself in such a way, particularly with someone for whom he had that much respect, and in a project that he loved that much, and a role that he felt in his bone marrow.

"Why," I said softly, "do you sabotage yourself, Walter?"

"I didn't sabotage myself."

"Yes, you did. You knew that Mozart was out of the question. And you knew that your playing Salieri would show that no matter how the public and the producers and money people had forced you into a comedy corner, this was your getaway. The way you went about it, Milos could not possibly have figured out what it is you wanted."

"Oh, no, you're wrong. Milos is brilliant. He knew, and he didn't feel I was right for Salieri."

"What do you mean 'he knew'? You asked him about Mozart."

"Milos knew I wanted to play Salieri *because* I said I wanted to play Mozart. If there had been even the slightest interest on his part, he would have said, 'Mozart? That's insane. Salieri, maybe.' But he did not say that. He just somehow didn't conceive of my playing Salieri. Listen, I always know who I'm talking to and how to talk to them."

But his bravado about his strategy and how he knew when to stop had a sad note in it. It was that sad note of fear. Fear of being a fool, fear of being rejected, fear of not being thought talented enough, fear of how others might perceive him.

This story reminds me of some awful book I read once many years ago, written by Hedy Lamarr, I think. But there was one great paragraph in it explaining how there's a time in one's life in the particular world of movies where one can do no wrong and everything one touches turns to gold and where life automatically sings to you whether you sing back or not. You don't have to do one thing, it's just the golden moment. And that golden moment is impossible to relinquish as you get older. As in the Mozart aria from *The Marriage of Figaro:* Where have they gone, the beautiful moments?

He has us locked up in a room with his jokes.

I'm so mad, I seethed to myself, I'm sick. I wish he had never been sick—at least then I could be mad at him. I can't show him that I'm mad because that will upset him and I'm so upset I think I'm going to get an ulcer and die.

That's it. I must get sick. I must get an exotic disease so he'll pay some attention to what I say. But what exotic disease?

But just because I'm well and sane, he'll keep making those rotten pictures and I'll just keep shopping. We'll keep going around in circles. Not even circles—just one circle.

He doesn't want to go back to the theater, he says, it's too tiring. He'd rather get tired with the bookie.

Why couldn't he have one intelligent conversation with a man like Milos? Why does he always come in on a slant and force people to translate him? Milos probably thinks he was making fun of him. He'll never know that he was making fun of himself.

And I can't stand it. I can't stand it. I can't stand it.

The Silver Frame

Walter likes to watch games on television—basketball, baseball, the horse races—anything he happens to be betting on. And now with cable, one can watch games twenty-four hours a day. Dinner is a time I usually like to talk about everything and nothing, big things and little things, but now I notice that if he thinks I have something to say he instantly turns the television on. At first I tried to do a few little things that would hint to him how rude I think that is, but he didn't pay much attention. Then I tried more things; I even gave myself a pedicure during dinner one night. He didn't seem to notice.

So now I simply leave the table and go upstairs and have dinner in bed and telephone anyone I know who is in any foreign country and speak to them for hours. He doesn't seem to notice this either.

He'll say a little something or two like, "You're always on the telephone."

To which I'll reply, "You're always on the television." And that is that.

Once we had a terrible, terrible fight. I don't remember what it was about. I don't know why I don't, but I don't. This is what happens when you have a fight. You remember the fight but you don't remember why you had it.

This fight was so terrible that it got to a point where I couldn't think of any more rotten things to say to him. So I went to bed and wrote him a lot of poison-pen letters, but they didn't seem to calm me down at all (and they usually do, although I know he *barely* reads them) and I was totally dissatisfied with what I had said in them. It just wasn't rotten enough.

This happened during the time when I was doing research on a man whom I regard as one of the most important men of this century, Admiral Wilhelm Canaris, the head of German military intelligence and one of the leaders of the 1944 plot against Hitler, among many other things. So I started to go through some of my books and make notes and became completely lost in that tragic time. I was thumbing through some of the pages and I came across Hitler's baby picture. And suddenly I knew exactly what to do.

I had a very beautiful sterling-silver frame exactly the size of the photograph, and I put the baby's picture in it and put it on his night table near his telephone and notepads and pens. It sat right next to a very rare paperweight that almost refracted the light from the room into a very special glow onto the photograph. It looked superb.

It articulated every single thing I was feeling. No words could possibly mean anything after that.

Walter didn't say anything about it the next day or the next week or even for the next seven months.

But one day he was on the telephone and was doodling on his notepad. Whoever he was talking to must have bored him terribly. As I listened to the conversation, I realized it was Lenny Hirshan from the William Morris office telling him how he couldn't get Walter a job. While sitting there listening and scribbling, Walter noticed the baby picture in the silver frame.

I was watching him from another part of the room, wishing to God I had a butler's ball so that I could see the expression on his face. (A butler's ball was used at parties in Victorian times. The butler would stand in the corner of the room with his back to the party, and by looking in a silver or gold ball, he could see the room reflected—and thus know who needed a drink refreshed. I wonder if that is why they always say the butler did it—he was always aware of things.)

He picked the frame up and looked at the photograph and the frame and the back of the frame, and he kept staring at the picture. If I know Walter, he was thinking, Who is this adorable baby?

because he thinks all babies are adorable. (I don't. I find very few of them adorable.)

When Walter finally got off the telephone, he turned to me.

"Do you like my hair this way?" I asked sweetly.

"What way?"

"All messed up. This way."

"Who's this?" he said, holding the frame up. "Whose baby is this? Is that Oona's baby?"

"Oh no, no, no, that's not Oona's baby."

"Why is it here?"

"Well," I said. "It's for you."

"What do you mean 'It's for you'? Why?"

"I thought you'd like it."

"You know I don't like presents."

"Well, I wouldn't exactly call it a present."

"Then what the hell is it?"

"It's something I just wanted you to have. It's a reminder."

"Who the *hell* is this baby? I think I've seen this picture somewhere. I think I know this baby, but I just can't seem to place it."

"I know. Nobody can. The baby's mother can't."

"Who is it?" he screamed.

"It's *Hitler!* It's Hitler's baby picture, and I feel it belongs to you."

He started to laugh.

"Jesus Christ," he said, "am I that awful?"

"Of course not. You happen to be perfect. I just wanted to make you laugh."

He then looked at me unsmilingly. "That's some terrific joke," he said.

But he has never taken it away.

Tunisia

I spent most of 1984 in Tunisia. Walter and I took two villas on the Mediterranean in hopes that some friends would come to visit us there, because we knew we'd be there for a rather long time. Walter was going to do *Pirates*. The director was Roman Polanski, who also wrote it with a collaborator.

I did not feel very well. I had started feeling sick in October of 1983, and now quite a few months had passed and I was getting sicker and sicker. It was strange because I had never ever been sick in my life and I didn't know how to be a sick person. So I made all the same moves I made when I was well. I started the day the same way, or at least tried to. I did not want to let the sickness overcome me. I believed I would overcome it.

I had been to quite a few hospitals in the States, and no one had been able to diagnose what was wrong. But I got weaker and thinner all the time. I went from one hundred twenty pounds to eighty pounds. Although I ate more than anyone else, I was always hungry. The food never took. (It wasn't until we came back from Tunisia that I was correctly diagnosed as having malabsorption, a disease that usually afflicts infants under one year of age and results in their death.)

My sister, who lived in London, had gotten the villas ready for us. She had made them very pretty and filled them with everything we could possibly need, and she did our villas within four days. She arrived on Monday.

We arrived that Thursday to a wonderful dinner that she had cooked for us. She was very excited. We hadn't seen each other in a long time, and as much as she tried to disguise it, I could see how shocked she was at my appearance. And because I was that thin, she could not believe how much I ate when we sat down to dinner.

"If you keep eating like that," she said, "you're going to look absolutely marvelous in no time at all. How did you ever get so thin?"

I told her truthfully that I didn't know. I just did.

But as time went on, she could see that I ate and ate and ate and got thinner and thinner. She was exasperated by that, and then said it was something she knew something about. Which she didn't. No one did.

Roman Polanski also noticed. "Carol," he said, "I know you're sick because I know what you really look like. You don't look like this." He wanted me to fly to Paris to see doctors. When I mentioned this to Walter, he said, "Then I won't finish the picture." He was looking for an excuse to get out, and I wasn't going to be it.

Also, I do try to be a great wife. I don't dare be in a bad humor with my husband; and I don't dare be sick. It was a great hardship for me to be sick on that trip to Tunisia, because I never wanted anyone to see me that way. I know how bored men are with women who take to their beds.

But as my energies waned, trying to live as I always had became increasingly difficult. I fell asleep all the time. One night I didn't, and Roman said, "God, it's lovely to have dinner with you when you don't fall asleep in the soup." My body was very bent and misshapen. I couldn't hear or see very well. Clumps of my hair were falling out. The caps on my teeth were jiggling.

I kept arranging for stronger glasses. The ability to read had seen me through my entire life—even through those early years in foster homes, where I found a book called *Honeybunch and Her First Little Garden* in the attic and read it over and over again. I loved it. And now all of a sudden, this ability was gone. I couldn't read, I just couldn't. It was the first time my body was shutting the world out.

I looked around Tunisia as well as I could under those circumstances, and I saw such poverty. It looked the way one imagines Fresno would look after a nuclear holocaust.

I kept noticing men, perhaps six abreast, walking around arm in arm and singing, particularly around the pier. There were very few women, especially at night. It was interesting because I don't think they were even gay; I think they just didn't consider women to be good company. And of course, they may have been right.

But I only saw these things sporadically, because I didn't leave the house very much.

Sometime in February, I woke up one morning and could tell from that sound that silence makes that no one was in the house. I looked at the clock. It was 1:30 in the afternoon. It was very hard for me to turn my head to the clock. It seemed to take a lot out of me. I had to go to the loo. I couldn't get out of the bed. I was in great pain all over.

Unable to get out of bed, I suddenly had the desire to let go. I thought, okay, I'll let go. I'll just let myself die. I will be dead in about ten minutes. Why not? I've had a long life, I've had a good life, I've known love, and I know Charlie. And when I got to Charlie's name, I said, no, I cannot let myself go. I must see Charlie one more time. He was in California, winning all kinds of prizes for his films at U.S.C.

"I've got to get out of this bed," I said.

I finally got down on the floor and crawled to the balcony door and tinkled on the balcony because I realized that the loo was too far away to make it there in time. I crawled back and began the long odyssey to the bath. It took me almost an hour to get to it. It was only a few feet away. It was a small, compact room, so I didn't have to move around a lot. I ran the bath water and brushed my teeth. I couldn't seem to get my hair up off my face, so I left it down. And after filling the tub, I got into it. It felt better to be in the tub. I washed my hair.

I got out of the bath and put towels around myself. I was somehow able to walk to the dressing table, and after another two hours I was dressed. Not to kill, but not to die.

I then went downstairs and sat in the living room. I think I heard a lot of bells ringing—doorbells, telephones. But I began to fall off to sleep again. Later that day, in fact it was in the early evening, everyone came back—my sister, Walter, etc. Suddenly, I felt good. I knew that by forcing myself out of the bed that day and not succumbing to a far stronger urge to go back to sleep, I had somehow survived a crisis during which I made the decision to live.

I made that decision because I suddenly knew that I was dying.

In the following days, I preserved my energies as well as I could, using them only for what had to be done, in order to hide the very real weakness and pain that I had. I usually sat somewhere by myself during the day and remembered things and people. I remembered love. I remembered not being in pain and how good that was. I even remembered feelings of physical well-being and strength. Although I couldn't really hear very well, I would go note by note through the Mozart piano concertos in my mind. It seemed almost as if I heard them.

So I sat in the villa in Tunisia and remembered and ate. And continued to get sicker, although the life-and-death crisis was over. I was very strong, though. I never allowed myself to really go to sleep after that, except in a very spotty way during the day or at dinner or maybe for an hour during the night. It scared me to go to sleep.

I didn't talk to anyone very much because I was only interested in myself—my thoughts and my project. My project was survival. My thoughts were about the past. I had some life-giving, happy times to remember, and I would think about them over and over again.

I started writing again for the first time since my book had come out. I put yellow pads and pens everywhere. It was all that was left to me, the only thing I could still do. I could take baths, I could sleep, and I could write.

I was afraid to look in the mirror, but when I did, I saw such a strange face—not a single wrinkle. The skin was tight on the bone. I guess there just wasn't an extra bit of skin anywhere. It looked very young and a little bit like glass, but much too sad. I *was* so sad.

Charlie and Michelle, his girlfriend, came for two days. I didn't want him to be shocked, so I went looking around for a makeup with a rosy glow. That was hard to find, but I did the best I could. Seeing Charlie so briefly made me know how right it had been not to allow myself the pleasure of oblivion but to struggle toward the sight of my heart's darling. And it renewed in me the determination to try even harder to make it home to see him yet again.

I found out later that Charlie had been shocked when he saw me, but he didn't let me know it. He wanted to take me home, but Walter didn't want me to leave. I think he thought I was going to die, and he wanted me to be with him. Anybody who saw me would have thought I was dying.

I guess, except for seeing Charlie, the aloneness changed who I was. We all know that we're alone. We are. It's just a fact. But when your nose is put in it like that, it makes it that much worse. Having time to go back through an entire lifetime gave me a chance to see all that had been wrong and, in a funny way, all that I might have avoided, had I had a certain strength of character. Which I had never thought of before. But I guess there is such a thing as character, and some people have it and some people don't. But I was going to have it.

If I lived through this, despite many of the hard times that were ahead, I now understood what I had known from the beginning. You simply are alone. You laugh alone. You cry alone. There can be people there, but you are alone. And there are no friends for sick people. Sick people are bores; they blight the fun. Fun—I kept trying to remember about fun. When was the last time I had fun? I then asked myself when was the first time, and then it was anytime. Did I ever have any fun? When did I have it and where was I and who was I with or was I alone?

So I played the game of fun. I played a game of friends. I played a game of enemies. I played a game of living different lives in different places with different people.

I just kept remembering everything. I remembered being a little girl. I remembered being a big girl. I found it strange to remember some of these things. They weren't sweeping memories of one's past, they were tiny details. I remembered the four-leaf clover I found growing out of some broken concrete when I was a little girl. How could it have come out of that concrete? It became a symbol for me of courage and valor and bravery against all the odds. It showed up where it was never meant to be. The whole notion of it made me happy.

I remembered a pink ribbon that I once found and tied around my hair.

I remembered the prettiest dress I ever had.

I remembered the first boy I ever kissed.

I remembered looking into a mirror once and seeing myself and I was beautiful. Just that once.

I remembered a little baby who crawled over to sit near me in the park. She sat there and she never said a word. Neither did I. Her nurse came to get her after a while. She picked her up and took her back to her carriage. The little baby turned her head and looked at me and seemed to wave, but I'm sure she didn't. But it looked as though she waved. I remember her also because she sat so quietly. I always wondered what she was thinking about, what dreams she might have had, what her name was. I wondered if she had come because she knew I was very lonesome. Maybe she was a very special baby and she could feel that. But of course, in thinking about it, I realized how accidental everything is really and how deeply we want to give it a value whether it is there or not. We want someone to look at us and say, "Oh, it's you. I know you. You're so special and I love you." I think that that may be the best how-do-you-do there could be.

And I spent all that time remembering my life, what I gave to it, what I took away from it, when I failed, when I succeeded. I thought that if I lived (and I was going to live), I would have a list that I inscribed in my bone marrow of the ways in which I was going to conduct my life.

When you take away the props and the tinsel and you turn your most intelligent eye to your own actions and those of other people, you find much wanting. You wonder about it. But past a certain point you can no longer afford to wonder why you did this or that or why they did that or this. You only know what you are going to do from that moment on. You know what you will never do again and you know why. Whatever intelligence I have, it had never been turned toward the way I lived my life. I lived my life in a much more accidental way, and I knew now that, given the chance that I was insisting on getting, there were certain "never agains." It is interesting that some of us have to be that sick and get so close to death before we know anything about living. Or to be even more truthful, before we even take an honest look at our-selves, no matter how wanting we are. When you hear the bell tolling, you know that if nothing else, you must set some things straight. Not for anyone but yourself. And you also know for the first time that you are worth something. Your own worth has never been in your thoughts before.

That is what I thought about.

There were bunkers all along the beach. There were Nazi bunkers, American bunkers, Tunisian bunkers, English bunkers. Each day I sat in a different one.

Whenever I sat in the Nazi bunker, I would have such terrible feelings of rage. It was rage about anyone daring to decide who would be allowed to live. I had felt it when Oona and Walter and I went to Dachau. And now, being as sick as I was, I did not handle this rage very well. It was so deep that it would keep me awake. It's a rage that permeates every cell of your body. I don't think it ever leaves you. It's always there. It's just that you live with it buried until you see a Nazi bunker on a beautiful Mediterranean beach, and then, for that moment, you feel it so deeply that it's very hard to go on.

Each day I saw the bunker from my balcony and I would get this slightly sickened feeling, on top of being sick already. One day, I decided I would pay the bunker a different sort of visit and leave my answer to it.

I put on a pink silk dress with white lace. I had pretty pink shoes and wore them with white lace stockings. And I had a pretty straw hat with a white ribbon around it that tied in a bow in back with streamers going down. It had a pink rose right in the middle of the bow. And, unbelievably enough, I had a pair of white lace gloves which I decided to wear. I wore a little makeup and my pink pearls. I was all dressed up. Except for one thing: I didn't wear any panties.

I went directly to the bunker.

I sat down and emitted a strange laugh that I had never heard from myself. It was a new sound, full of that rage. And all at once, I was sure I was going to say what I had to say.

I decided the bunker or anything with a Nazi emblem on it was really a loo.

So I lifted up my skirt and jumped around the bunker using it as a loo. I was laughing uncontrollably—laughing, laughing, laughing. I had never laughed before during such an activity and now I couldn't stop laughing.

And the more I laughed, the more I did.

A few days later, I did hear a bit of talk about what someone had done in the Nazi bunker, which usually was kept quite clean. I, of course, became more of an invalid than ever. The minute I heard the words "Nazi bunker," I pretended to be sound asleep. Also, everyone knew I never left the house.

But I thought to myself, There is one brave person on this Mediterranean beach and I am that person.

I thought to myself, What other fun can you have if you're in a Nazi bunker? I couldn't think of one other thing that would have meant more to me.

It sustained me for a while.

Having spent a lifetime being a person who would rather not do anything like that even in the most perfect place to do a thing like that, it was surprising that I didn't think any less of myself because I was now capable of a human activity in an inhuman environment. It was my moment of glory—the only fun I had that year.

In your lifetime, how many definite things do you feel strongly and need to say in your own way? Life changes so many of the things you once thought you wanted to say. But there seem to remain possibly two or three things that you will feel deeply all your life, and mostly you do not get the chance to express them.

This was my message. It always will be. And being sick in Tunisia gave me a chance to say it.

Truman

Walter was working steadily now and we hadn't been going East, but Truman came and went a few times. He usually came with his friend John O'Shea, who was another example of Truman's obsession with the everyday. He was a low-level bank vice president on Long Island in the proper-color gray suit and that college boy puce-colored hair and Truman fell in love with him.

But John could be very cruel. His sadistic self would show itself at a dinner table or in front of people who really cared about Truman. And Truman would be very embarrassed about what would be said in front of me because he knew how I felt about him.

Once Truman came out and we went to the old Swiss Café on Rodeo Drive in Beverly Hills. We used to go there all the time and sit way in the back late at night. This night, he was sobbing, curled up in the fetal position, and I held him in my arms in the middle of the night in the dark, as the restaurant was closing. He was like someone without a skin—every part of him was an exposed raw nerve. I had seen him very, very upset quite a few times over the years, but never to this degree.

He was in pain about John O'Shea, about the way their love affair was going. "How can you stand him?" I said. "He's not attractive at all."

"Oh, honey, you don't know, you don't know," he said. "You're not attracted to that kind of man." Because Truman did have this absolutely fantastically overwhelming unbelievable fascination for the ordinary.

I told him that and he said, "Honey, you're right. But I have it, so what am I going to do?"

Physically and emotionally, Truman worsened. He could not afford the sleazy people he was seeing. He needed a gentle life, one that Jack Dunphy alone could have provided. He was a person of beauty and compassion, and he dearly loved Truman. And Truman loved him back. But as Truman became more and more successful, the demands of his friends became too much.

The last time Truman came to California, he stayed with Joanne Carson, one of Johnny's ex-wives. She made things very convenient for him. She was like the porter, the cook, the chauffeur, the secretary. She was the way I had been for Bill. She didn't exist.

Once he arrived, Joanne called. She told me how anxious Truman was to see me.

"Oh, well, I'm anxious to see him. May I speak to him?"

"He's resting," she said.

I heard her enjoyment through the wires.

"Well, I'll call him a little later."

She told me that he was quite tired from the trip and suggested that perhaps I should wait a day or so.

Before the day or so passed, he telephoned and we talked. He sounded wrong.

We talked about the big fuss that was being made about whether Truman's *Answered Prayers* was a complete manuscript or just random chapters. I knew of the many terrible distractions he had had while he was writing it. I knew about *Answered Prayers* from the nights we had spent at the Gold Key Club, where he had described it as "my big one." Shortly after, he stopped to do *Breakfast at Tiffany's*. Later, when he saw a piece in the newspaper about the two men who killed the Clutter family, he stopped again to write *In Cold Blood*.

I knew that it struck him as insane (as it did me) to imagine that someone who had been a writer of his caliber for all those many years would be accused of lying about whether or not he was really writing *Answered Prayers*. He was a writer who had broken ground for other writers, who had combined remarkable journalism with brilliant creative talent, who had never played it safe at any time—

as he could have—and had taken his place as a wonderful and precious little southern writer of the Eudora Welty school. (This is not said with anything but admiration for Eudora Welty—I think she's a wonderful writer, who went deeply into the human heart, but her stomping ground stayed where it started. Truman, on the other hand, was everywhere and wrote about everywhere he went.)

As I remember him and his amazement at the idea that anyone would ever doubt that he was writing a book, it still breaks my heart. I think he was deeply wounded by that notion, and that was a deep wound. It was the old domino theory—little by little, everything for him began to fall from grace, everything but his beautiful mind, which is, in the end, all one really needs.

When I think about Truman, I think of him as one of the most serious people I've ever known. About politics. About people. He had an eye like no one else in the world. He was strong. He was honest with himself. He was very dignified. And there was nothing about anyone that escaped him. But Truman had a party personality that played right into everybody's expectations.

I understand that. I've done it myself. When I was young, I looked so vacuous, like a piece of pie. And when people thought I was dumb, I was dumb for them; I gave them the whole bit. I didn't want to disappoint them. I knew Truman was the same way, because we used to talk about it. He didn't mind playing the fool because he didn't take himself that seriously.

"The only thing that's going to be left is what's between the pages and that's all I care about," he would say. "If I want to have fun and fool around the rest of the time, why not? What am I going to prove?" He rarely thought people were wonderful, and boy, he had a point.

I remember Joanne Carson on the phone one last time. Evidently she had been making many calls to tell people that Truman had died during the night, that she had found him dead in the morning, and that she had arranged a service for him.

She asked if I knew of anyone she might have missed who should be informed and would want to pay their respects. This was all done in a slow, businesslike way.

I went. Walter had to go to another funeral that day, so Felicia

Lemmon came with me. Truman adored Felicia, because whenever he began to tell stories, she would fall asleep like a little cat.
He would watch her sleeping and drone on and on to keep her
asleep.

"Look at that precious thing, that precious little girl sleeping.
Isn't that precious?" he would say.

"Yes, she is precious," I would say.

But of course she wasn't asleep on that day. No one was.

It was an abomination to hear people who barely knew Truman
speaking of him. I remember one man describing the "high point"
of Truman's life as the Black and White Ball (an unthinkable thing
to say about a man as serious and brilliant as Truman).

I did ask Joanne to ask a few writers, not just the richest people
in town. Christopher Isherwood spoke about Truman, laughing
very hard as he told how much Truman had made him laugh.
Knowing the little I knew about Christopher Isherwood, I knew
he was wetting his pants, because Charlie Chaplin once complained terribly that every time Christopher Isherwood visited, he
would laugh so much that he would wet the chairs, even the rugs.
Charlie simply couldn't stand it and finally stopped inviting him.
Now I watched as Christopher Isherwood couldn't keep himself
from laughing through his eulogy for Truman.

As we filed out, John Gregory Dunne said, loud and clear, "I
don't want anyone to tell jokes or anecdotes or be funny at my
funeral. I want them to be sad, to miss me, and to say that they
loved me and to cry at my funeral. Not laugh."

And of course, he was righter than anyone could have been. It
was quite terrible.

Truman did something in his later years that I often think about.
He was very upset when Tennessee Williams died and he went on
The Dick Cavett Show and asked Dick Cavett if he would mind if
he was not funny because he had something to say that he felt
should be heard by as many people as possible. Dick Cavett said
that was fine. And then Truman spoke very seriously about what
America does to its artists.

He spoke about how Tennessee Williams had spent the last

twenty years of his life being out of fashion. He said Williams was out of fashion in a way that was particularly American and that he knew that every single day of his life, and yet he still went into the room he wrote in and spent at least four hours writing there each day.

Truman explained the pain of doing that when one is an artist who is out of fashion and knows it. Truman said Tennessee was very brave because he knew that if he wrote the very best piece of work of his life—something that went beyond *Streetcar* or *The Glass Menagerie*—that they would still throw cabbages at him simply because he was out of fashion.

The critics still encourage writers and artists when they are getting started, but at a certain point they start throwing poison darts at them. It is so intimidating for writers to grow and come into their own or to do anything different from the formulas that originally worked for them.

There was never anything that Tennessee Williams wrote that did not at least aspire to beauty and I don't think anything is good if it doesn't do that, even if it fails. No one had higher aspirations than Tennessee Williams, and that's what counts.

It was nice that he knew how good he was, but it was tragic that he knew he was destined to fail in the eyes of the critics for the rest of his life.

Truman is gone, and it seems such a long time to me. Yet it isn't the way it is when other people go. I don't think I have read anything since his death that has not made me think of him and wonder what his opinion would be. He was a wonderful critic. I know that there will be all sorts of things said about Truman for a long time, and then everything will settle and what will be left will be his work. I think that will endure, because of his very special gift of simultaneous lightness and depth.

I miss him in the rain. We often took walks in the rain—we both loved the rain.

I miss his advice. And I hate and despise the fact that the people who knew him the least are such authorities on him. What do they know of his broken heart, his tears, his loneliness, his astonishing aspiration, or his sense of beauty? These so-called authorities know nothing of Truman.

Good-bye, Truman. I'll always think of you as the boy who wrote, "As for me, I could leave the world with today in my eyes."

The Celebrity Bus

I am very upset because that celebrity bus that used to stop in front of our house is nowhere to be seen. I have told Walter if it does not come back, I'm going to leave him.

Everyone complains about the bus but you have no idea what it's like when it doesn't come anymore.

But that is an actor's life. It's so clear in *The Day of the Locust:* That crowd can go any way in any direction at any time—it is crazed—a combination of Coney Island and the French Revolution. It's funny about Walter: The same thing that catapulted him to *big movie success* and *big movie money* is what imprisons him now.

Permanent Transients

When the whole wide world is going his way and everything he ever wanted is around him and his life is becoming more and more perfect, he loves *you.*

When the drought comes and the beautiful fresh water is receding and there are dried white skulls seen here and there on the landscape, memories come. Memories of his beginnings, his escapes. He hates *you.*

That is why life in a company town is so sad. That is, if you love him. If you don't, it doesn't matter. But I do.

Actors often describe their professional life as being so very
unprofessional. In most other professions, there's room for failure
because one has already built something up by one's past accom-
plishments. Whereas an actor's last gross is his whole story.

If he built a beautiful house, and then a few miles away he built
an ugly one, the beautiful one would still be there. That is supposed to be real life (if there is such a thing). In the movies, he
doesn't get any gold stars for stretching or trying to grow. "They"
like him to stay in one recognizable slot. He has no past, he doesn't
know if he has a future, he has only the fear of right now.

And that's what makes it a hard life, an unsure life. He becomes
a chorus boy waiting for the telephone to ring with news about a
job. His chances to be a person decrease, and anyway, he doesn't
know what a person really is after a while. That is what keeps an
actor tense and nervous and, depending on the kind of person he
is, it can spoil the rest of his life. I mean, the other part of his life
that is always waiting for him. He has nothing left to give to it. He
is drained by the anxiety of his profession. He doesn't know who
to kiss—the writer, the director, the producer, the makeup man,
the hairdresser. Who's holding the cards?

He knows it's not the head of the studio, because the head of the
studio has two minutes left before he's fired by the board of
directors. He doesn't know where or who the board of directors
are. They change a lot too. Everybody's moving, but in what
direction? Who's going where? Who should he follow? Who
would he be great with? Who should he spit on?

He is ambitious.

He has a family.

He wants to live, too.

He must rest sometimes.

Most actors at the finish of a picture wonder if they will ever
work again.

That is why the houses on the street look as they do. You can
drive down a very beautiful street with well-tended lawns but they
are all the wrong color green. This is a desert, and green grass does
not grow in a desert. It's a movie set. There are southern mansions
like Tara in *Gone With the Wind* next to split-level ranch houses
next to bastardized Tudors next to Cape Cods next to Spanish

haciendas next to Spanish Monterey colonials. It's all there, not belonging. If the weather gets hot, the houses burn down. If it rains, the houses float away.

It's pretty much a wartime mentality. Nothing really belongs here, but it's here in H Wood, U.S.A., anyway, in a transient way. It won't last.

There are great American stories about families spending Christmas in houses that have been there for years and years on the kind of terrain where they belong. There is a world like that out there someplace. But it's not his. And his family is not in it. His life is here and he's wondering, Will I hit or miss? Is he making it? Is he failing? If he is, how does he get to be a success forever and ever? How does he become remembered? That would be nice, he'd love to be remembered. And that is what would keep him alive because, like most people most of the time, he's dying of fear—the fear of not being wanted.

When he is turned down for a job as a street cleaner, it's because they have enough street cleaners at the moment, or perhaps they're going to give one of their own street cleaners another chance. But when he's an actor who is turned down, it means they hate him. They hate "him."

They hate his eyes, his nose, his mouth, his hair, his build, his voice, his dreams, his money, his family. It's him they hate.

That is why being turned down for an acting job is like dying, whether you're at the beginning, middle, or end of your career. You cannot live if they don't love you.

Who are "they"? Who are "they"? Who are "they"? Who are "they"? Who are "they"? They, they, them, them, them, them.

Who did Clifford Odets mean when he said, "Look what they did to me. They did it. I'm a fine artist. Look what *they* did to me!"?

There is no "they." He is "they." You are "they." We are "they." No one is out there. He is all alone. He is "they," he is him, he is it, he is a studio. He is a movie theater, he is money. Someone, someday will write the real book about Hollywood, but it will have to be written by a C.P.A.

The telephone is ringing. It's the idiot—the agent. "Hello," he lies. Maybe it'll be all right.

Christ, these are big swings. Things happen, big swings. It could be a job. It could be the job he's waited for all his life, paying ten million dollars. Maybe he's still up there. That's the great thing about life. You don't know. You simply have no way of knowing what's coming next. It may be that his number came up.

There's no question in his mind that he's getting an Academy Award the next time. They better be more careful with him because he has the one thing they need—talent. But more than his talent, they need real writers. They don't really know what a writer is. In this town, the writer doesn't get the prize. The hairdresser takes it.

Norman Mailer cannot make a successful movie. He's got more guts and elegance and journalistic brilliance and poetic ability than any other writer in this country. He's a giant.

He must play this game. This success game. The success syndrome. The success story. Success. Money. Recognition, without which he cannot love his wife or child or neighbor or give one fuck about anything. They made him a golden boy. They can't stop now.

Where are they? He's hungry. He's angry. He's alone. In the middle of they. He has no one to talk to. Christ, do you know what it means to have no one to talk to? Endlessly, for days that go on and on. Do you know what it means to be over forty? Over sixty is the end of the world. That's what they mean when they say dying. Dying. I am dying of degradation. I don't read John Donne anymore. I am an island.

. . . .

Gloria and Oona and I

. . . .

Gloria and Oona and I were the closest of friends. By that I mean our pasts were shared in certain ways. We lived far away from one another—Gloria in New York, Oona in Vevey, I in Pacific Palisades. But tender feelings know no distance. I feel that they are still each a part of me—deep, true, and loving. How they felt about each other I don't really know. I think sometimes they were close, and much of the time they were not. They were girls together, women, and then widows.

It's like being part of the same space capsule, more than it is an everyday "I love you." I was closer to either of them than they were to each other. And the three of us lived very different lives— each disconnected in its way to the other—and yet there was that closeness that is hard to describe. We were drawn together. Our lives started together. It was the eve of the war. After that didn't matter. There are so many changes in women, all the silly, sad, obvious arguments. They will always have my love, in very different ways.

As I think back, it seems that when Oona's life was great, Gloria's wasn't. When Gloria's life was great, mine wasn't. My life is my life—but Walter has and does make it a real life, which it never was before. They both loved Walter because of that and because they felt that in some way I was protected. They were very dear. They wanted things for me that I never thought of for myself.

They were those opalescent girls who danced through those beautiful, romantic nights. They both had wonderful minds, though utterly different. They both could have been anything, but more than making decisions about how they wanted their lives to go, their lives showed up. I think that is true of a whole generation of women.

Gloria has made more choices than Oona or I. In a way, she has lived more. She has tried more. She has been interested in more. But Oona and I were luckier. Gloria is very brave. She is even surviving the ultimate tragedy, the death of her son, Carter Cooper. She knows that while she cannot really survive it, she's healing that part of her that she can save for her other children. For her sense of life. For her belief in believing. It is possible that she may lead a whole new life, be a whole different person, and start again. Oona could not do that. I don't know if I could. Gloria dares.

If Wyatt had lived, he and Gloria would still be together.

If Charlie had lived, Oona would still be alive.

Charlie

When Charlie was born, I was more awake than I had been for the other two births, and Dr. Greeley held him up in the air and said, "It's Charlie! It's not Amy Rose. It's Charlie!"

I looked up at the absolutely luminous pink and white perfect little baby and Dr. Greeley put Charlie in my arms and said, "Now you can both rest for a while. I'll be back."

It was perfect. Charlie fit so sweetly into my arms and there was an immediate, unmistakable bond and I knew it would be that way forever. I felt it. There he was—our love, in person, in matter. I was looking at love, this little boy was made of pure love.

And from the very first, he brought happiness to Walter and to me, in a way neither of us had ever had before. Every once in a while, when we would be driving somewhere, I'd say, "Let's talk about Charlie," and Walter would smile and we would talk.

There were always so many sweet things about him. One night, I had just given Charlie a bath and as I was drying him, and powdering him and putting on his fresh nightclothes, I said all the stupid things in the world you could possibly say—things like "What a cutesy sweetsy babykins you are. You're my perfect little baby. You're my perfect goodness. Oh, I just love you and love and love you," and went on and on in that way. At some point, I looked at Charlie's face and I felt embarrassed. He looked like the wisest and most tolerant man on the Supreme Court, and I felt like a perfect fool. But then there was that other thing of Charlie's—his little twinkle. So of course, I hugged him and kissed him. There simply was great pleasure in living with Charlie, in being with him. He was so utterly civilized.

As he grew, many things happened. I knew how smart he was—he began investing in the stock market at age eleven, pretending to the Chicago Stock Exchange that he and another boy were men, saying things like, "Gotcha" and "I'll get back to you."

I could go on and on. He was so industrious and he was very interested in money, possibly because of Walter's gambling and my spending, which I believe is a result of Walter's gambling. It's so corrupting. I remember when we moved to California, into a house, Charlie made lemonade to sell—as much as he possibly could. He used fillers like sugar and cherry juice to make it look bigger. He set himself up in front of the house with a chair and bucket of ice and paper cups and napkins and the bottle of lemonade. There was a little cup with change in it and he was dressed all in white. He wore a little white baseball cap, onto which he had painted a lemon.

He sat there for a long time. He had a little bell he kept ringing, but no one stopped.

He looked disheartened, then suddenly I saw his face change. He didn't know that I was watching him from just a small distance away, behind a weeping willow tree. He suddenly had an idea. He took his cup with the change and went to Walter and said, "Poppy, please do me a favor. Could you stand behind me, because maybe if you did, some of the cars might stop just to see you and get interested in my lemonade."

So there they were, the two of them in their baseball caps, except Walter had "Mozart" written on his. The cars were all stopping.

Charlie couldn't keep enough lemonade outside. It was going so fast we had to make some more and after a while, the stars came out and the night fell.

Charlie then began to count his money before anything else. He had made almost fifteen dollars and was really thrilled, as was Walter.

What pleasure we had from living with Charlie and learning about his projects and watching him begin to understand things, and then to know things that I didn't know, and Walter didn't, either.

He was funny. I think the first funny thing he said was about van Gogh. He and Walter were talking about him. He told Walter how he had cut off his ear and sent it, as proof of love, to a girl.

"How did he send it?" Walter asked.

"Ear mail," Charlie said.

But my favorite of all the things that Charlie ever did (and he did wondrous things every day) was when he had a little pail and a ball and was playing in the playpen. He would throw the ball to me or to Walter and we would throw it back into the pail and he would throw it back to us. This game went on and on, and he enjoyed it. But one time when I threw it back, I missed the pail. The ball went into the playpen, so Charlie picked it up and put it in the pail and then took it out and threw it back to me.

That was one of the most enchanting events of my life. I associated it with a definition of genius I'd read long before in the *Saturday Review*. It was a rather long and arduous piece on genius (a very dangerous word). It said that the real definition was someone to whom it was not enough to solve a problem, the problem had to be solved elegantly.

I've had a lifetime of pleasure from that memory.

· ·

Oona Is Dead

· ·

Oona's death waves like a red flag back and forth, night and day. Waves in the rhythm of "Oona is dead."

I cannot make the regret stay still. At best, I sleep very little—but now my sleep has been invaded with the music of many memories and her tears have become mine. Dreams make everything more so, happiness is heightened, sadness goes to the core of you. When the dream is happy I forget that she is no more. When I wake up I don't remember for a few seconds, and then, as I do remember, the grief crashes all over me, and the red flag waves widely back and forth, so fast that all else is covered.

My Ice Cream Is Melting

I do know that life is not good enough at any age, but when one gets older, one is expected to assume a proper attitude about aging, about being something somewhat less than one was yesterday or last night. I can't quite do this. I have tried and I have affected wonderful things about getting old, such as how freeing it is. It really does free you in a certain sense: You can make big mistakes and you simply don't have that many years left to pay for them. So one is certainly less afraid to make mistakes. But I don't think I've ever been afraid of making mistakes. I just wouldn't feel alive if I didn't feel free to make them.

But I must say the bonus stops there. The freedom to make mistakes is the one and only bonus of getting old. I try to affect a polite obliviousness about it, but it is totally unreal. I find it sad to get old. And to be slowly drifting over to the dark side of the moon. I don't think about being young in terms of what I might have done, and whether I would have done something differently or anything like that. I don't think I would have. We all know that old saw about how death begins for us as soon as we are born. We've also been told that we never again learn as much or as quickly as we did in the earliest years of our lives. What is left out is what it is that we learn. I think the things we learn later have a deeper importance and a greater horror. If I regret anything (and I do) it has to do with what I did not do.

But one doesn't really set out to learn, one sets out to live. Of course, you learn as you live. But overall, when I think back to my earliest years and all the way right up to now, I like to remember when I was happy.

Some days my thoughts go all over the world, all over my life, and all over what might happen, what did happen, and I have a feeling of not having really survived. I did not survive everything. No one ever does. Little pieces of you—sometimes the best of you—get lost in a little lie here, a little joke there. And of course, the aftereffect is the tiny sob—unseen, unheard, deeply felt.

I'm sad for all those unlived hours, years. I'm really sad that I didn't say certain things to certain people at certain times. I'm sad that I didn't make a run for it once or twice.

I think about so many worlds that I never inhabited, certain people I miss a lot.

Laughter—that was—can make you sad if it is no longer.

I guess I want everything all the time. I believe that to be the truth about everyone.

I have tried to live in different ways at different times in my life, and I have never really felt natural in any of them. That doesn't mean that I am unaware that life is a gift. I'd like to celebrate it more, but I still know that it isn't good enough. It's very possible that what I mean is that I'm not good enough. I could be better, and I know now that life can.

Somehow, there were far fewer happy times than there were just ordinary times. On the other hand, they are the most unforgettable. They are not necessarily times of great accomplishment. They also are not necessarily times of great love affairs. There is only one perfect love affair and that is when the girl dies young. Short of that, they hold some happiness and also some of the saddest times. Love that lasts forever is the greatest achievement any of us can ever have in our lives. That is the rarest, but not necessarily the happiest. Laughter and love affairs are not always partners, although they should be.

One of my happiest moments was when I saw a tiny plastic boat peeking out of a Cracker Jacks box. It was as though all the world had opened up for me and the stars were with me.

The first "I love you" that you ever hear is a landmark of relief rather than happiness. I think that falling asleep in someone's arms is one of the ultimate happinesses, far more than the erotic tension and the sensuality and the whispered words that precede it (despite the pleasure of it all). None of this stops with age—or at least so far.

Music and literature continue.

So what does stop that counts? One's own physical and mental abilities and attributes. One is less beautiful, one is less able, finally one is unable, finally one is a mass of rivulets and chasms and has a face that one tries to conceal. But I have seen beauty in certain old faces. Actually, as I have already said, one finally shows up on one's own face after a certain age, and it is that appearance of you on your face that makes all the difference. There is no old age. There is, as there always was, just you. There's nobody out there. There's no one else and, once again, there is no they.

It really is strange how used to being young one is. I always tried so hard to be older, but never to the degree that I now try to be younger.

There are a few things that let you know that you have gotten old. You don't go to Central Park and jump on the carousel and try to catch the gold ring. You don't go ice skating at Rockefeller Center. You don't wait for the Good Humor man. And you have stopped waiting for that great big shining life that you thought would be yours. That doesn't mean that the life you are living doesn't have its wonders. It's just that there is the beginning of a shadow.

To be honest, I cannot be honest. More of my life is out of this book than in it. But a book is only a book, and a life is a lifetime.

I really don't care what people think of me. I only care how they act to me in front of me because I know that I will never really know much about someone else—about another person's deepest, darkest, or most beautiful feelings. Those are all private things. No one ever really tells them. So because of that, I have easy friendships and a much easier life.

I have a deliberately developed lightness of manner, because of which a lot of people I've known (particularly when I was younger) thought I was very dumb. I would always catch that and play it all the way for them. I'm talking, of course, about people who didn't really mean anything to me—people who were not really part of my life.

But I have cared and loved deeply in my life a few times, and those are the times that I really have been the most alive, because that is all I really cared about. And in that way, I must say, I've been very spoiled. And very, very lucky, with the exception of my first and second marriages.

But to have met Walter and to have had a real, whole second chance at life is so unexpected. It is in him and through him that I really became a woman, that I learned how to be happy, and most of all, that I learned the pleasure of making someone else happy. I think it's very hard to stay in love with someone you cannot make happy. That simple word, that scoffed-at, sniffed-at word— "happy."

The day the war ends and soldiers and sailors and girls and old women and young men and young women and old men run toward Times Square and kiss one another and hug one another— these people are alive. They love one another. For that moment. For that time. For that second. However long, it is love. Those are the highest points of one's life. I don't mean by being in Times Square; I mean by being with that one person who envelops all kinds of love—Times Square love, baby love, friendship love, every love.

When love is a memory in the solitude of age, it fills it with pleasure and pride.

Because it's so brave to love and that valor of trusting gives even that final aloneness an echo of a heart once filled—that final whisper of pleasure haunts us with sweet secrets from all those many years ago.

We know that we lived.

Acknowledgments

I want to thank:

Louis Jourdan, because it was he who sent me *The Basic Writings of Nietzsche*—underlining the Schopenhauer quote—and telling me about things I never heard before in such a gracious and fascinating way that we could have been sitting anywhere in the world.

Joni Evans, for her elegant honesty and taste and sweet laughter, and for trusting me.

Kenneth Turan, for his confidence in me, his help, his sensitivity, and his impeccable manners.

Barbara Roberson, for her decency, patience, honesty, and all the qualities that go with a very underused word, *character*. Also, she's a pleasure—a young and pretty pleasure to see—her heart beats with yours when it is breaking or when it is filled with laughter.

I have a special thank-you for my brilliant and darling friend Lillian Ross, who told me many of the facts of writing.

George Christy, for telling me to write every time I saw him, which was practically every time I went out.

Bruce Kaplan, for his brilliance, taste, and wit.

Charlie Matthau, for sticking around.

With Eli Wallach on Broadway in *The Cold Wind and the Warm*

My first book, with the wrong title

Finally, an Avedon

Walter and I getting married at City Hall, 1959

Total happiness, 1967

Charlie and Walter wrestling for Oscar

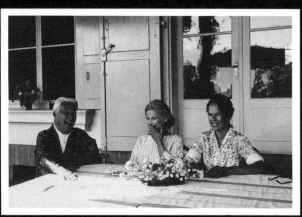

With Oona and Charlie
in Vevey

In Southampton for the weekend, 1979